CW01096106

'This is an important and valuable book. L; and holistically so as to expertly guide critica and being physically active in early childho highly readable text makes a compelling case childhood development, as the primary source of joy, health, resilience, learning and development. Through focusing upon clearly argued principles for movement-centred practice, it provides a fresh, logical and creative resource that demands a response from us all.'

– Professor Jan White, author of Every Child a Mover *and*
Playing and Learning Outdoors, 3rd Edition

'In this book Dr Manners has distilled a lifetime of observation and research into a very necessary, practical manual. Now, more than ever, we need tools based on sound foundations that can effect positive change for children. Dr Manners is in the unique position of being able to combine physical and cognitive and developmental knowledge to help impact skill progression. A lifetime of experience is now made applicable through her research. This book allows practitioners the privilege of replicating results through an enjoyable, multi-layered appreciation of the value of each child's unique developmental journey.'

– Lesley Johnson, speech and language therapist and allied health lead

'Dr Lala Manners' latest book *The Early Years Movement Handbook* brilliantly connects the dots between physical play and learning. Movement is an essential requisite to early childhood development and an often missing critical element to the body and brain's formal learning preparation. Lala cleverly dissects important research and gives practical ideas of how adding movement to children's daily learning diet can enhance their learning experience. If ever there is a time for making a case for movement-based learning it is now when childhood as we know it is under threat.'

– Gill Connell, globally respected child development and
movement specialist, co-author of A Moving Child Is a
Learning Child *and* Move, Play, and Learn with Smart Steps

'This timely book by Dr Manners provides an accessible text for early years practitioners and students about the crucial importance of physical movement for holistic development. With both theoretical perspectives and practice application, *The Early Years Movement Handbook* is essential reading.'

– Dr Eunice Lumsden, Head of Early Years,
University of Northampton

'This book is a wonderful and timely reminder of the need to let go of our adult agendas and free children to follow their innate drive to move, explore, learn and simply enjoy themselves, each other and their world. Drawing on philosophy, science, child development theory and inspiring practical examples, Lala Manners shows us how to create the conditions in which young children can flourish through developing their physical confidence.'

– Kim Roberts, Chief Executive, HENRY
(Health, Exercise and Nutrition for the Really Young)

'This book is hugely helpful in putting the wider discussion about physical development into a historical and pedagogical context. It confirms the importance of all teachers knowing more about why and how we offer children relevant and enjoyable experiences that build their confidence to use their bodies to explore the changing world. The book is divided in two with Part One establishing eight guiding principles that inform and support practice in physical development and Part Two focusing on "How do I do it?" The book avoids becoming a checklist because it is written in such a way as to enable you to drop in and out, expanding learning on broad questions such as "What is movement?" and more specific issues such as spatial reasoning. It will certainly be used as a key text at LEYF.'

– June O'Sullivan MBE, Chief Executive,
London Early Years Foundation

'A much-needed resource at a time when childhood obesity has reached a crisis stage and children are more and more often treated as though they exist only from the neck up! Brava, Lala, for answering the question, "Why bother?"'

– Rae Pica, early childhood consultant and author of
the Moving & Learning *series*

'A must-read book for any practitioner working in early years education.'

– Mike Loosemore MBE, Lead Sports Physician (South of England) for the
English Institute of Sport and Lead Consultant in Sport and Exercise
Medicine at the Institute of Sport, Exercise and Health

The Early Years Movement Handbook

of related interest

Create, Perform, Teach!
An Early Years Practitioner's Guide to Developing Your Creativity and Performance Skills
Nikky Smedley
Illustrated by Sam Greaves
ISBN 978 1 78592 431 6
eISBN 978 1 78450 799 2

Observing and Developing Schematic Behaviour in Young Children
A Professional's Guide for Supporting Children's Learning, Play and Development
Tamsin Grimmer
ISBN 978 1 78592 179 7
eISBN 978 1 78450 450 2

Learning through Movement and Active Play in the Early Years
A Practical Resource for Professionals and Teachers
Tania Swift
ISBN 978 1 78592 085 1
eISBN 978 1 78450 346 8

Helping Children Develop a Positive Relationship with Food
A Practical Guide for Early Years Professionals
Jo Cormack
ISBN 978 1 78592 208 4
eISBN 978 1 78450 486 1

Supporting Toddlers' Wellbeing in Early Years Settings
Strategies and Tools for Practitioners and Teachers
Edited by Helen Sutherland and Yasmin Mukadam
ISBN 978 1 78592 262 6
eISBN 978 1 78450 552 3

The
EARLY YEARS
Movement Handbook

A Principles-Based Approach to Supporting Young
Children's Physical Development, Health and Wellbeing

LALA MANNERS

Foreword by Professor Gareth Stratton

Illustrated by Tilly Power

Jessica Kingsley *Publishers*
London and Philadelphia

The epigraph on page 24 is reproduced from Robinson 2007 with kind permission from TED. To watch the full talk, visit TED.com
The epigraph on page 39 is reproduced from Connell and McCarthy 2014 with kind permission from Free Spirit Publishing.
The epigraph on page 60 is reproduced from Fortunati in Pace 2014 with kind permission from Bloomsbury Publishing.
The epigraph on page 90 is reproduced from Malloch and Trevarthen 2010 with kind permission from Oxford University Press.
The epigraphs on page 106 have been reproduced from PSLA 2013 with kind permission from Pre-school Learning Alliance.
The epigraph on page 195 is reproduced from Manning-Morton 2017 with kind permission from Early Education.
The epigraph on page 232 is reproduced from The Carpenter's Pencil by Manuel Rivas, translated by Jonathan Dunne. Published by Harvill Press. Reprinted by permission of The Random House Group Limited © 2001.

Every effort has been made to trace copyright holders and to obtain their permission for the use of copyright material where necessary to do so. The author and the publisher apologise for any omissions and would be grateful if notified of any acknowledgements that should be incorporated in future reprints or editions of this book.

First published in 2019
by Jessica Kingsley Publishers
73 Collier Street
London N1 9BE, UK
and
400 Market Street, Suite 400
Philadelphia, PA 19106, USA

www.jkp.com

Copyright © Lala Manners 2019
Foreword copyright © Gareth Stratton 2019
Illustrations copyright © Tilly Power 2019

Front cover image illustrated by Tilly Power.

Library of Congress Cataloging in Publication Data
A CIP catalog record for this book is available from the Library of Congress

British Library Cataloguing in Publication Data
A CIP catalogue record for this book is available from the British Library

ISBN 978 1 78592 260 2
eISBN 978 1 78450 546 2

Printed and bound in Great Britain

To Harriet and Kate

Contents

Part Two: Into Practice

Foreword

This text captures a lifetime of thinking and practice by Dr Manners focusing on her passion for growth and development in the early years. Lala beautifully captures the challenges of the time, the stresses placed on children by an ever more demanding, managed world in the age of the internet and information communicated to every corner of human existence including early childhood.

The pervasion of technology into the lives of young children and the peers and adults who nurture them has disrupted the normal processes of human development. Development is optimal when all senses are challenged in physical and social environments that afford interactions to occur at a pace appropriate to physical and psychological needs. As a result the 'space for the physical' seems to be ever diminished and to an extent has lost its value.

The Early Years Movement Handbook returns the reader to the deep rooted philosophical principles of Descartes, Merleau-Ponty, Locke and Rousseau bringing us forward to the current debate about 'Physical Literacy', a concept created by Margaret Whitehead that is being further developed by academics and practitioners across a range of disciplines.

The UN article 31, 'The rights of the child', is central to the essence of this text. Starting 'where children are' is so important and ways of providing environments and affordances through which children may explore and challenge themselves physically and emotionally are uniquely explained through the 'movement canopy' principle included in the text.

The simple and effective examples of the use of apparatus, music and the environment are timeless. Professionals may explore and develop these approaches whilst also providing easily accessible ideas for parents and families to properly support young children's overall development, health and wellbeing.

Having a strong academic background in child development, Dr Manners also expertly crafts the theoretical underpinnings of Froebel, Montessori, Steiner, Pikler, Goldschmied and Gascoyne into the text, and extends these abstract academic underpinnings into the 'real-world', providing tangible examples and processes critical for ensuring optimal child development.

While this text is wonderfully crafted it also captures the 'quantity and quality' debate. The quantity debate (primarily driven by the childhood obesity epidemic) is really one where children are simply expected to 'move more'. There are international guidelines that quantify the amount of time that children should be moving. Three hours daily (accumulative) is apparently optimal whilst reducing the time young children should spend restrained in highchairs, buggies, and car-seats – and engaging with hand-held screens.

But 'moving more' often undermines the endless opportunities for adding a quality dimension to movement. *The Early Years Movement Handbook* critically addresses quality in movement, so that children may effectively engage in quality physical experiences while growing up in a hugely complex world. One in which 'outside' is perceived as dangerous, yet inside seems to become ever more 'cyber dangerous'.

This is a wonderful book, there is no text quite like it and it's a 'must read' for any person interested in giving children the best possible start in life. I am particularly drawn to Plato who said that 'you can discover more about a person in an hour of play, than a year of conversation'. Dr Manners expertly *identifies the value* of movement and *values its identity*. She places this as the most central, constant pillar in the development of children, physically, socially and emotionally. This makes it a seminal contribution for all policy makers, professionals, practitioners and parents – congratulations, Lala.

Gareth Stratton
Professor of Paediatric Exercise Science
Deputy Pro-Vice Chancellor
Physical Activity, Sport, Health and Wellbeing
Head of School of Sport and Exercise Sciences
Swansea University

Acknowledgements

So many wonderful people have influenced this book over what seems a lifetime of teaching, training, educating and writing. Observing the power of movement to extend and illuminate learning has always been a privilege and pleasure.

My particular thanks go to Gareth Stratton and Lesley Johnson – both have been instrumental in providing the forensic questioning and analysis needed to create a clear and focused argument for movement as the basis of learning and development in young children.

Thank you also to my many friends and colleagues in the field – you know who you are. Your unwavering support, generosity, advice and belief have been hugely appreciated. I hope I have done our work justice.

Most of all, thank you to all the children I have had the joy of being with – you have taught me so much, and without your inspiration, this book would never have been written.

Introduction

How children's bodies are perceived and valued, and the status accorded to childhood generally, has a significant impact on a wide range of policies. Environment, housing, transport, health, education and welfare initiatives are directly affected by the priorities established by stakeholders and agencies engaged with young children's physical health and wellbeing.

Inevitably, these priorities vary greatly between countries and change over time. For some, nutrition, hygiene, shelter, vaccination, water and medicine are the focus. For others, it may be obesity prevention, access to outdoor play, ensuring the availability of sporting opportunities and supporting mental health and emotional wellbeing.

On a macro level, children are physically affected and protected by the following global agreements:

- In 1989, governments worldwide adopted the United Nations Convention on the Rights of the Child (UNCRC).[1] Children should be treated as 'human beings with a distinct set of rights instead of passive objects of care and charity'. These rights describe what a child needs to survive, grow and fulfil their potential in the world. All agencies must work together to protect and ensure their physical and mental health.

- In 2000, the United Nations Educational, Scientific and Cultural Organization (UNESCO) 'Education For All' (EFA) initiative was adopted by the World Education Forum.[2] The subsequent 'Dakar Framework for Action' included six goals – the first being: 'To expand early childhood care and education.'

- In 2015, the Global Strategy for Women's, Children's and Adolescent's Health 2016–30 was reviewed by the World Health Organization (WHO).[3] This 'envisions a world in which every woman, child and adolescent in every setting realises their rights to physical and mental health and wellbeing, has social and economic opportunities and is able to participate fully in shaping prosperous and sustainable societies.'

Early childhood is now considered a critical time for learning and development, a period of emerging agency and personal responsibility, years in which physical health and wellbeing must be protected, supported and maintained. Global initiatives agree that Early Childhood Development (ECD) is important, that 'it is about the foundation for individual and societal progress that has an economic payback for all'.

However, global investment in ECD is limited and is sourced mainly from health and/or education foundations. In developing countries, less than 5 per cent of government budgets are allocated to education, and only 2 per cent to health. On average, 0.5 per cent of funding is directed at young children.

Interest in children's bodies over the past 100 years has led to a marked decline in mortality and disease and an increase in height and weight related to age. Physical development, physical activity, movement, health and wellbeing are, in various combinations, present in a range of Early Years curricula.

Three issues have emerged that present a significant challenge to children's health and wellbeing and impact on practice related to children's physical development and physical activity.

First, obesity. In 1990, globally, 32 million children aged 0–5 years were obese. By 2014, this figure had risen to 41 million. The predicted figure for 2025 is 75 million. In developing countries, there has been a 30 per cent increase in childhood obesity in the last ten years. In the UK, it is estimated that 12 per cent of 3-year-olds are overweight or obese, rising to 26 per cent at age 5 and 32 per cent at age 11.[4]

Despite the dire warnings, we were not adequately prepared for the effect that obesity and weight status issues would have on all areas of childhood development. Should we now factor into all provisions related to health and wellbeing an element of obesity prevention? Is moving for movement's sake – just for fun and enjoyment – no longer of value? Must children demonstrate a level of engagement with physical activity that has proven quantifiable benefits for their physical health? Does our remit now include ensuring that the dispositions and behaviours that impact on long-term habitual physical activity are embedded and visible?

Inevitably, a level of tension has arisen between different approaches to young children's physical activity. Is 'moving to learn' as they 'learn to move' most important or is the priority to ensure they experience the optimum level of physical activity for health reasons as a prescribed early preventive intervention?

Second, the prevalence of digital technology (DT). Factual and anecdotal evidence (see Chapter 11) suggests that the explosion of availability and use of handheld devices has led to a significant increase in early eyesight problems (particularly short sight), behavioural issues (notably, listening and concentration), difficulties in engaging in mainstream curricular activities that demand a high degree of fine-motor skills, and an unhealthy interest in body image for children so young.

Third, curricular demands. Despite global frameworks that stress the importance of smooth physical development and physical activity, and the presence of Physical Development as a 'prime area' in the current Early Years Foundation Stage Curriculum (EYFSC),[5] it is becoming increasingly necessary to justify time and resources spent on supporting this developmental domain. It is no longer enough that physical development is *present* in the framework; it has to *earn* its place, pincered by planning and timetabling demands that, in turn, must accommodate frequently changing central directives and priorities.

This book has been written to present 'the case for movement' as a profoundly important factor in ensuring children's smooth overall development, health and wellbeing.

Approaches to supporting physical development in the Early Years and establishing provision for physical activity fall broadly into two camps: programmes and principles. They are not mutually exclusive by any means and, in practice, are used equally by teachers as they adapt and react to changing needs and situations.

More so than any other domain, physical development must accommodate a wide range of variables, and in the absence of a cohesive strategy or rationale for provision it is vitally important to appreciate the difference between these approaches so that informed decisions may be made that support best practice.

The programme approach. Historically, physical activity programmes have been designed for sport, gymnastics and dance. However, many programmes now make explicit links to the EY curriculum and the issue of 'school readiness'. Whatever the specific focus, physical activity programmes share these characteristics:

- The acquisition, rehearsal and refinement of discrete physical skills/ competencies is central to the design and delivery of practical sessions.

- Skills are acquired sequentially and enhanced through repetition over time.

- A graded syllabus with accompanying assessment procedures is followed.

- Apparatus will be skill-specific and linked to teamwork or competition.

- Teaching resources often include laminated cards and manuals that may be shared between professionals.

- Rewards may include stickers, certificates, cups and medals.

There are many advantages to using this approach. Activity programmes are generally simple to deliver, monitor and assess. They use time efficiently and immediate results are evident. Uniformity of movement is assured, and children become adept at replicating movements on demand. They also become very competent at processing complex verbal instructions. A direct teaching style is adopted that suits a range of physical disciplines.

The programme approach has its disadvantages. Creativity and self-expression are not generally encouraged, and it is often difficult to successfully accommodate variations in development and ability within a specific age range. The focus on physical performance and an end product rarely accounts for other areas of development that are profoundly affected by children's physical experiences.

The principles approach has a long and illustrious history. Central to mid-twentieth-century pedagogical thinking, physical development was never considered as separate or distinct from other developmental domains. It was recognised as informing and supporting all areas of learning, and from this understanding clear principles emerged.

Provision for physical development was seamlessly threaded through daily practice as young children were afforded a range of physical experiences that encouraged self-direction and discovery.

The positive habits, behaviours and dispositions that engagement in physical activity supported (generally considered as important 'life skills') were fully appreciated and considered to share parity of status with the physical skills children were acquiring.

There are very sound reasons for implementing a principles approach:

- Physical experience affects all areas of learning and development – particularly communication, language and emotional domains.

- Opportunities for movement and physical activity are many, varied and may be embedded in daily practice – they are not confined to specific times or places and are not reliant on particular clothing or equipment.

- It is not primarily performance- or goal-focused. Progress may emerge in unusual or unexpected ways and regressions and plateaus have equal value.

- It allows for differences in children's interests, abilities and levels of engagement.

- Inclusion is supported by adults and children at all times.

- Children's contributions are actively acknowledged and valued.

- A wide variety of resources and materials are used that are familiar, easily accessible and manageable.

- Physical activity is an organic part of daily life, not an 'issue' that requires continual monitoring and formal assessment.

Part One of the book presents the eight guiding principles that inform and support practice in physical development. They are not designed to be part of a checklist or slavishly followed in any way but aim to provide material to answer the fundamental question, 'Why bother?'

Why bother to focus on physical development when 'it happens anyway'? Young children obviously have boundless energy and never sit still – so, why make such an issue of creating opportunities for them to move and be active? Why give ourselves more work when the pressure to deliver on other curricular areas is so great?

Much has changed in a generation, and we can no longer assume that children will experience the variety, quality and quantity of physical activity that properly supports their overall development, health and wellbeing. We now need to be much more proactive and assertive in making the case for physical development practice. Understanding these principles will provide essential material to support the argument that movement matters.

Some chapters will no doubt be more interesting and relevant to you than others. This is to be expected. There may be sections that affirm and validate your practice, others that may puzzle or provoke. At different times you may need information or inspiration, and often a simple increase in underpinning knowledge leads to greater motivation and confidence.

Part Two answers the second question, 'How do I do it?' How can movement and physical activity be embedded in daily practice? How can a wide variety of opportunities be provided that *all* children can engage in? How can different approaches to planning support provision? Chapter 9 focuses on the 0–1 'Foundation' year – in which critical early movement skills are acquired. Chapter 10 highlights how these foundation skills are further refined between 1 and 3 years to support the body as the primary 'Enabling' environment. Chapter 11, 'I Move, Therefore I Am', presents a range of possibilities to ensure this maxim is effectively supported in practice with 3–5-year-olds.

Evidence from a particular study is included in Chapters 1–8 to create a common thread and maintain focus. This project took place over a school year in a language unit attached to a mainstream nursery. Initially, Nina, the resident Speech Language Therapist (SLT), worked alongside me to deliver a ten-week movement intervention programme (the term is used *very* loosely here) to a group of five children aged 4–4.6 years. The following term, she delivered the programme independently to the same group, while I worked with a second group of children who were also in her care. The project was multilayered and multifaceted, so, although the evidence included here gives just a glimpse of the whole picture, it has been chosen specifically to reflect how the eight principles may work in practice.

This book is not a manual or a programme. It may be picked up as and when needed to affirm, inspire or guide. Interesting nuggets may be found for further exploration, to be shared with others, including parents, carers and fellow professionals. Deliberate echoes between Parts 1 and 2 are also included that are designed to reinforce critical points.

What we should try to remember is that:

> *Despite all our best intentions, we cannot get everything right for children all the time – and ultimately life's challenges, triumphs and disappointments will be experienced and managed in an entirely individual way. What we can do for children is provide the quality and quantity of movement experience that ensures they are physically able to respond positively to all opportunities and that they can depend on their bodies as a reliable resource in an ever-changing world.*[6]

Ultimately, we need to do what's right for children, what's needed and what works. This book aims to provide valuable material to help you make these decisions.

Part One

THE PRINCIPLES

1

The Body Is the Primary Source of Learning and Development

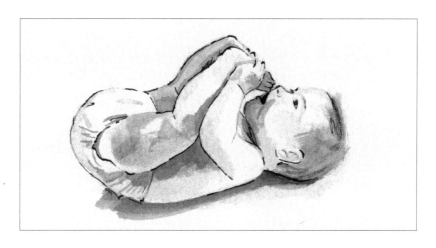

What happens is, as children grow up, we start to
educate them progressively from the waist up. And then
we focus on their heads. And slightly to one side.

Sir Ken Robinson, TED Talks[1]

I am smart precisely because I am a body. I don't
own it or inhabit it; from it, I arise.

Guy Claxton, *Intelligence in the Flesh*[2]

Joseph Tobin suggests that the body is disappearing in early childhood education. He proposes a range of reasons for this: the emergence of 'moral panic' related to sexual abuse (the emergence of 'safe touch' training), the declining influence of psychoanalysis (the ego replacing the body as a core concern) and the rise of brain research (the brain being the 'favourite organ' of the new millennium).[3]

Certainly, evidence of awareness and understanding of the critical role the body and movement skills play in young children's lives and the profound importance they have on overall learning and development is becoming increasingly scarce – in both policy and practice.

Even the terms used in various Early Years curricula differ as priorities jostle for pole position. In England, this component is called 'Physical Development', in Scotland 'Health and Wellbeing', in Northern Ireland 'Physical Development and Movement'. Is the status of the body as a primary source of learning also being undermined by the drive to address acknowledged health issues and the demands of increasingly formalised curricula – both areas that demand reliable, quantifiable data to justify expenditure on creating initiatives and training opportunities?

EDUCATION AND HEALTH PERSPECTIVES

The education and/or health approach to children's bodies is not just a domestic issue. Historically, Finland has always been more interested in supporting children's physical health through providing a wealth of resources for active outdoor play in the community. In response to new research data, however, this focus is changing. Movement skills are now considered to be a critical component in promoting learning – and there has been significant investment in training teachers to value the opportunities movement provides to nurture this. In contrast, South Africa always valued movement as a source of learning – particularly in supporting rural mothers and their children to become competent English speakers. In response to growing concerns about increasing rates of childhood obesity, the health benefits of engaging in regular physical activity have now become the prime focus.

To make the two approaches explicit, let us examine a simple task from both perspectives:

- Sit or stand comfortably.

- Rub your hands together – start slowly – then rub as fast as you can until they are hot.

- Take a deep breath, blow slowly on your palms.

- Repeat.

From a *learning* perspective, there is much to consider within this very simple task:

- The body must be in the correct position to start: balanced and poised for action – the arms and hands placed at exactly the right distance from the body to gain traction – the movement of the hands must be equal for both sides.

- Instructions need to be processed: What does 'rub' mean – or a 'deep' breath?

- How much force and speed is needed to create friction and heat? What is the best timing and rhythm for this action?

- What happens when you blow on your palms? Cause and effect – do they cool down? Why?

Now, let us look at this sequence from a *health* perspective – what areas are being highlighted:

- Strength is needed in the core muscles of the trunk to sit or stand still.

- Balance is necessary to keep the head and body correctly positioned.

- Strength is required in the shoulder joints and hands to rub hard enough to create heat.

- Coordination is important to ensure both hands are moving at the same time and at the same speed.

- Taking a deep breath expands the lungs – maximises oxygen intake.

- Blood flow increases with effort – the heart must pump harder.

So the actions are the same. Viewed from a learning perspective, the content is significant: this is not just 'active learning' but a meaningful physical experience that fuses learning across all developmental domains. In terms of health, the impact is probably minimal. I wouldn't go as far as Tobin, who writes that 'preschools are now a battle-zone in the war against the body, sites where the bodies of children and the adults who care for them fall under increasing scrutiny and discipline', but we have definitely arrived at a crossroads and must decide which road we take – and what works best for us. How can we acknowledge the undoubted benefits of the Finnish approach – but address issues shared by South Africa? How can we best support the enormous learning potential of the body and movement, and yet, take seriously the health issues that impact so negatively on children's lives?

HISTORICAL PERSPECTIVES

Maybe a historical perspective is useful to consider.

Historically, the body has played a central role in education (derived from the Latin verb *educere*, 'to lead out'). For the Ancient Greeks, education was inherently practical – and physical. Boys' education started at aged 7, when they learned to wrestle, run, throw and develop the specific skills included later in the Pentathlon. Dancing, in religious rites, military drills and civic processions, was considered to promote 'harmonious action with others' on and off the battlefield. Interestingly, performing the movement correctly, maintaining perfect posture, being a good loser and keeping temper under control all had parity of status with winning and receiving prizes.

Although the Romans appropriated much of Greek culture, after 146 BC, their attitude to the body was much harsher and more disciplined. Dancing and gymnastics were rejected in favour of brutal military drills and lessons in warfare. Education, though an apprenticeship system, was highly practical and based on supporting the principles of 'good citizenship'.

Descartes

The philosopher and mathematician René Descartes (1596–1650) is possibly the thinker most responsible for the radical change in the status of the body in education – from a significant and valuable source of learning (across all developmental domains) to a muted presence that is often misunderstood and undervalued in practice.

The phrases 'Cartesian split', 'Cartesian dualism' and 'Cartesian dichotomy' are frequently used to convey the separation of mind and body that Descartes advocated.

He was writing at a time when the authority of the Church was in decline and a predominantly religious understanding of the world was waning. New styles of knowledge were emerging as secular authorities took over roles previously assigned to the Church. His now famous dictum, 'I think, therefore I am', assumed that the 'higher truths' – previously bestowed by God – actually originated and existed outside the body. The only way to achieve these 'truths' and achieve 'body transcending rationality' was to engage in abstract, rational thought – to 'do science', then to refine this further by 'doing mathematics'. For Descartes, the only divinity that counted was the process of human thought that 'seemed to be able to float free of this earthly and bodily existence'. As many critics have pointed out, however, this 'process' actually happens to be the product of his 'specific, historically embodied life'.

Ian Burkitt writes that, 'This transition from an authoritarian to an autonomous mode of thinking led people to examine themselves more carefully and to view their bodily sensations and emotions as objects that were to be scrutinised, categorised, regulated, controlled and tested by doubt.'[4]

For Descartes, all knowledge, thinking, knowing, concepts and understandings are completely disconnected from any material or cultural body. For him, the sense of self – what constitutes the 'I' – lies in the *idea* that we exist: because we are capable of having this idea, herein lies our inner being, the essence of us. Descartes was so convinced that his own essence as a person was distinct from his physical body that he claimed he was what he was despite his body – his existence did not depend on his 'corporeal presence'.

Ultimately, for Descartes and his fellow 'Rationalists', the body is simply an object – something that entraps the 'I' and is quite distinct from the mind and thought.

He wrote the following with absolute certainty: 'There is nothing included in the concept of the body that belongs to the mind – and nothing in that of the mind that belongs to the body – the mind is a disembodied space – the organ of intelligence.'

A total separation between mind and body is thus effected, leading to a definitive division between 'an embodied knowledge of the world as it exists in space and time' and the thought processes that actually support understanding of its order.

Merleau-Ponty

In his theory of 'embodiment', the twentieth-century phenomenologist Maurice Merleau-Ponty (1908–61) challenged Descartes' 'rationalist' thinking by arguing that the body is the source of all knowing, and that sensory perceptions can, and should, be trusted: 'all human knowledge draws its sustenance from corporeal roots'.[5] For phenomenologists, everyone perceives the world from a unique perspective based on accumulated previous experience – we make sense of the world as it appears to us. They do not believe that there is anything concrete or objective 'out there' for us to understand; what individuals perceive are 'phenomena' ('appearances' in Greek): 'things as they appear to us – not necessarily things as explained by scientific discovery'.

The mind, to Merleau-Ponty, is inextricably biological and embodied; action is the key to understanding what it means to be human; we are not passive spectators in the world, we are 'enmeshed in a living relationship with it – through the medium of an active body'.

He suggests that thought is not structured in a mind that is distinct from the body, 'it is acquired bodily actions or habits that make thought possible'.

How these opposing philosophies play out on the educational field is interesting. For Wayne Bowman, there is growing evidence that 'intelligence' remains the abstract, mental, cerebral, disembodied construct it has always been; that there is still a stubborn divide between 'knowing that counts' and that can provide visible proof (e.g. worksheets) and 'that which does not'.[6]

He expresses concern that instead of valuing movement for its own sake – as something of intrinsic merit to children – we are slowly being lured into making claims for it in terms of cognitive benefits that are not only unfounded but should not be necessary.

Margaret Whitehead also makes an interesting point: that despite a robust rebuttal of Descartes' 'dualism' by academics, the language used about the body in daily life reaffirms the 'body as object'. She asks why we always refer to the body as a noun, as something that we can do things 'to' or 'with' or 'on' – we clothe, wash, feed 'it'? How difficult would it be to say, 'I *am* my body' rather than 'I *have* a body'?[7]

What did the great pedagogues, on whose legacy our practice is built, make of this debate? Curiously, there is little evidence in their work that it had much impact. They seemed to know instinctively that children's bodies are a profound source of learning, that there is no mind/body divide in their lives, and that movement is a magical source of imagination, creativity and positive energy.

Locke and Rousseau

John Locke (1632–1734) and Jean-Jacques Rousseau (1712–78) have much to say about children's bodies. Locke determined that 'curiosity' and 'liberty' are the prime motivating principles for children. Curiosity about themselves and their world drives children towards knowledge and it is the responsibility of parents to try and answer all their questions. Liberty in this context is the sense of independence in action – that children must be afforded the freedom to create and participate in their own active play. 'Education' therefore means supporting children to use this liberty wisely and productively. Locke was also very keen on dancing, 'that gives children manly thoughts and courage and encourages good manners'. Being physically active would train children to acquire lifelong healthy habits, and through daily interactions with adults, peers and the world, they may learn to manage their bodies and deal with 'social restraints and expectations'. There is not much evidence of enjoyment or fun here. Locke emphasises that bodies must be disciplined, tamed and organised: freedom to choose is fine up to a point, just so long as the status quo is preserved and compliance maintained.[8]

For Rousseau, education emerges from three sources: nature, men and things. All three must work together, coincide and lead to a common goal. He concluded that nature must determine the level of influence of the other two as it is the element over which we have the least control: in effect, nature must be answerable to education. When nature and society appear to be conflicted, society must decide between 'making a man' and 'making a citizen'.

Rousseau believed that children should be removed from the pressure and diktats of society and engage with nature in order to develop personal moral standing. The publication of *Émile* in 1762 was enormously influential. He considered reading to be 'the greatest plague of childhood' and any formal instruction for children younger than 5 years was not advocated. Education should be a 'joyful celebration of childhood' and children must learn through engagement with the natural world, through all the senses:

Give nature time to work before you take over her business, lest you interfere with her dealings. You are afraid to see him spending his early years doing nothing. What! – is it nothing to be happy – nothing to run and jump all day? He will never be so busy again all his life long.[9]

What an extraordinarily perceptive statement – and how apposite it remains as we determine how best to support young children's physical development within the current educational climate.

So, essentially, Locke wants to produce effective social beings who fit in and acquire the skills to navigate life with ease – citing successful leaders in political and social arenas who actively support democracy and liberalism. Locke's child is to become a man of action in society. Rousseau's concept of 'education' was not primarily about training up future citizens. He emphasised that 'becoming a man' should be viewed as a valued process in itself – as being of intrinsic merit to individuals – not just a means of producing a necessary, fully functional societal resource. Rousseau's child therefore is educated to lead a natural life of beauty and simplicity apart from society – which all sounds a bit elitist and impractical now, but his thinking had a significant impact on future provision for children's health and education. His fictitious child Émile ushered in the 'great and innocent age of the child' by loosening the vice-like grip that adults had previously maintained over every area of children's lives. His work later influenced doctors in Germany, the USA and England to reconstruct health standards for children based on his belief in the importance of proactively engaging with the outdoor environment, physical activity and the wearing of comfortable clothing and shoes.

Johann Heinrich Pestalozzi (1746–1827) was influenced by Rousseau in his determination that children's 'innate faculties' must be developed in accordance with nature. Children should be given 'real' experiences and engage with 'real' things to ensure their smooth overall development. In a nod to Comenius (1592–1670), he emphasised the importance of including all the senses in educational provision. For Pestalozzi, life is about action. Schooling should be focused on 'interdependent action and fitness for life'. In his schools, swimming, walking and good food were all considered important, and provision was well made for them.[10]

For Robert Owen (1771–1858), fresh air and physical activity (particularly marching and dancing) promoted 'cheerfulness and contentment'. Promotion of physical wellbeing was considered important as a means of reforming 'vicious habits'. This may seem harsh to us, but his acknowledgement that the discipline and effort required to maintain a healthy body may have a positive impact on other life skills actually fits in well with modern thinking.[11]

Friedrich Froebel (1782–1854) believed that physical play underpinned children's smooth overall development – that they learn by doing. In his settings, children from 1 to 7 years were encouraged to garden and enjoy nature. Nature walks and the freedom that outdoor activities provided were considered enormously important while singing (the 'mother songs'), and activities in a circle created opportunities for increased social interaction.[12]

Rudolf Steiner (1861–1925) proposed that learning should be based on the 'three Rs': rhythm, repetition and reverence. In this approach, children's physicality is a vital element. Rhythm helps to harness energy, provides a structure for movement and makes children physically confident, strong and secure. Repetition increases the sense of security and stability whilst also supporting memory and learning. Reverence applies to interactions with other people and the environment and also includes a positive approach to nutrition and care for the body.

Again, we see an emphasis on the intrinsic value of practical experience: gardening, cooking, cleaning and constructing. The habits and dispositions that children acquire as they engage in these activities are considered to have parity of status with the physical skills they are practising. The affective, physical and cognitive domains are all equally important. There is enormous respect for children's individual capabilities and self-direction in the Steiner approach, and the physical element of their lives is truly valued in practice.[13]

Maria Montessori (1870–1952) was also influenced by Rousseau, Pestalozzi and Froebel. She emphasised the importance of concrete, real experiences and materials in ensuring children's understanding of abstract principles. Her science background supported her acute observational and evidence-gathering skills that suggested children learn most effectively through movement and use of all the senses. In common with the Steiner approach, caring for and respecting the physical self, the environment and others is fundamental to Montessori practice.[14]

All these great educationalists support the importance of the body in education: not just in terms of health – that fresh air, good nutrition and physical activity are of benefit – but also in recognising the immense learning potential inherent in all movement experience.

As a robust defence against the perceived lingering influence of Cartesian dualism in education, and in a concerted effort to ensure the body is properly valued by policymakers, Merleau-Ponty's theory of 'embodiment' is gaining traction.

Chris Shilling describes embodiment as 'persons experiencing them-selves in and as their bodies'.[15] Bowman describes it as a state in which 'the body is minded, the mind is embodied, and both body and mind are culturally mediated'.[16]

Bowman is right when he says that breaking free from the mind/body dichotomy in practice requires decisive action and that this means addressing two very fundamental issues. First, we must vigorously refute the assumption that 'sensing and acting in the world' are not cognitive achievements. Second, we should question very seriously the claim that language alone comprises the ultimate or ideal measure of cognition.

Embodied learning considers the mind as an 'activity' emergent from, structured by and inseparable from bodily experience. The idea that intelligence can be embodied in physical structures and that such structures can therefore take some of the strain off minds and brains is central to the science of 'embodied cognition'. Guy Claxton makes a pugnacious case for embodied learning: that on a cellular and molecular level, the mind and body are intricately related; that feelings are somatic events; that the brain is servant, not master, of the body; it is a 'chatroom', not a 'directorate'; seeing, thinking, deciding and acting are not 'strung out like different departments in a factory' – they are inextricably entwined. He proposes that the physical body is a critical vehicle through which we relate to the world because of its vital role in language acquisition and in moderating emotions.[17]

PHYSICAL LITERACY

The emergence of 'physical literacy' is an interesting development of the 'embodiment' debate within the teaching of physical education. The word 'literacy' was initially chosen as not only is this a well-known concept but it also ensures that physical education can move away from a purely performance- and skills-based approach to something that is wider, more holistic and interactive with the environment.

Rebecca Lloyd gives physical literacy more context here: 'The body is the medium through which we have a world. Motility is how we attribute meaning. Embodiment is the key to the world: how we relate to it, make sense of it and adapt it to our design.'[18] Whitehead and Lloyd are clear that the concept of physical literacy is designed to underpin and inform practical approaches to embodiment and physicality. Whitehead describes physical literacy thus: 'As appropriate to each individual's endowment, physical literacy can be described as the motivation, confidence, physical competence, knowledge and understanding to maintain physical activity throughout the lifecourse.'[19]

Lloyd concurs that physical literacy is an embodied approach to physical activity that 'prioritises the thinking and feeling learner'. Movement should be considered as a 'body-mind world phenomenon', not simply a set of techniques that must be acquired, rehearsed and refined for a predetermined purpose. In her 'function-to-flow' model, she determines how teachers can imbue practice with an emotional and sensible element.

How does the physical literacy approach manifest itself in practice? As yet, this remains undefined. 'What does it actually look like in practice? What makes it different?' are questions yet to be answered in any cohesive way. The flexibility of the approach is a significant strength, but it means that interpretations of the central tenets become many, varied and endlessly debated. Canada 'Sport for Life' defines it as: 'the mastering of fundamental movement skills and fundamental sports skills that permit a child to read their environment and make appropriate decisions – allowing them to move confidently and with control in a wide range of physical activity situations'. In South Africa, physical literacy for children lies in 'possessing the competence and confidence in fundamental movement skills and fundamental sports skills combined with the ability to read their environment and make appropriate decisions'. In Northern Ireland, it is 'the ability to use a range of fundamental movement skills in a competent manner, with the capacity to apply them with confidence in a range of settings that can lead to sustained involvement in sport and physical activity'.[20]

Dominic Haydn-Davies suggests that, 'In essence it is a disposition rather than a product or a process.'[21]

For Gavin Ward, however, physical literacy is 'limited to an exclusively philosophical understanding of human movement – [it] becomes less useful because it simply swaps a dualist position (mind/body) for a monist (unified whole) position'. He goes on to say: 'Developing physically literate pupils requires the development of competency and efficiency in moving. As a consequence the debate spirals back to the tensions created when dominant ways of moving are privileged.'[22]

How useful is the physical literacy approach to Early Years practice? It may be more relevant to adults – to support their personal 'physical journeys' and hence promote positive attitudes towards children's physicality and movement skills rather than as an effective framework that informs practice. We will see.

Young children are by their very nature embodied. They do not experience the mind/body dichotomy in the same way as adults. Their lives are mediated by physical experience – by immediate and continual contact with people, places and things. For them, all learning is embodied. Their bodies are not merely objects to be presented to the world in a particular way – to be battled over and fought with, or compared to ideal representations as seen on social media. I agree with Jennifer Thom that there are 'no sharp boundaries to bodies – bodies are nested in bodies – bodies of knowledge unfold from – and are enfolded in the bodies of knowledge: knowing, doing, being are ultimately indistinguishable aspects of the same whole'.[23]

Some writers go even further – that not only is embodied learning important for children, but that their very concept of self is fundamentally related to movement and the body.

Shaun Gallagher suggests that from the very beginning of life there exists a 'primary notion of self' – what he terms the 'proprioceptive self': meaning 'a sense of self that involves a sense of one's own motor possibilities, body postures and body powers'.[24]

Ian Burkitt also writes that:

The original sense of 'I' is the 'I can' – a practical sense of the body's capabilities and therefore the sense of identity possessed by humans is not based on disembodied thought, nor in early visual representation of self. Instead the sense of self we develop is primarily based on the feel we have of our body and the way it connects us to the world.[25]

For Maxine Sheets-Johnstone, all thinking is:

consummately wedded to bodily life; indeed it begins in, and with, bodily experience. In the most fundamental sense, it is modelled along the living lines of our bodies… We make sense of ourselves in the course of moving… Our capacity to make sense of ourselves, to grow kinetically into the bodies we are is…the beginning of cognition.[26]

The neurobiologist Daniel Wolpert concludes:

We have a brain for one reason and one reason only: that's to produce adaptable and complex movements. Movement is the only way we have of affecting the world around us… I believe that to understand movement is to understand the whole brain. And therefore it's important to remember when you are studying memory, cognition, sensory processing, they're there for a reason – and that reason is action.[27]

The Spatial Reasoning Study Group

As an example of the embodied approach to learning in action, it is useful to look at the work of the International Spatial Reasoning Study Group in the field of Early Years mathematics. Initially based on the work of mathematician Dikram Tahta, the group advocates that spatial reasoning, not simply awareness, is intimately linked to locomotor and manipulative skills, and that it is the reasoning element in mathematics that is being compromised due to endless paper-based testing and demand for quantitative evidence of achievement. Being able to manipulate shape and pattern, being confident to make errors and use appropriate mathematical language may be effectively supported by using children's bodies to 'illuminate knowledge as concrete (em)bodied and live(d)'.[28]

Spatial reasoning is learned through movement and engagement with the real, physical environment. It is a specific aspect of nonverbal reasoning, seeking answers to 'why, when and how'. It does not require visible proof of learning via worksheets or specific assessment procedures, but advocates the idea of 'conceptual blending', in which there is 'the conceptual combination of two distinct cognitive structures with fixed correspondence between them'.

Thom uses the concept of a circle as an example: children will first make circles individually with different body parts, then experience this shape in a group, use it in a dance sequence and finally recognise it in 2D form on a page. They will also be able to talk about circles and draw or paint them in vivid, energetic presentations.

For this group of academics, embodied cognition is critical. Movement and bodily experience provide the anchor and primary reference point for all conceptual frameworks. Motor development, not age, determines children's spatial readiness ability. Their spatial skills aged 3 are acknowledged to be strong predictors of mathematical ability aged 5.

THE STUDY

The idea of 'conceptual blending' that they advocate was a very useful tool throughout the study. Between the movement sessions that Nina and the children experienced with me, their daily therapeutic language interventions continued. She began to appreciate that a less rigid approach to working with the group had some unexpected benefits.

In conversation with me during Week Four of the initial ten-week programme she revealed the following:

Interestingly, we were doing 'long' this week, and I thought about how to combine the concept of 'long' with some communication work. So we stretched our bodies out long on the floor, and then everybody helped make a long path of bricks. They were much more able to grasp this concept having performed it physically, and they were much more sensitive about space and each other's ability too.

She also added the following insights a few weeks later:

The last time I did something with sound, we did 'loud' and 'not being loud' and 'being Mr Noisy'. I was trying to make them listen rather than lining up the language with direct experience, and I'd never connected up using their own force for sounds. I'm always having to stick to specific vocabulary and work on the paradigm of being something and not something, like being noisy and not being noisy – so I can really see now how using their bodies makes it much more relevant and fun for them.

A movement approach to therapeutic intervention gave Nina additional tools to support the children's language needs. Aligning concepts with physical experience provided relevant and meaningful material on which future mainstream therapeutic provision could build.

To paraphrase Howard Gardner: we desire a world in which all children have the chance to raise their own questions, create their own answers and to approach them in ways that are their own. Of course, the Early Years health agenda must be properly accommodated, but this will be much easier to do if children are afforded continual opportunities to learn in which their bodies play a central role – and in which their generic interest and enjoyment in all things physical is proactively supported.

Children's physical experience and embodied learning should never become part of yet another box-ticking exercise. Much of it is profoundly personal and ephemeral, and it should be respected for its intrinsic merits – not for any proof of progress it may provide for adults.

Janice Ross reminds us that:

The parameters of language are not the parameters of knowing. How applicable is this to young children, for whom movement experiences are profoundly vivid, meaningful and life-changing? Do we interfere with their reflection and ordering by continually asking them to talk about it, by urging them to write things down? Is there not merit in leaving it there as an experience in its own right that has intrinsic merit and validity at that particular moment on that particular day?[29]

For the body to reappear in early childhood education means recognising fully the historical precedents and pedagogical thinking on which a movement approach to learning is based. As children learn to understand and value their bodies they will appreciate the benefits to overall health and wellbeing that movement and physical activity offer.

The Canadian 'Futurist' Hans Peter Moravec – despite his work in robotics and artificial intelligence – writes the following:

> *Encoded in the large, highly evolved sensory and motor portions of the human brain is a billion years of experience about the nature of the world and how to survive in it. The deliberate process we call reasoning is, I believe, the thinnest veneer of human thought, effective only because it is supported by this much older and powerful, though usually unconscious, sensorimotor knowledge. We are all prodigious Olympians in perceptual and motor areas, so good we make the difficult look easy.*[30]

2

Start Where They Are

They are where they are – start from there.

Gill Connell and Cheryl McCarthy, *A Moving Child is a Moving Child*[1]

Children themselves are remarkably adept at gauging where they are in terms of physical competency. Watch a group of mixed-age children closely as they engage in physical play: you will see how the younger, smaller, weaker and less confident children will carefully calibrate when and how to join in. They seem to have a peculiar sixth sense as to success or failure, enjoyment or struggle. If they *can*, they *will* run faster, climb higher, shout louder, balance for longer; design their own challenges, take risks, manage their bodies in differing environments in ways that are right for them at that particular time, with a complete understanding of why they're doing what they're doing.

It is we as adults who often misjudge and afford them opportunities that don't support, inspire or enthuse. We may get the environment wrong (too big, too small); offer inappropriate equipment (too heavy, too large, not enough); use confusing language; include instructions that are too long and complex or implement programs that minimise noise and risk, and may be unsuitable for developing bodies. The lure of stickers, certificates, specialist clothing and equipment often disguises the fact that children are experiencing a narrow range of movement possibilities that bear minimal relevance to daily life or encourage wider engagement in physical activity. We often misjudge because *we* don't know 'where they are'. Attached to ages and stages and developmental norms and panicked about obesity issues, are we forgetting the intrinsic importance to children themselves of the smooth acquisition, rehearsal and refinement of movement skills?

If you really want to know what physical skills mean to children, where *they* think they are, ask them three questions: 'What are you good at? What are your friends good at? What are you not so good at?' I conducted a small-scale study of 35 children between 3.9 and 4.6 years, 20 boys and 15 girls, across a range of settings. Top of the list of replies for the first question was 'playing outside', followed by 'catching [playing "It"], running, jumping and hiding'. The answers to the second question prompted similar replies, even though some of these friendships were undoubtedly imaginary. Not one child mentioned reading, writing, numbers or puzzles. In answer to the third question, their replies were: 'concentrating, doing my work, sitting still, listening and tidying up' – all significant elements of the adult agenda.[2]

In a range of sociometric status studies in which children were asked to rate their peer group, the degree of peer acceptance emerged as a powerful predictor of current and future psychological adjustment. So what makes children popular? Mostly, being active, leading activities, making suggestions and structuring activities.[3] Daniel Walsh suggests that, 'Young children's friendships are profoundly physical. They develop their sense of physical self in physical contact with others.'[4]

Children inhabit bodies that are a constant source of puzzlement, mystery and enjoyment but, as Chris Shilling writes, they must also 'accept constantly changing bodies and changing institutional contexts in which meaning is given to these changes'.[5] Parental delight in the first pointing finger, wobbly steps and new teeth all too soon informs children's dawning realisation that an 'acceptable body' must be controlled and controllable. Children's bodies begin as 'objects', as parents endlessly engage in 'managing the exterior' through buying clothes and shoes and changing hairstyles. Shilling again: 'The child who is clean and dressed exhibits the social status of carers. The child becomes the symbol of adult creation and a moral statement of adult achievements.'[6] Harsh perhaps, but he makes a valid point. Young children deal daily with the challenges, irritations, pleasure and pain, of their changing bodies. Shoes get too tight, nappies become unnecessary, teeth fall out, hair and nails need cutting, yet their priorities often seem quite different from their parents' and carers'.

In our questionable need for children to conform to adult agendas, do we, consciously or otherwise, buy into intrusive monitoring, assessment and measuring procedures? Have we perhaps overlooked the base: are children's bodies in danger of being acted upon, regulated, disciplined and monitored to such a point that what *they* feel and understand about their bodies has disappeared into the ether and is no longer considered a valuable source of information for the planning and provision of physical activities?

Shilling also remarks that, 'Schools are involved in the production of particular forms of bodily control and expression, which can serve to obtain from children and adults forms of consent that the mind could otherwise refuse.'[7]

There will always be tension between adult and child agendas regarding physicality and physical skills. This is apparent in adult approaches to children's health, wellbeing, growth and development.

'HEALTH' – DERIVED FROM THE OLD ENGLISH WORD 'HÆLO', MEANING 'WHOLE'

In a Harvard paper, 'The Foundations of Lifelong Health Are Built in Early Childhood', the authors write that:

Health is more than merely the absence of disease. It is an evolving human resource that helps children and adults adapt to the challenges of everyday life, resist infections, cope with adversity, feel a sense of personal wellbeing and interact with their surroundings in ways that promote successful development.

Health is a state of being that is subject to wide individual, social and cultural interpretation and results from the interplay between individual perceptions and social influences.[8]

'Childhood' as a specific timespan emerged in the nineteenth century through the development of mass schooling and the grouping of children by age. Understanding of the child's body was central to the rise of philanthropic and political reforms. For the McMillan sisters, poor children could be 'rescued' through positive educational experience, fresh air, exercise and good nutrition to become 'agents of the new social future'.[9] Over time, the welfare of children's bodies became intricately linked to the overall welfare of the nation. In 1908, the School Medical Service was established in England; treatment and inspection clinics were offered within a medical framework and poor health became an explanation for *educational* failure.

In the reports by Frank Field (2010),[10] Graham Allen (2011)[11] and Dame Clare Tickell (2011),[12] the relationship between children's physical health and their ability to achieve in educational settings is made clear.

Where does movement and physical activity fit into this overall picture? In a systematic review of the link between physical activity and health, the New Zealand authors write the following:

In infants there was low to moderate quality evidence to suggest that increased or higher physical activity was positively associated with improved measures of adiposity, motor skill development and cognitive development. In toddlers there was moderate quality evidence to suggest that increased or higher physical activity was positively associated with bone and skeletal health. In pre-schoolers there was low to high quality evidence on the relationship between increased or higher physical activity and improved measures of adiposity, motor skill development, psychosocial health and cardiometabolic health indicators.[13]

A report for the New Zealand Ministry of Health also includes this statement:

Some have compared a child's evolving health status in the early years to the launching of a rocket, as small disruptions that occur shortly after take-off can have very large effects on its ultimate trajectory.

Thus, 'getting things right' and establishing strong biological systems in early childhood can help to avoid costly and less effective attempts to 'fix' problems as they emerge later in life.[14]

WELLBEING

The health and wellbeing of young children are intimately related – but what do we really mean by 'wellbeing'? Thomas Weisner describes it as, 'The ability to successfully, resiliently and innovatively participate in the routines and activities deemed significant by a cultural community.'[15] For some, evidence of wellbeing includes: 'facial expressions such as smiling, bright sparkling eyes, body movements such as running, jumping, dancing, clapping hands, being bouncy, and moving about happily with purposeful movements'. For Anne O'Connor, 'Children who understand the benefits of physical activity and delight in using their bodies in creative ways for activities and movement indoors and out will achieve a sense of wellbeing.'[16]

For many, physical activity is connected to emotional wellbeing, a way of connecting with others in the world. O'Connor cites the 'Jabadao' project, a ten-year longitudinal study to determine the possible relationship between movement play and children's wellbeing. Using the Leuven Involvement Scale for Young Children[17] (see Chapter 7 for futher discussion on this),they suggest that children experienced 'increased levels of enjoyment, relaxation and inner peace, vitality, openness, self-confidence and being in touch with oneself' through engaging in movement play'.

A recent Norwegian study (part of the wider 'Stavanger Project: The Learning Child') explored the relationship between the 'variables' of children's wellbeing, play, social competence and movement skills.[18] Over a three-month period, 1084 children (530 girls and 554 boys) aged 30–33 months were observed regularly during play and everyday activities. They were assessed using valid and reliable instruments. The team conclude that:

Poor motor ability makes the physical activity associated with social engagement more demanding and may reduce a child's ability to deal with the social environment.

It is possible to understand movement skills as a necessary precondition that enables a child to participate in a play context where the child uses his body and at the same time participates in meaningful social interaction.

Evidence for a positive relationship between the variables was gained. Motor skills play a significant role in supporting social competence and play, which, in turn, is a major determinant of wellbeing in children at this age.

The researchers point out that, although 'it is reasonable to believe that gross-motor skills are more decisive with regard to social competence and play', the 'lack of a valid and reliable instrument to measure these was an issue'.

GROWTH

The health and wellbeing of children are intricately related to movement and physical activity. In turn, both are influenced by adult attitudes to their growth and development. Consider these statements:

- Growth is change of physical aspects of the organism.

- Growth is cellular.

- Growth is the change in shape, form, structure and size of the body.

- Growth stops at maturation.

- Growth is quantitative in nature and may be measured accurately.

The measurement of growth begins long before birth, as mothers' weight gain is monitored and babies' progress is charted through ultrasound scans. Birth weight assumes enormous importance as family members compare notes and possible genetic predictions are fully discussed.

Babies are weighed and measured and their head size checked regularly during the first year. By using centile charts, it may be determined whether these measurements are increasing within 'normal' margins. 'Normal' is decided by comparing individual patterns of growth with larger cohorts of children of the same age and gender.

Although these charts may provide reassurance – and flag up any specific areas of concern – growth rates vary widely and almost all are considered 'normal'. For children of any age and gender, only two-thirds will have measurements that fall within this range. Perhaps 'typical' and 'atypical' would be more useful terminology? 'Normal' is such a loaded word and 'typical' is more sensitive and descriptive.

For children themselves, getting physically bigger, rather than older, is possibly the most important aspect of their lives. In a recent interview with a nursery teacher, I asked her what attribute she thought had the most currency with the children in her group. Her reply was, 'Being big – definitely.' This exchange between two boys was later overheard in the playground: 'Your birthday is before mine.' – 'Yeah. I'll be 5 and I'll be bigger than you then.'

DEVELOPMENT

Consider these statements:

- Development is overall changes and progressive changes of the organism.

- Development is organisational.

- Development is structural change and functional progress of the body.

- Development is qualitative in nature.

- Development is subjective interpretation of change.

Two processes determine children's motor development that we should be aware of:

1. *Cephalocaudal* development refers to development that is 'top-down' – meaning it starts from the head and ends at the toes. If we think of a newborn baby: the head is well-developed to house the brain, whereas the feet and toes are relatively undeveloped, weak and not yet able to support the body or effect mobility. Muscular development starts with control of the head; this then spreads to the shoulders; once the infant can hold the head up unaided, the muscles surrounding the spine strengthen and the sitting position is achieved. Once crawling begins, the legs and feet are in continual motion, strengthening the muscles and ensuring the joints are in the optimum position for future standing and walking.

2. *Proximodistal* development describes the process of movement control emerging and extending from the 'proximal' (closest to the body) out to the 'distal' (furthest from the centre of the body). Motor control starts with the large muscle groups in the trunk, arms and legs as infants roll, crawl, sit, climb, push and pull, and spreads slowly to the smaller body parts of hands, feet and, finally, fingers.

Ignoring this developmental process can have very profound consequences – particularly if we ask young children to engage in activities for which they are simply not physically ready. A good example of this is the insistence on introducing writing exercises with small implements while the musculature in the shoulder girdle, elbows and wrists is still being formed and strengthened.

Historically, much of our knowledge about children's physical development has depended on theories based on milestones – or 'ages and stages'. Led by the American physician and psychologist Arnold Gesell (1880–1961), the 'maturationist' approach took pole position amongst developmental theories in the early twentieth century, claiming that the maturation of the nervous system (not the environment, culture or genetics) was the principal driver of physical, motor aspects of human behaviour.[19] The Griffiths Scales, the Bayley Scales of Infant Development and the Peabody Developmental Motor Scales are direct inheritors of this approach and are still widely used today in some form or other.

How useful are these frameworks really?

We should remember that Gesell's original research was based on a very narrow demographic – mainly white, male, middle-class children of European extraction – so, there is little acknowledgement of the differences in experiences, environment and culture that have such a significant impact on physical development. As Linda Pound points out, 'These highly detailed descriptions of norms of what some children *actually* do, have, however, come to be regarded as prescriptions of what children *should* do.'[20] Daniel Walsh also warns us that, 'The norms themselves become constraints that both enhance and restrict as society sets strong expectations about what children can and cannot do and should and should not do.'[21]

The developmental 'norms' Gesell established were also based on a very limited range of skills – that he claimed were 'lawful sequences that are never normally circumvented'.

But children *do* sometimes miss out on stages in their physical development and arrive at the same point as their peers at roughly the same time: there are many children worldwide who must learn to swim, climb or ride before they walk, or who are swaddled and miss the crawling stage completely – evidence suggests that they all 'get there in the end'.

This blog post from a parent beautifully illustrates the tension between our ongoing attachment to 'norms' and the reality of children's lives:

Eating implements, footwear and modes of transport are cultural artefacts. It's important for children to use both hands simultaneously, to protect their feet and get from A to B – but in many societies people don't use both hands to eat, wear shoes with laces or ride bicycles – so you wouldn't notice if children couldn't do those things. In addition –

some children are never going to be able to do those things. At what age 'should' a child be able to use both hands simultaneously and balance on two wheels? At what point do you stop trying to develop a skill and adopt an alternative method of getting the job done (fork, spoon, Velcro-fastening, scooter)? Clearly there must be reasons why some children pass developmental milestones later than other children, but we don't know how many developmental hiccups would spontaneously resolve given time.[22]

Are we losing sight of the bigger picture – forgetting to ask ourselves *why* we consider certain skills more important than others? Do our priorities always align with those of children – for whom 'getting the job done somehow' is essential? 'Critical periods' have morphed into 'sensitive periods' and 'windows of opportunity or achievement' that definitely reflect an increasing sensitivity and understanding of children's overall development – but we remain stubbornly attached to scales and norms when it comes to physical development. Maybe a more poetic approach is needed:

Young children's development is perhaps best thought of as both personal and structural, both internal and external, both continuous and discontinuous, open and bound… a 'rhizome' that defies the regularity of linear growth.[23]

How is physical development treated within the canon of Early Years literature? Priorities vary, as does the significance of environment and culture in supporting children's physical development.

Shilling determines that cultural stereotypes about what constitutes a 'normally developing' body are very important for both children and parents and that different cultures have specific 'techniques of the body that provide identity and govern infancy, adolescence and old age'. In the West, as children develop, the more autonomous, responsible, unique and individual they are expected to become. For many other cultures, development is about learning to fit in and function as a supportive, proactive, effective member of a carefully defined community.[24] Gaile Cannella points out that, 'As a field we have continued to ignore the ways that young human beings have been fully functioning members of diverse cultures and societies for thousands of years, without the so-called benefit of Western child development knowledge.'[25]

How do differing cultural attitudes to children's bodies affect their physical development? In contrast to children growing up in the UK, who are particularly subject to the vagaries of politics and curricular demands, young children in Japan experience a relatively long, pressure-free period of 'familiarisation' before formal schooling begins. This includes a significant amount of rough-and-tumble free play outside using challenging equipment to push their physical boundaries. In Walsh's essay, 'Frog Boy and the American Monkey: The Body in Japanese Early Schooling', he writes that: 'Cultural beliefs about children's physical capabilities and about the importance of physical activity informed this developmental context.'[26] In Japanese culture, young children are viewed as essentially and profoundly physical. Their physical development is central to early education. Japanese teachers believe that intellectual development requires the support of a strong, balanced, agile and coordinated body and that this is achieved through prolonged, vigorous physical activity.

Walsh is interesting in his examination of the cultural constraints related to children's physical development. He asks: What do we expect and allow of young children physically, what do we consider possible, what do we make accessible, what do we value and what do we support? He determines that Japanese culture really values physical activity and that 'the body' is central to their cultural narrative. Being 'genki', meaning 'fit, strong and healthy' is a highly valued state, so Japanese children are expected to be tough and resilient. 'The young Japanese self is seen as, and accepted as, a physical self, developed on the playgrounds and in rambunctious interaction with others from an early age. They are given the time and space to persist and practise.'[27]

A critical point to note is that the adult role in children's physical development is deliberately muted. Japanese teachers and parents afford their children an extraordinary level of freedom to rehearse and refine their physical skills, on the basis that if they formally supervised activities, children may become dependent on them and this dependence, in turn, would make them less careful and responsible. Playgrounds are therefore mainly unsupervised and development is considered to happen in the time and spaces where adults don't interact with children.

However, it is unclear precisely what the legacy is of this extended period of physical play. Does this exposure to independent, fearless daily physical activity instil a lifelong engagement and interest in all things physical, as the physical literacy approach would suggest, or do the later strictures of formal educational environments minimise any long-term effects? Does this period of self-efficacy and agency in the physical domain translate successfully to long-term dispositions and behaviours towards work, relationships or play? It would be interesting to find out.

In their latest book *Do Parents Matter?* the LeVines examine the possibilities afforded for children's physical development from an anthropological angle. They cite the Hopi and Navajo tribes in South-West America, who swaddle their infants and use cradleboards to manage the demands of challenging environments. They conclude that despite the obvious physical restrictions, 'There is no evidence to suggest that the experience of either compromises motor development, and that observable differences between babies on cradleboards and those raised without them are transient.' On the whole, they take a very relaxed approach to physical development: 'It will happen when it happens.'[28]

In *The Body Has a Mind of Its Own*, the Blakeslees mention two very different cultures and the value they place on specific elements of physical development.[29] Malians strongly believe that babies with 'crooked' legs are unattractive. From birth onwards, Malian mothers embark on a therapeutic regime to straighten the legs that involves vigorous stretching, stroking and holding the child upside down. The result is that many of these children are walking by 7 months. The Blakeslees suggest that this is because the movement parts of the brain have been hyperstimulated. In contrast to this intrusive, corrective approach they also cite a research study conducted with Romanian children who had spent their early years between 12 and 24 months in orphanages, deprived of touch and attention and not allowed to crawl. What was the long-term effect of not experiencing the crawling stage? At age 3–4, the IQ scores of these children were normal, but in eight domains of motor development, all 22 were 2–3 standard deviations below the norm. Only 1 per cent of children worldwide should score that low. They were asked to put one hand on a shoulder, one hand on the waist, change sides and stand on one leg. Further tests were also undergone by 18 of the 10-year-olds from this same group. The children were unable to balance on a beam or on the floor and swing their opposite arm to leg.

What we value, support and afford in terms of children's physical development is critically important. We should be aware of what informs or compromises our vision and ability to provide children with the movement experience they need to support their smooth overall development.

BODY SYSTEMS

Physical development is fundamentally dependent on well-integrated and functioning body systems:

- *Touch*: This is related to pressure and vibration.

- *Thermoception*: This is linked to heat – the deep tissues in bodily organs have receptors that manage core body temperature.

- *Nociception*: This relates to receptors that deal with perception of pain.

- The two that are most relevant to young children's physical development are the *vestibular system* (balance) and *proprioception* (intuition).

The vestibular system

Sally Goddard Blythe writes that the vestibular system is possibly the oldest and most primitive of all the sensory systems.[30] The human ear may well be an outgrowth or development of the 'lateral line receptor', a sensory system found in many fish and some amphibians that informs the animal of water motion in relation to body surface. In mammals, the ear has evolved into a highly complex system that houses the vestibular apparatus. This is located in the inner ear and must monitor and make adjustments to any movement of the head. It is the very first system to be fully developed, becoming operational at 16 weeks *in utero*, providing the foetus with a sense of direction and orientation. It also helps babies accommodate gravity at birth and affects their cycles of sleeping and waking.

Goddard Blythe claims that 'vestibular input is necessary for static and dynamic balance development, eye-tracking ability and motor planning'. It tells us, 'Is it me moving? How fast am I going? What direction am I going in? Am I upside down?'[31] 'Movement is critical to the smooth development of the vestibular system as it constantly challenges the brain to adjust and record its understanding of what it *feels* like to be in and out of balance. Movements that include turning, spinning, swinging, tumbling, rolling, rocking and sliding all 'refresh' the vestibular system on a continual basis. A well-modulated vestibular system is vitally important for keeping us in a calm, alert state and it helps to maintain a balanced level of arousal in our brains. Children with a poorly developed vestibular system dislike going on swings or roundabouts; they may also experience difficulty climbing up and down stairs; and may be very cautious when entering open spaces.

O'Connor writes that the vestibular system is intricately related to emotional wellbeing because: 'The part of the brain that generates emotionally based behaviour is the limbic system and this depends on the vestibular system to help modulate input from the senses.' She also talks of 'gravitational security' – the feeling of 'groundedness' that is so important for children to feel emotionally safe and secure. The soothing motion of rocking is a typical example of the close link between vestibular refreshment and emotional wellbeing.[32]

The vestibular system is also closely related to the development and processing of language. The auditory system is present in the ear receptors – so, too, are the mechanisms for the vestibular system. As O'Connor clarifies, 'being able to hear isn't the same as being able to process what we hear – this is linked to comprehension and our ability to understand what we are hearing – which we acquire at the same time as we learn to integrate vestibular sensations through our interactions with the environment'.[33]

Finally, vestibular development is also closely related to the effective production of speech. Speech is a physical skill that is dependent on the smooth functioning of the muscles in the tongue, throat, lips and jaw. The vestibular system 'influences motor control and motor planning that are necessary to use those fine muscles to produce intelligible speech'.[34]

Proprioception

Sir Charles Scott Sherrington (1857–1952), who won the Nobel Prize for Medicine in 1932, discovered and named the proprioceptive system – describing it as: 'The feeling of forces of the moving self inside the body'.[35] He also described muscles as 'organs of sense' and how the 'distance senses' of sight and hearing are used for proji-science, or 'reaching out to anticipate the properties of the environment and the objects that the body takes up'. The physiologist Henry Charlton Bastian (1837–1915) further developed these insights and created a theory for the sense of movement that he named 'kinæsthesia'.[36] In 1913, the psychologist George Dearborn (1878–1955) concluded that: 'Kinæsthesia is about to come into its own as the primary and essential sense… the very meaning of protoplasm, physically speaking – is motion'.[37]

This was an important moment, because – as Dearborn suggests – 'experience in the discourse of kinæsthesia was neither an indiscriminate registering nor a careful filtering of sensations' (as found in empiricist theories) but 'experience was theorised as the enjoyment of the immediate effect felt on the body's musculature… kinæsthesia understood as a uniquely corporeal self-consciousness was the only kind of reflection possible in this model of experience'. Kinæsthesia thus referred only to sensations that emerge when muscles are contracted and in motion.

The neurologist Oliver Sacks has described proprioception as the 'vital sixth sense' – an essential element in ensuring individuals are 'fully embodied in the world'. Goddard Blythe describes proprioception as a 'compound sense', derived from the Latin root *proprius* meaning 'one's own'. The receiver of multisensory information, it also forms an information channel of its own. It oversees all sensations involving body position either at rest or in motion and unlike kinæsthesia encompasses *all* sensations involving the position of the body – both in motion and at rest. The proprioceptive sense of where the body is in space or position develops *in utero* from around four months onwards, as the growing baby explores its tightly confined environment. Gill Connell suggests that we:

> *Think of it as the body's internal GPS system. It provides us with a sense of our physical selves by answering important questions such as, 'How big am I? What shape am I?' In turn, this gives us the intuitive sense of how to navigate the space around us. 'How tall is that step? Will I fit through that tunnel?'*[38]

Proprioceptors are located throughout the body in joints, tendons and muscles, and are activated by all bodily movement. One type of proprioceptor cells is embedded in muscles and tendons to register stretch (so the brain can work out where different body parts are located). Another type is found in the cartilage between skeletal joints (so the brain can be told about the speed and direction of movement the joints are experiencing).

Jan White writes that: 'The development of the proprioceptive sense is an incredibly important and complex process – it helps fit bodies into spaces and surfaces around us – and to navigate successfully both environments and interactions with people or objects.'[39] Movements that include pushing, pulling, digging, lifting, carrying, stretching, hanging (by arms and legs), throwing and jumping will all support the development and maintenance of the proprioceptive sense.

If proprioception is poor, children may appear to fidget constantly, need to be held tightly, provoke altercations that ensure a high level of sensory input, and experience poor posture and a range of visual issues. The overuse of 'containers' – baby-bouncers, walkers and sitting devices may also have a negative impact on proprioceptive development as young children cannot see or feel the lower half of their bodies when restrained. These are children who may also dislike sleeping in the dark – and need to see what they are doing all the time – especially when managing fiddly things like buttons and zips.

The concept of 'body schema' was first proposed in 1911 by two British neurologists – Sir Henry Head and Sir Gordon Holmes. They described body schema as 'organised models of ourselves' that are closely linked to the proprioceptive sense.[40] What is fascinating about their work is the suggestion that body schema actually expand to accommodate the clothes we wear, the implements we use, the materials we play with and the devices we use to travel. Wearing hats, holding an umbrella, using a spade or riding a bike become extensions of the self through continual exposure. If you have ever seen Brazilian footballers playing futsal, skateboarders in parks or professional cooks working, you will know what I mean.

We should be aware of the demands on children's body schema in the different environments they experience. They are constantly managing extensions of themselves every time they hold a pencil, use a paintbrush or a ball, carry a bag or wear their wellies. It explains why they are so interested in and often confused by their shadows: 'Is it a part of me – is it mine – or is it something completely separate? And where does it go?'

In 1935, Paul Schilder introduced the concept of body image, claiming that body schema did not convey adequately the full nature of bodily experience.[41] The body image, Schilder concluded, was the mental picture we have of our bodies: the way our bodies appear to us. Body image has become less dependent on body schema because it can be modified, created and manipulated – particularly since the emergence and prevalence of social media. In this climate, it is ever more critical that young children manage their body schema through movement experience that will then inform and underpin a positive body image.

A well-developed and integrated proprioceptive system leads to the establishment of a dynamic 'sensory motor map' of the body – a unified sense of self that ensures the physical properties of the body may be managed easily and economically within different environments and whenever physical challenges are encountered. Well-ordered body maps are particularly important for young children to acquire as their bodies change rapidly within a very short time. They must continually adjust to changes in height, weight and size – and accommodate the emergence of new skills and abilities.

Brain development/neuroscience

The neuroscientist Susan Greenfield claims that: 'If we didn't move, we wouldn't have a brain,' thus making a clear link between movement experience and brain development.[42]

What is now widely accepted is that early movement experience ensures that the 'architecture' or 'wiring' of the brain is built on sound foundations. These foundations may then properly support the later, higher-functioning, cognitive skills on which successful curricular engagement depends.

What do we know:

- A healthy newborn baby's brain has all the neurons needed. Penelope Leach points out that:

  She does not need to make any more now or in the future. What she needs is not more neurons but more connections to link them up and make them work for her; complex connections between different areas of the brain and a growing ability to use particular areas of it.[43]

- Robin Balbernie reminds us that, 'The potential number of connections is unimaginable, and these must become refined down to create an efficient match with their individual environment.'[44] This necessary 'pruning' to match demands very quickly fits the structure of the brain to the wide variety of environments in which children grow, learn and develop. These connections proliferate and prune in a *functional* order. Although the *timing* of this 'pruning' is genetically determined, the biological imperative to adapt affects which eventual neural networks are weak or strong.

- 'The strength and vulnerability of the human brain lie in its ability to shape itself to enable a particular human being to survive its environment. Our experiences, especially our earliest experiences, become biologically rooted in our brain structure and chemistry from the time of our gestation and most profoundly in the first months of life.'[45]

- Different areas of the brain are formed in a hierarchical fashion – beginning with the life-support, automatic nervous system circuits then moving up to the more complex sensory pathways including vision and hearing. The conduits needed for babies to connect to people are the first to develop after birth – followed by early language skills, emotional regulation and higher cognitive functioning.

- Early positive experiences increase glucose production that increases the richness of the neural connections. There is a dramatic burst of synaptic connections around six months when caregiving relationships are at peak importance, and at nine months infants are beginning to integrate the internal state of their bodies with the environment.

- By age 1 most of the windows of brain development are open. Balbernie writes that 'Many of the neural networks that lie behind a lifetime of skills, responses and potential are beginning to take shape. This is the time of a child's love affair with the whole world – unless we spoil it with teaching.'[46]

In an editorial for the *European Early Childhood Education Research Journal*, Michel Vandenbroeck questions the 'brainification' of early childhood education.[47] He cites the growing pressure put on neuroscientists by psychologists eager to garner evidence for their latest theories. An increasing number of neuroscientists criticise how their work may be misinterpreted by some developmental psychologists who insist on the existence of 'critical periods', while neuroscientists themselves are finding new evidence for the flexibility and malleability of the brain throughout later stages of development. He also highlights the irony that, despite this growing scepticism within the scientific community, the influence of neuroscience continues to increase in early childhood care and education and may eventually become the prime driver for policy and provision.

The justification for pursuing this route is that intervening at an early age is deemed to reap significant economic benefits for society long-term. Later aberrant behaviours and unemployment rates will be positively affected if we invest in good-quality early childcare and education. The danger here is that the economic argument ends up claiming pole position: that somehow we must prove that what we do has a measurable effect; that the profound and intrinsic importance of the early years gets lost in the drive to produce future labouring citizens of a meritocratic society.

Joseph Tobin warns that: 'It's too early to tell what the long-term impact will be of brain research on the field of early childhood education, but early returns are, at best, mixed.'[48] For Tobin, the application of brain research to early childhood education is a 'bridge too far', leading to spurious claims by settings that offer a 'brain-based curriculum' and 'brain-rich activities' – listening to Mozart, use of 'BrainBoxes' and 'brain gym' being offered on a daily basis. Mine Conkbayir also makes a very valid point here: 'no evidence (as yet) exists which elicits the thoughts and opinions of professionals from the early childhood sector about the relevance of neuroscience to education.'[49] So why don't they ask us?

What happens to children's physical experience in all this debate is that its *intrinsic* merit is in danger of being ignored. Do we end up trying to justify its inclusion in the curriculum by claiming a range of effects that are, frankly, difficult to support? We simply don't know for sure if upping children's movement provision and physical activity *will* make them better readers, writers, mathematicians – the current evidence is 'primarily weak in quality' – but there is 'some preliminary evidence that higher duration/ frequency of physical activity may have beneficial effects on cognitive development'.[50] Despite this caveat, many commercial activity providers continue to base their advertising on claims for which there is (as yet) minimal supporting evidence.

The Pikler approach

A refreshing alternative approach to children's physical development was developed by Emmi Pikler (1902–84). Initially trained as a doctor in Vienna, she was influenced by two paediatricians: Clemens von Pirquet (1874–1929), who was exploring the support of healthy development through nutrition, and Hans Salzer, who promoted the concept of a 'respectful relationship' with his young patients. Magda Gerber (d. 2007) trained with Pikler and in 1957 introduced her work to the USA, where she founded the organisation Resources for Infant Educarers (RIE).

The central tenet of the Pikler approach to early physical development is to afford infants and young children complete freedom of movement: that, in the long term, it is more beneficial for children to learn how to roll over, crawl, sit up, stand and walk according to their own inner timetable without unnecessary adult support or interference. As she wrote: 'If we provide enough space and possibilities for moving freely, then children will move as well as animals: skillfully, simply, securely, naturally.'[51] For Pikler, it is not up to adults to teach children to sit and walk, because they are perfectly capable of guiding their own motor development and moving according to their inherent ability – they do things when and how they can. Children do not need artificially constructed, complicated interventions to help them move, because they will do so whenever they are willing and able. Teaching them skills before they are ready often masks the level at which they are actually operating.

Does our anxiety about 'ages and stages' and visible milestones, and our stress concerning any child being 'left behind', render some of our behaviours unnecessarily intrusive? To Pikler, any aid that supposedly facilitates the development of motor skills is unnecessary and interferes with the natural emergence and unfolding of children's physical capabilities.

If allowed complete freedom of movement, infants will creep on their tummies and crawl on hands and knees *before* they come naturally to the sitting position. In one Pikler study of 591 children, the children crawled at 44 weeks average, sat and stood up at 49 weeks, took their first step at 15 months and walked with ease at 17 months – significantly later than when we have now come to expect and consider typical.[52]

Film of infants who attend the Pikler setting in Budapest demonstrates how calm and peaceful they are. The atmosphere is one of quiet purposefulness as adults and children go about their daily business. The infants are afforded their own contained floor space where they practise their emerging movement skills together. Adults rarely enter this space; it is *theirs* – they own it. They practise rolling over, crawling, sitting and wobbling as they begin to stand. There are no tears or dramas – nobody 'swoops and scoops' to sort them out – they just quietly and with great determination explore all their movement possibilities.

The second major tenet of the Pikler approach is the importance of tactful and respectful care as adults and infants physically interact with one another during care routines. Viewing footage of nappy-changing, dressing and applying sun cream is a profoundly moving experience. The level of trust, enjoyment and gentle cooperation apparent between children and attendant adults is extraordinary. The approach to care routines in Pikler is highly skilled, competent and multilayered. Bodily care is treated with huge respect because, as Dorothy Marlen writes: 'What we do in the routine, repetitive tasks of infancy, undertaken several times a day over several years, ripples into adult life. These repeated care moments will be, without exception, unconsciously taken in on a bodily and emotional core level by the child.'[53]

As she so rightly says, 'World peace starts on the changing table.'[54] During changing time, the adult is fully present and engaged with the child's physical experience. There are no distractions such as music, toys or mobiles. The carer describes in detail the sequence of changing: it is a very special time where gentle attention is given – it takes as long as it takes. No feet are yanked into the air. The hand is carefully placed across the back of the thighs so children can still move. All care routines are carried out *with* the child's full cooperation – they are not intrusive actions done *to* them.

What do Pikler children turn out like? They tend to be very calm, physically very confident, brilliant climbers, toilet-trained easily and very strong. Jane Swain writes: 'Pikler babies are graceful and do not fall. They find perfect balance. They develop perfect posture, core strength, agility and awareness.'[55] Yes, this approach to physical development is time-consuming and labour-intensive, but it has undoubted long-term benefits for both adults and children.

Interestingly, the presence of retained primary sensory motor reflexes (see Chapter 7, Reflexes) that Goddard Blythe points out may cause issues with children's later successful engagement with the curriculum is unknown at the Pikler Institute. Because Pikler children are afforded open-ended opportunities for daily movement experience, there is ample time for the primitive reflexes to naturally fade between 6 and 12 months, and the emergence of difficulties with fine motor coordination and sensory perception is therefore avoided.

In an article for *The Conversation* (2016), 'Are children who walk and talk early geniuses in the making?' the answer is: not really. There may be a tentative connection in that early walkers may engage at a younger age with the wider environment, but there is no conclusive evidence that children who hit motor milestones early will retain this head start later in life. It possibly gives them better language skills in the short term (as the world opens up when they can move independently) which *do* make a difference, but, for motor skills, the evidence really isn't there.[56]

The Touchpoints approach

Another alternative approach to childhood development, the Touchpoints Model of Development, has been created by T. Berry Brazelton and Joshua Sparrow in Boston.[57] Touchpoints are 'periods, during the first years of life during which children's spurts in development result in disruption to the family system'. Thirteen 'touchpoints' have been identified between pregnancy to three years. The beauty of this model is that it focuses on caregiving themes that matter to parents – feeding, sleeping, toileting, discipline – rather than traditional milestones. Essentially, to be forewarned is forearmed. If parents know when and why a touchpoint is looming – e.g. a baby at four months is likely to be a difficult feeder and wake more at night due to a burst in cognitive awareness of the environment and visual skills at this time – then they will react to behavioural changes in supportive and positive ways rather than become paralysed by a perceived inability to cope, or distressed if their child is not 'hitting their milestones'. Bursts, regressions and plateaus in development are expected and embraced in this model and the 'overflow' from one area of development to another is respected and understood. This approach supports a more positive model of observing and valuing parental successes and promotes a collaborative rather than prescriptive relationship between health and education professionals. There is scope to explore this model. It may mitigate parental anxiety and provide a more positive and less medical approach to growth and development that benefits all parties.

'Starting where they are' means taking a very holistic view of children's growth and development. For young children, the acquisition, rehearsal and refinement of physical skills is of profound importance to their relationships with peer groups, to the successful exploration of the environments they encounter and to navigating complex community interactions. Early movement skills do not need to be forced, rushed or taught; they will emerge at the appropriate time if we provide a range of supportive and interesting environments for this to happen. Let us also remember that physical development is rarely entirely linear and is full of progressions, regressions and plateaus. Many children need time to get used to a new skill and to work out how to use it most effectively – alone or with others; with or without apparatus; at what speed and for how long? Some will happily practise in private or talk about it endlessly until they are absolutely sure they are ready to reveal themselves as physically competent. Progression may also appear in a different developmental domain – a new friendship is created, repetition of vocabulary at home or in the playground is noted or a sudden interest in specific equipment may appear. Curiously, even with children who experience asynchronous development, however advanced their maths, music or language skills, their gross motor and locomotor skills tend to remain at a level broadly commensurate with their chronological age.

Neuroscience may well provide evidence for innovative educational approaches in the future, but, as Conkbayir points out, 'As yet there is a lack of consensus from neuroscience, insufficient collaboration across disciplines and inconsistent application of neuroscience-informed practice across early childhood practice.'[58] We should remain open and adaptable to findings from neuroscience and psychology but treat both fields with caution. Of course, a sound knowledge of children's physical development is important – but 'ages and stages' are simply useful guidelines; they are not a pass-or-fail framework designed to cause upset or anxiety. We should do all we can to avoid reaching the point at which 'we now have a new neurotic national pastime – raising a scientifically correct child'.[59]

3

The 'Enabling' and 'Immediate' Environments Support Learning and Development

*The environment is not an 'other' to us. It is not a
collection of things we encounter. Rather, it is a part of
our being. It is the locus of our existence and identity.
We cannot – and do not – exist apart from it.*

George Lakoff and Mark Johnson, *Philosophy in the Flesh*[1]

Trust in the richness of your own context.

Aldo Fortunati, in Martin Pace, *I Love Forest School*[2]

The environment in which children grow, learn and develop is seen increasingly as the prime determinant in their lives, one that has a profound impact on mental health, social wellbeing, life chances and future school success. Initiatives are created to mitigate the effect of 'disabling' environments on emotional health, language acquisition, knowledge of the natural world and predilection for weight gain.

Pia Haudrup Christensen writes: 'That childhood is, and should be, a nice protected world in which the only problematic external forces from the environment, or perhaps from malevolent adults, sometimes intervene is an important component of the perception of Western childhood.'[3] Many of our policy decisions are based on this: that children deserve a fit and healthy, 'good' childhood; that they are entitled to opportunities for play, and their rights are enshrined in international law. The environments they experience are expected to fully support their individual needs, growth and development. If deemed to be failing, organisations and central bodies are on hand to support and facilitate change. As adults, we like to feel important – that we can *do* something, that through our own efforts we may provide our children with enough positive experiences to ensure they flourish and thrive in the varying environments they encounter along the life course.

THE 'ENABLING' ENVIRONMENT

Amidst all the talk of what constitutes an 'enabling' environment, what is often unacknowledged is that, for young children, the primary enabling environment they experience is their unique physical body: a well-balanced, strong, coordinated, competent, confident, agile body is the most enabling environment of all with which they could possibly engage. Adapting and reacting with ease to continual changes in body size, shape and weight, this is what enables them to navigate the demands of adults, cope with shifting peer group loyalties and embrace the opportunities offered by varying landscapes. The enabling environment of a reliable body is also critical to children's ability to acquire and use language effectively. They communicate by doing, through being physically active. Language emerges from a shared sense of purpose and through experiences that may be remembered and talked about. It is no surprise that the most socially confident children also have the most mature physical skills and that obese children, who are undoubtedly compromised physically, score 30 per cent lower on the Social Competence domain in the Australian Early Development Census.[4]

Although there are shared understandings among educationalists as to what constitutes 'the environment', curiously, the physical body is rarely mentioned. For Jennie Lindon, environment 'usually means the physical features of the location in which children are raised, but is sometimes used interchangeably with experience'.[5] For June O'Sullivan, environment includes 'not only the space the children use and the furniture and materials within that space, but also the adults and children who spend their days with each other'.[6] For Penny Tassoni, the term 'environment' does not simply refer to available resources or the layout of the room; it also refers to the emotional environment that is created.[7] For Kathryn Solly, the indoor environment is 'much more than the physical setting: it includes all the external facts and conditions which potentially can influence a child'. She adds the people within it, how time is structured, how behaviour is encouraged or discouraged, and how roles and responsibilities are distributed.[8] The FrameWorks Institute talk about the 'total' environment: meaning *everything* about the child's environment, 'from the chemicals in paint to interpersonal relationships'.[9] A range of possibilities are included here, from physical features, experiences, adults, other children, emotional needs and resources.

In his exploration of Forest School, Martin Pace widens further the constitution of the environment: 'Forest school is more of a philosophical, value-based approach giving scope for children's freedom, choice and risk-taking rather than a woodland environment. It has become an ethos rather than a place.'[10] The outside environment thus becomes much more than its physical features by including a conceptual framework of how children may learn to be in the world. Pace also reminds us that: 'When children feel confident in the environment, they are willing to try things out knowing that effort is valued.' Undoubtedly true, but feeling confident in the environment primarily means having confidence in the physical skills that determine enjoyment and engagement in new opportunities.

BRONFENBRENNER'S ECOLOGICAL AND BIOECOLOGICAL MODELS OF DEVELOPMENT

Urie Bronfenbrenner's Ecological and Bioecological Models of Development are useful frameworks in which to place children's physical development. Bronfenbrenner's original 'ecological' model stressed the importance of the interactions between individuals and the multiple environments they experience as being key contributors to overall development.

Criticised for 'not giving adequate consideration to social and cultural constructs or to power relations between contexts', [11] Bronfenbrenner subsequently extended and refined this model to become the 'bio-ecological' model, in order:

> to emphasize that a child's own biology is a primary environment fueling her development. The interaction between factors in a child's maturing biology, his immediate family/community environment, and the societal landscape fuels and steers his development. [12]

The bioecological model outlines four elements – person, process, context and time (PPCT). The context element of the original 'ecological' model remains – with the four interconnecting systems (micro/meso/exo/macro) sharing parity of status. Time was included as a new core element and was systematised into the theory through the introduction of the chronosystem. The five systems are as follows:

- *The microsystem*: This includes family, school, peer groups, neighbourhoods and childcare. It encompasses the relationships and interactions children have with their immediate surroundings and contains the structures with which they have direct contact.

- *The mesosystem*: This is the system that *links* experiences and environments, e.g. a child's home and school.

- *The exosystem*: This includes external environmental settings that are tangentially related to children's development, e.g. the parental workplace.

- *The macrosystem*: This is related to the wider cultural, economic and political contexts that affect their development.

- *The chronosystem*: This refers to 'the dimension of time as it relates to a child's environments'. It describes the broad social changes that affect childhood over time and that lead to 'perspectives and advice being revisited and reviewed'. Elements within this system may be external (e.g. bereavement) or internal (e.g. physiological changes that occur as children mature). Continuity and change are equally relevant. The chronosystem is broken down further into microtime (the consistency of interactions between people, objects and symbols), mesotime (how often these interactions occur) and macrotime (historical time).

How do these systems affect and support the 'primary enabling environment' of children's bodies?

The chronosystem

There is increasing evidence that children's overall health and wellbeing remains compromised. Obesity levels, behavioural issues, oral health and emotional wellbeing are of continuing and serious concern. Advice, initiatives and resources are available to support a 'healthy environment', 'a place or social context in which people engage in daily activities in which environmental, organizational, and personal factors interact to affect health and wellbeing'.[13]

Yet, we know that roaming distances for children have fallen by 90 per cent in a generation (from five miles in Sheffield in the 1950s to 300 metres in the same city today), that the average roaming distance for a child in the UK is now reduced to 500 metres from home and the amount of time children spend in unstructured play has decreased by 50 per cent.[14] School playing fields continue to be sold off for development. In 2016, there were 27 sell-offs recorded – the highest number since 2013. Local authorities in England have closed 214 playgrounds since 2016 and are planning to close another 234 in the future. In the London Borough of Wandsworth, three adventure playgrounds were demolished in 2013 and in Lambeth only six of the fifteen adventure playgrounds are currently open.[15] As Jennie Lindon writes, 'It takes serious discouragement from key adults and a depressing learning environment to create young couch potatoes.'[16] Why is our chronosystem so poorly equipped to support children's physical development and need for physical activity? With all the experience, knowledge, research data and expertise available, the quality and quantity of children's physical activity remains stubbornly low and this will continue to have a negative effect on their overall development.

The microsystem: 'the layer closest to the child'

If we take children's bodies (their own biology) as the primary environment they experience, how does the physical development of their bodies relate to the bioecological framework?

The poet Samuel Taylor Coleridge was probably correct in his observation that: 'The history of man for the nine months preceding his birth would probably be far more interesting and contain events of greater moment, than all the three score and ten years that follow it.'[17]

Sally Goddard Blythe writes:

From the very beginning of life there is movement. Just a few days after conception, inside a tiny ocean, an acrobat starts to perform. Beginning with gentle rocking movements in response to the ocean's tide, small primitive movements and reflex responses gradually unfold. These early movements will eventually become part of the dance of development, the stages of which have been choreographed over the course of many millennia through the evolution of humankind.[18]

There is a growing body of evidence that conditions within this tiny ocean are of critical importance to the long-term health and wellbeing of our future acrobats. At 21 days after conception, the inner ear begins to develop – laying the foundations for the vestibular system. At 5 weeks, the embryo begins to respond to external stimuli and between 7 and 8 weeks, taste buds will start to grow. As the embryo develops, it will respond to touch on the upper lip by flinching and withdrawing like a little snail. The palms of the hands and soles of the feet soon become equally sensitive. Eventually, the whole body surface responds to touch. The foetus is also exposed to a rich and varied spectrum of tastes via the amniotic fluid that is affected by whatever the mother eats and drinks. Babies in the womb initially experience sound by feeling vibrations and are highly sensitive to the 'dominant acoustic environment' of their mother's internal body rhythms. By 6 months, they respond through movement to their mothers' voices talking and singing. Even *in utero*, Guy Claxton's observations are pertinent: 'I am, through the body, intimately, intricately related, embroiled in, the environment, both physical and social, and it in me.'[19] Mine Conkbayir also points out, 'The foetus is not a passive occupant of the womb, but one which responds, grows and develops directly in response to the stimuli it receives.'[20]

These stimuli may be positive and negative. Diet and stress are two critical factors that are known to have a long-term effect on children's physical development. It is now accepted that mothers with a high Body

Mass Index (BMI) before pregnancy are three to four times more likely to have obese children. It is suggested that the reason for this is related to the foetus developing a compromised metabolism due to the increase in material insulin levels. Rapid weight gain by the foetus between 37–38 weeks has also been linked to obesity in children between 2 and 7 years. About 43 per cent of mothers exceed the recommended weight gain during pregnancy; 67–70 per cent of obese women do the same.[21] We now know that towards the end of pregnancy, babies swallow the amniotic fluid, whose makeup is affected directly by maternal input and that this may adversely influence their later nutritional choices. There will be children we teach and care for who may be compromised in terms of obesity and weight status by the environment they experienced *in utero*.

Vivette Glover writes: 'The environment in the womb can alter the development of the fetus with a long-lasting effect on the children. Many types of infant and child outcome can be altered by antenatal stress both neurodevelopmental and physical.'

Her pioneering research into the effect of the stress hormone cortisol on the developing foetus suggests that, as early as 17 weeks after conception, higher cortisol levels in the mother's blood are reflected in higher levels in the amniotic fluid surrounding the baby. As amniotic fluid is mainly produced by the foetus, it is a good indicator of what factors and substances the foetus is being exposed to.[22] However, she cautions that: 'We do not yet know what biological changes in the mother caused by stress, anxiety or depression are most important for fetal programming. Cortisol may be involved but other factors are likely to be at least as, if not more, important.' One of these factors may be the change in function of the placenta, because if the mother is stressed or anxious there is less of the enzyme available that breaks down cortisol in this organ. Evidence of depression suggests that there will be more of the receptor that responds to cortisol – so the mother's mood 'may alter the fetal exposure to cortisol, independently of raising cortisol levels in the mother. And increased exposure to cortisol can affect the development of the fetal brain.'

Evidence suggests that if mothers are in the top 15 per cent for antenatal anxiety or depression, the risk of their children experiencing a mental disorder at aged 13 years is doubled – from 6 to 12 per cent – 'even after allowing for a wide range of confounding factors'. Female adolescent children of mothers who experience antenatal stress may be anxious or depressed, whereas boys may suffer from Attention Defecit Hyperactivity Disorder (ADHD), be aggressive or have learning difficulties.[23]

In a 2017 Norwegian study, researchers focused on 112 infants (average age 23 months) in 85 childcare centres. All the children had been in childcare for 5–6 months before cortisol sampling. Saliva samples were collected at 10am and 3pm on two consecutive days, one in the setting and one at home. Cortisol levels increased in the setting from 10am to 3pm and decreased in the home setting. Researchers concluded that the number of hours spent in childcare with different caregivers and separation from parents were the principal causes of stress.[24] An earlier study, conducted in 2004, that focused on children aged 11–20 months in daycare, suggests that levels of cortisol remained elevated even after five months of attending.[25]

We should be aware of these findings and appreciate that we may have children in our care whose bodies have been exposed to high levels of cortisol from the very beginning. It is therefore imperative that these children are not exposed to additional stressful situations in their early learning and care environments and they have the physical skills in place to manage the demands of daily life.

Brain development *in utero* is rapid, extraordinary and dependent on a supportive and nourishing environment. Early in the first trimester, the neural tube begins to grow, eventually forming the forebrain, midbrain and hindbrain by 6–7 weeks. The most primitive part of the brain, the brainstem, is formed first. This focuses on survival and controls foetal heartrate, breathing and the fight-or-flight response. By the end of the second trimester, the brainstem is almost entirely mature, and neurons and synapses appear in the cortex that enable the foetus to make the first voluntary movements.

At birth, everything changes. Goddard Blythe reminds us that: 'Being born introduces the baby to an entirely new set of challenges… Babies must accommodate the sudden change from a warm, aqueous, relatively quiet, secure environment to one where sensory stimulation is vivid, intrusive, alarming and often overwhelming.'[26] Sam Gill writes that: 'Our body is the entry point into the world – the medium through which, and in which, our reality is constructed.'[27] How babies react to and accommodate different stimuli has led researchers to explore the possible relationship between innate temperament and the later development of personality.

Temperament includes inborn, biologically based, behavioural and emotional patterns that are observable in infancy and early childhood – considered 'the foundation'. Personality is the complex brew that emerges after cultural influences and personal experience are added – considered 'the building'.

The difference between temperament and personality may be important to factor in when affording children opportunities to support their physical development. In 1989, Jerome Kagan gathered 500 infants aged 4 months in his Laboratory for Child Development at Harvard, predicting on the strength of a 45-minute evaluation which babies were predisposed to be introverts or extroverts.[28] Each baby was exposed to four carefully chosen stimuli: tape-recorded voices, balloons popping, colourful mobiles and inhalation of a drop of alcohol on cotton swabs. Around 20 per cent cried loudly, kicked and flailed: Kagan called this group 'high-reactive'; 40 per cent stayed quiet and fairly placid, labelled 'low-reactive'; 40 per cent fell between the two extremes. He followed many of these children through at 2, 4, 7 and 11 years, each time testing their reactions to different stimuli: age 2: a lady wearing a gasmask, a man in a clown costume, a radio-controlled robot; age 7: play with children they had never met; age 11: an unfamiliar adult interviewed them about their personal lives. Their reactions were noted for body language, laughter and speech, and parents were also interviewed to gain an additional perspective. As Kagan predicted, the original high-reactives became serious, quiet and careful individuals; those in the low-reactive group were observed to be relaxed and confident. He determined that because the stimuli he used were not 'people-based', babies were profoundly sensitive to their environments from the very beginning. High-reactive children feel their environments acutely, and we should be aware of this when creating opportunities to support their physical skills.

In 2003, Avshalom Caspi and colleagues studied 1000 children aged 3 growing up in New Zealand. Each child engaged in a 90-minute session and was rated on 22 characteristics. These children were clustered into five types: well-adjusted, confident, inhibited, reserved and under-controlled (impulsive, restless). Of this original group, 96 per cent were followed up when they were 26. Those in the under-controlled category aged 3 scored highest on Negative Emotionality: they were tense and anxious; the confident ones scored low on Self-Control; and the inhibited ones scored high on Constraint. It is interesting to note that he had also assessed these children at 18 years and the characteristics that were noted at aged 3 were very evident at this later developmental stage.[29]

By the time infants are 4 months old, it seems that we may have a pretty good idea as to what sort of children they may become, and at 3 years how they may emerge as adults. Considering what is now known about the foundations of temperament, it is likely that for a significant minority of children (who may include those placed in some kind of daycare for ten hours a day, five days a week) the environments they experience may be less of a 'nest' and more a source of significant stress.

In 2016, an international research team gathered evidence to suggest that adults who display similar behavioural characteristics tend to move their bodies in the same way. Each person has an individual motor signature (IMS) that, if aligned to others that are similar, will result in 'more organised collective behaviour' and easier interpersonal interactions. Although primarily designed as an approach to supporting adult mental health, it is interesting to relate this to our observations of children when they engage in free physical play – to observe who takes the lead in organising activities – whose strengths are played to – are groups always formed by those whose skills and interests align?[30]

The exosystem

This 'defines the larger social system in which the child does not function directly but feels the positive and negative forces involved with the interaction with his own system'. Many of the dispositions, habits and behaviours towards physical activity (that have a profound long-term effect on physical development, health and wellbeing) are laid down in these early years and are informed by adult agendas. Anne O'Connor writes that dispositions are environmentally sensitive and that children's ability to trust and discover the world is 'intrinsically linked to their physical competence and confidence'.[31] Jyrki Reunamo's evidence from Finland suggests that young children are very physically active for only 47.5 minutes each day between 8 a.m. and 4 p.m. They are most active when outside and engaging with their peer groups. Interestingly, they were observed to be least active when the teacher determined the opportunities to be physically active. As he writes, 'Children's peer relations are the key for a physically active life. The teacher needs to value peer relations, give children possibilities to spend time together and to provide space and tools to enhance physical activity.'[32]

The exosystem includes not only the care experienced in settings and outside the home environment but also the nutritional environment experienced by children. This has an undoubted impact on their eating habits and possible emergent obesity issues. Although we do not yet have firm evidence of a link between early onset obesity and physical activity (currently the available evidence is labelled 'limited and observational'), high levels of sedentary behaviour (on average 6–7 hours daily) are considered a significant risk factor for weight gain. Children's long-term dispositions and habits towards food and physical activity are embedded at a very early age and are heavily influenced by the attitudes and behaviours of adults.

O'Sullivan describes the range of pedagogical thought that has influenced the environmental presentation of all London Early Years Foundation (LEYF) nurseries. For Montessori, the physical environment should be 'a place of beauty and order, stimulating, child-centred and multisensory'. She was also adamant that children should take responsibility for the care of their environment, tidying up in particular. In LEYF nurseries, the colour schemes and lighting are neutral and soothing; a calm, homely atmosphere is reflected in comfortable and familiar furnishings. Froebel's influence may be felt in the opportunities for self-directed activity afforded the children, and Steiner's principle that cooperation is more beneficial than competition is evident in the time and energy spent on collaborative projects. The New Zealand Te Whāriki approach is also factored into provision. In this framework, childcare and pre-school settings are expected to be an 'integral part of the community' and LEYF nurseries 'will always be sited right at the heart of the community'.[33]

The macrosystem

This 'refers to overriding beliefs, values, ideology and practices that exist within a culture'. How may this apply to the enabling environment of children's bodies and the wider environment in which they are learning and developing? Currently, there is renewed focus on children's physical health that is reflected in initiatives to combat obesity, a commitment to outdoor play and an emergent interest in the impact of physical development on other domains of learning.

The 'prepared environment' is not a new concept in early childhood education. In the Montessori and Steiner approaches, it is very clear that, although children are encouraged to choose their own activities and are given the freedom from adult direction to engage with materials, these resources are carefully calibrated, often prescribed, and the prepared environment is rarely prepared by the children. In the Pikler approach, a conundrum emerges. Éva Kálló and Györgyi Balog write: 'The play area is one of the essentials for the development of free play.'[34] Yet, Pikler's principles stipulate that each infant needs 'at least a square metre of space such that she actually has more room to move'. The floor of the play area consists of a sheet of wood elevated about 5 cm, whose hardness is vital for the development of infant muscle growth and future independent mobility. This wooden sheet may be covered with a thin cotton blanket and secured. So, despite the emphasis on free, active play, a very precisely prepared physical environment is considered an essential support.

The use of the immediate environment as an integral component of the learning process has close links to the principles of the Dutch 'Activity-oriented Observation, Registration and Evaluation of Basic Development' (HOREB) learning model. This model proposes that children should be actively involved in the process of learning through use of the environment, and that teachers are proactive partners in their development: 'The process of continuing and renewing relevant meanings occurs in a negotiation of meaning between the participants in an activity. It is a process of collaborative meaning construction in which heterogeneity is needed and discourse is essential.'[35]

The question of ownership and agency within a prepared environment is one that exercised me greatly during the study at the nursery. The changing relationship between the primary enabling environment of the children's bodies, the immediate environment of their peer group and adults, and the physical space surrounding them emerged as a significant theme. Aldo Fortunati's maxim to 'Trust in the richness of your own context' was one we referred to frequently.[36]

THE STUDY

The five children (four boys and one girl, aged 4 years to 4 years 6 months) rarely played or worked together as a group and each attended a daily individual 20-minute therapy session with Nina in a room 10 ft by 8 ft. This environment was tightly controlled, regulated and unchanging. There were rules about time, resources and space that were non-negotiable and the door was kept firmly shut. There was no evidence of any children's work (posters of oral motor exercises were stuck on the wall) and no sign that they enjoyed either ownership or agency of this space.

Inside the large, open-plan nursery, the usual 'corners' had been created: home, writing, nature and sand play. The children were observed to avoid any activity they knew would be a struggle and at which they may be seen to fail, e.g. writing, threading and cutting with scissors. They were given no specific role when activities were set up or tidied away, and tended to spend their time in solitary play with manageable materials, such as washing the dolly's hair or playing with the cars, sand and water. Sitting still and listening during circle time and the music lesson was challenging. They couldn't remember the words of the songs or keep to a steady beat. They knew precisely which situations were manageable (e.g. playing alone) or threatening (e.g. taking the register) for them.

Outside they fared better. They were not confronted with difficult activities and the adults were more relaxed with them. Only the parachute session proved challenging: they couldn't hold the parachute very easily because the gripping action was hard to maintain, the timing of different activities was unmanageable within such a large group and processing shouted instructions at speed was overwhelming.

It became clear that they would benefit from developing some level of agency, ownership and responsibility within their therapeutic space. How was this effected? The first change was to keep the door of the therapy room open as the children arrived in the morning and afternoon. Any member of the group could then pop in and see Nina with their friends and show them the resources and materials we used. The chairs and table were also removed during the movement sessions, not only for reasons of space, but it made the room feel 'special' to the group and provided a relaxed time in an environment they often found stressful.

Throughout Nina's and my movement programmes, the enabling environment of the children's bodies and the immediate environment of participating children/adults and the physical space were used to explore a range of different themes that supported the approach introduced in Chapter 1.

Here are two examples. During one session, we used socks to explore the theme of 'strength'. The children put socks on their hands (a very strengthening activity) and rubbed, scrubbed, polished, wiped and cleaned many different objects and surfaces in the room. They used a range of communication strategies as they discussed with us which resources needed attention and different hand actions to make the room 'sparkle'. In another session, 'sound' was the chosen theme. As we all lay on our tummies with eyes closed, Nina made different sounds with objects situated around the room, and we had to guess what they were (pulling Sellotape, opening drawers, closing the blinds, sharpening pencils, turning the lights off and on). We then asked the children to reproduce these sounds independently. This generated much talk as they tried out different possibilities and negotiated solutions.

During a discussion with Nina about the children's engagement with the physical space, she gave this very honest reply:

I was initially very worried about you changing the room and how they would react. In a therapeutic session we stress calm and focus, and having them all jumping around and muddling up the room wasn't easy for me to accommodate. It's been good for them to really observe each other and to use the space and me in a different way.

It was a challenging adjustment for her but, as she also noted later in the project:

They're much less fearful of coming in now, and they're always moving around the room, touching and feeling things, while they're here talking to me. I think they feel a need to do this to get in touch again before we start the main therapeutic stuff. It was so good too that pictures of me were on the wall every week. They really feel that it's our space that we've all shared, and it's given them something to engage with immediately they come in. I think using the room in a different way has given them a feeling that they belong somewhere, that this really is a place they have a good time in with their friends. It's quite difficult now, though, to keep their hands off things, because they're just so curious and they immediately notice anything in the room I've changed around.

And finally, this was the reaction from the head teacher:

They seem to be much calmer in the nursery, and they're easier to deal with now because they're not disappearing every time someone wants them to do something. They're definitely more confident to do things now, and at least they'll try and join in.

An interesting finding emerged that related to their drawings. During phrase three of each session, the children created a paper-based record of their experience that included a representation of themselves engaged in the activity they had most enjoyed. As early as the 1800s, Cooke and Ritchie established that children's drawings change as they develop, and that their developmental status may be determined by the level of quality and detail presented and portrayed.[37] In 1921, Burt noticed that developmental progress and delay were evident in children's drawings, and in 1926 Florence Goodenough linked children's drawings to levels of intelligence through her Draw-A-Man Test. Dale B. Harris revised this test in 1963, and it is now known as the Goodenough-Harris Drawing Test.[38] The Draw-A-Person Test (man, woman, themselves) is commonly used as a measure of intelligence in children, although experts have found a very low correlation between this test and the Wechsler intelligence scales. Although we were not using any specific scales, I was curious to discover if the children's two-dimensional representations of themselves would change and develop as they became more confident and competent physically and engaged more closely with the immediate environment. Molly Davies had also used drawing as an assessment procedure in her study.[39] She asked children to paint their climbing, jumping and balancing activities, and found that the degree of accurate and detailed verbal descriptions of their activities (that she already knew matched the detail and complexity of their movement), in turn, related to their ability to represent these actions pictorially.

What emerged during the study was a significant change in the children's representations of themselves that began with small, indecipherable smudges high in the corners of the page. Over time, larger bodies with necks emerged – facial features were added – hair appeared in abundance – as did enormous hands and feet. I cannot say for sure that the movement intervention programme alone was responsible for this, but their increasing physical competence led to a higher level of confidence to operate effectively in both inside and outside nursery environments and the confined therapeutic space.

Considering the body as the 'primary enabling environment' is useful. It may even claim to be the mesosystem of Bronfenbrenner's bioecological model: the glue that binds together the different components of the microsystem experienced by children.

In physical development terms, agency and ownership start with the body. Ensuring that the enabling environment of the body really does enable children to engage effectively with the immediate environment of others and varying geographical spaces requires effort, application, patience, perseverance, nurture and time. Lilian Katz is absolutely right when she reminds us that dispositions are 'habits of mind and patterns of behaviour that are directed towards a broad goal'.[40] They may be encouraged by adults, but they cannot be formally taught. She also makes the important point, reiterated by Jennie Lindon, that 'the methods practitioners use to promote specific learning for children must protect and encourage the children's disposition to use those skills out of choice'.[41] For physical development this is critical. There is no point in offering children opportunities to engage actively with the environment if the dispositions, habits and behaviours that ensure continual positive engagement are not properly and positively supported.

Wendy Thompson writes that: 'Proponents of an experiential learning model argue that young children are capable of demonstrating sophisti-cated levels of complex thinking when provided with an appropriate learning environment.'[42] If learning begins with the enabling environment of a balanced, coordinated, strong and agile body and directly related to the immediate environment of others and the physical space, then abstract concepts and attendant language become relevant and meaningful. Thompson also reminds us that: 'It is sustained engagement with experience that leads to a different relationship with the world from that based on a succession of brief encounters.'[43]

THE BRIC PROJECT

For children to really appreciate the physical properties of the spaces in which they are learning, they should be afforded the time and space to investigate and explore. In January 2015, a project was created to 'involve preschool teachers, young children and parents in exploring democratic engagement in public and civic spaces'. The Young People, Public Spaces and Democracy Project (BRIC) 'aims to raise the profile of young children as stakeholders within local communities by taking children out to explore three public spaces: the pavement, an outdoor green space and an indoor space that is not at school'.[44] Tim Waller, who leads the UK team (the other two are in Sweden and Italy), explains: 'The most important thing is working with the community to acknowledge that young people have a part to play, and helping the children become aware that the space is theirs as well.' The UK practitioners have kept it very local, going on regular walks in the immediate neighbourhood, taking the bus to the local library, and moving around with cameras to photograph whatever interests them. Children are out and about exploring, looking at and listening to what's happening in their community. They have also explored making chalk marks on pavements and walls. Interestingly, the mixed reaction this activity provoked led to further learning experiences – the children had to wash off the marks they made on private property, but this led to a positive discussion with the local council to determine where they could create new artworks.

How refreshing and inspiring to see practitioners really 'trusting in the richness of their own context'. Forest schools are enticing, particularly if you live and work in an urban environment, but as Thomas Weaver points out: 'Dependency theory states that those with a perceived paucity, or placed on the periphery, will tend to distort themselves to fit the dominant value set.' He claims that the UK, in particular, finds itself both geographically and conceptually on the edge of the Scandinavian cult of outdoor learning and as a result has created a 'mutated version' of *Skogsmulle* ('if children are taught to love nature, then they will cherish and protect it as adults').[45] He writes that a 'return to the poetry of the back garden' is needed. This BRIC participant teacher would agree: 'Public spaces are versatile places for children when they can explore and play through their bodies, their sight, through touching and smelling and, regarding community involvement, it is always good to smile.'

Children's identity is informed and supported by their physical competencies. Mark Johnson proposes that: 'The environment as a whole is as much a part of the identity of the organism as anything internal to the organism.'[46]

Having a reliable and competent 'primary enabling environment' leads to enjoyable and proactive engagement with the 'immediate environment' that others and physical spaces provide. Exploring wider geographical environments may then become a source of profound delight and wonder – leading to long-term life-enhancing interests, hobbies and careers.

4

Music and Rhythm Support Learning and Development

*Music is the literature of the heart – it
commences where speech ends.*

Alphonse de Lamartine (1790–1869)[1]

*Rhythm is our universal mother tongue
– it is the language of the soul.*

Gabrielle Roth (1941–2012)[2]

Archaelogical evidence dated to 40,000 years ago strongly suggests that the early Cro-Magnon people were engaged in some sort of music-making. Bone pipes and flutes fashioned out of bird skeletons, that were uncovered in acoustic-friendly caves, point to a society that may well have used music to support group identity, encourage collective thinking and to frame celebrations related to hunting and harvest. As Ian Cross writes: 'Music appears to be something of a universal social fact.'[3] Wayne Bowman would agree: 'Music plays a crucial role in the creation, maintenance, and negotiation of identity – both individually and collectively. It acts powerfully on the body, activating, guiding, facilitating, enabling, and shaping.'[4]

CONTEXT

Across cultures and eras, the forms and significance of music are extremely diverse but 'all known cultures have, or have had, something that can be regarded as music'[5] employed for purposes of entertainment, ritual, courtship, marking milestones and seasonal change. What is interesting is that there are some societies 'that have no word for music or whose concept of music has a significance quite different from that generally associated with the word "music"'. Cross cites the Igbo people of Nigeria, for whom the word 'Nkwa' denotes music and dance. As he says, it seems the practices that are recognisable as music in societies beyond contemporary global Western culture are characterised by their use of sound and movement together.[6]

Defining what music is provokes heated debate amongst experts. Cross points out that 'notions of music reveal themselves to be ideological constructs rooted in the workings of broader socioeconomic and political forces, which are dynamic, changing processes'.[7] He urges that we should remember the alternative, and often older, ways of engaging with music, particularly as an active element in everyday life. Bowman encapsulates this well when he writes that: 'Music is a valuable cognitive resource not because of what it teaches us about the disembodied metaphysical realm of feeling but what it shows us about the profoundly embodied and socioculturally situated character of all human knowing and being.'[8]

Theories linking music to manifestations of cosmic harmony beyond human nature are ancient but influential. Pythagoras's natural law, known as the 'Harmony of the Spheres', connected music, the theory of numbers and astronomy: since the celestial bodies, including earth, move in perpetual orbits, they must therefore create tones whose pitch may vary, in the same way that strings of different lengths produce different sounds. Followers of Pythagoras believed in the importance of music to spiritual wellbeing; that changes in rhythm and melody had the capacity to influence emotions. 'It leads the soul to excitement, relaxation, amusement, pleasure, suspense, drowsiness, stimulation, vivification and enthusiasm.' These archaic theories of cosmic harmony, music and number are now at the forefront of biomusicological and neuroscientific research, 'converging on a new synthesis of ideas concerning the mathematical regularities of nature, in which the Pythagorean whole integer ratios and resonance phenomena indeed emerge as the rock bed upon which music scales, harmonies and tonal relations appear to rest'.[9]

The roots of music-making and the rationale for its presence in societies are primordial and profound. But how may Cross's suggestion that we return to earlier, older ways of engaging with music play out in our lives and our professional practice, considering the influence of digital technology, the fragmentation of families and communities, and the sheer pressure of time?

Martin Clayton talks of *entrainment*: that the contexts in which music occur are active and participatory. An integral part of this 'entrainment' is that it 'involves the coordination in time of one participant's musical behaviours with those of others'. This is fundamentally related to rhythm, 'the regularities in both temporal and intensive patterns', the 'strong, repeated, regular patterns of movement or sound'.[10]

Rhythmic organisation is an essential component of music, language, movement and cultural practices, yet an accepted definition of rhythm is elusive. Plato linked the Greek word *reo* ('to flow') with bodily movements and rhythm was defined as 'order in movement'. Aristotle, however, linked his exposition of rhythm to the atomists Leucippus and Democritus, for whom rhythm meant form: the characteristic arrangement of parts of the whole; that this form is 'improvised, momentary and changeable'. Henri Lefebvre makes an interesting point regarding rhythm when he writes that: 'It appears as regulated time governed by rational laws, but in contact with what is least rational in a human being: the lived, the carnal, the body.'[11]

Charles Bell's work on proprioception and Henry Charles Bastian's on kinæsthesia is reflected in the literature of early twentieth-century psychology in which rhythm is explored primarily through the relationship between muscular tension, kinæsthesia and consciousness.

Wilhelm Wundt (1832–1920), an early experimental psychologist, was fascinated by this relationship and wrote that:

Consciousness is rhythmically disposed, because the whole organism is rhythmically disposed. The movements of the heart – of breathing, of walking – take place rhythmically. Above all, the movements of walking form a very clear and recognisable background to our consciousness.

His work in linking bodily and psychic rhythms and the ways in which external rhythms may influence internal ones proved a fruitful research field for his followers.[12]

How does the link between music, rhythm and consciousness begin? We should begin at the very beginning.

Bowman writes of the 'intra-uterine symphony', life in the womb 'where we first begin to discover the world around us and our place within it, a world dark and ambiguous, yet filled with vivid sound'.[13] The physical apparatus that supports hearing begins formation during the fifth week of gestation, and by six months *in utero* the foetus is able to hear muffled sounds through the mother's abdominal wall. Surrounded by rhythmic patterns of internal sound, including digestion, breathing and heartbeat, babies are also continually exposed to their mother's voice and the external rhythms of daily routines. Michael Lazarev writes:

Before birth, although the baby is protected from many external environmental stimuli, he still experiences many of them in a different way. One of the main sources of external stimulus is sound. Sound stimulates development of the prenatal brain, and for nine months of prenatal life the child, subject to acoustic influences, experiences the primary elements of socialisation.[14]

Alfred Tomatis, (1920–2001), a French Ear Nose and Throat (ENT) surgeon who developed a sound therapy intervention to treat a range of disorders, observed that rhythm and sound are processed through different parts of the ear. The vestibular apparatus is involved with the feeling and production of rhythm; the cochlear apparatus addresses pitch and sound.

Using fibre-optic cameras, Tomatis discovered that the foetus will move a specific muscle in response to specific sounds (phonemes) sounded by the mother. This varies from baby to baby, but the same sound produces the same muscular reaction. This would suggest an early link between action and language, a critical relationship that supports later effective learning.[15] Through the vestibular system rhythm also takes a functional role: 'Where there is movement, there is frequency; and wherever there is frequency, there is sound; so that sound is a product of anything that moves.'[16] Tomatis also suggests that as the rhythm, cadence and timbre of mothers' speech remains constant throughout the pre- and postnatal phases, this acoustic link will be a seminal influence in the later development of speech and language. Lazarev's work with mothers and babies (followed through to aged 7) suggests a profound link exists between the experience of sound and rhythm *in utero* (particularly through the mother's voice) and later improved functioning in children's immune systems, motor and language development.

Ellen Dissanayake argues that infants are born with 'protomusical capacities'.[17] As a result of walking upright and possessing an enlarged brain, human infants must experience an extended period of dependence. To ensure mutual interaction and interest, parents and children engage in 'dyadic species-specific interactions that serve to coordinate behaviour and emotions'. Niki Powers writes that 'a baby starts the journey an innately musical, poetical being, moving and hearing with pulse and rhythm, immediately sensitive to the harmonies and discords of human expression in the Self and in companionship with close Others'.[18]

This is what Stephen Malloch and Colwyn Trevarthen term 'communicative musicality'. This is much more than the simplified singsong of motherese or infant-directed speech; it includes 'concurrent special facial expressions and movements of the head and body'. They describe it as 'the ability that allows both infant and mother to sustain a coordinated relationship in time and to share a jointly constructed narrative of moving'.[19]

Trevarthen also suggests that parent–infant communication is:

> *greatly facilitated by the mutual coordination of rhythmical, temporal patterning, or kinematics of vocalisations and gestures, and the expressive use of faces and hands. Therefore the mechanisms of sympathetic engagement are adapted and come to life and function within a cultural framework of meanings, and facilitate learning how to behave in meaningful ways.*[20]

New research suggests that key to these exchanges is rhythm. Infants perceive other people as living, proactive partners and respond in highly adaptive, directed and coordinated ways, communicating expression, initiating intentions and sharing consciousness and emotions. Evidence suggests that as early as 6 weeks, infants enter into a rhythmic communicative partnership with parents, sharing in syllable and phrase elements for three seconds on average, and by 6 months can sustain mutual interactions for ten seconds. Katerina Mazokopaki describes infants' rhythmic expression in movement as 'a series of events in time produced by activity of the body, where a stable beat can be perceived and the various elements have a degree of regularity and organisation'.[21]

Daniel Stern writes that infants and mothers use their voice tones cooperatively with communicative musicality to sustain a harmony and synchronicity of 'emotional narrative envelopes'.[22]

These 'emotional narrative envelopes' play a significant role in supporting effective communication and are equally relevant to all age groups, not just babies. Recognising what constitutes an 'envelope', who is involved and why, what the 'terms of engagement' are, who plays what role, for how long does the narrative last and what the expectations are in terms of cultural practices are all aspects that children need to absorb as they acquire communication skills. For those who experience language difficulties or who are new to English, they are particularly important. Forming safe and secure 'emotional narrative envelopes' within which mistakes may be made, different strategies tried and a range of skills employed to gain results is critical for children who may be highly sensitive to possible exposure of their language issues.

Froebel

There are two pedagogical luminaries for whom music and rhythm lie at the centre of their work. For Friedrich Froebel (1782–1852), education should be continuous, seamless, know no boundaries and be embedded within communities and family. In 1843, frustrated by a lack of attention from his (male) peer group regarding his work, he began training women to become kindergarten teachers, and published a book of songs and instructions for mothers of babies and young children, *Mutter und Koselieder* ('Mother Songs').[23]

He argued that singing to babies was a fundamental way for mothers to convey love and care, that 'latent emotions may be stirred' and that the content of the songs would help both parties 'to understand their place, role and purpose in the world and connectedness to their surroundings and their (divine) creator'.

Froebel emphasised that singing was not only a pedagogical tool but also an invaluable emotional conduit. The songs are designed for children to become aware of their bodies, particularly their hands when performing the finger-play songs. Travelling or 'wandering songs' are aimed at children who are walking and the original versions may be extended into more complex stories and plays as they mature.

Sacha Powell and colleagues conducted a study to determine how singing may support interactions between practitioners and babies in their care.[24] Seven daycare settings and 23 staff participated. They determined prior to the study that specific barriers existed that affected the quality and quantity of verbal interactions between adults and the babies in their care. These related to the pressure of sticking to routines, the general 'busyness' of baby rooms and a simple lack of appreciation of the best times to interact: e.g. nappy-changing, nap-time and feeding. Evidence suggested that practitioners *did* sing with the babies, but usually these moments included action songs and not lullabies. They were using songs as a means to manage the babies' behaviour: as a distraction, to quieten them and to signify changes (e.g. leaving time). When practitioners reviewed the film evidence, they understood how much more engaged the babies became when lullabies were sung to them. However, they also realised that they only ever used songs they had inherited through their own experience and family connections; they had never sourced songs from the different cultural backgrounds of the babies.

What the practitioners reported enjoying most was the feeling of a shared social event with the babies and the creation of happy 'emotional narrative envelopes' that singing lullabies to them created. They reported an increased level of eye contact and ability to successfully interpret the babies' individual reactions to likes and dislikes.

Froebel's views about singing as a medium for emotional expressiveness seemed to resonate with the practitioners here. Although they did not pick up on his insistence that the content of songs is as important as the delivery, they concluded that singing may be a useful additional skill to encourage 'emotionally companionable exchanges'.

Steiner

Rhythm in its broadest sense lies at the centre of the Steiner curriculum. The following statement forms part of the Steiner prospectus:[25]

Working with rhythm helps children to live with change, to find their place in the world and begin to understand the past, present and future. It provides a very real foundation for the understanding of time – what has gone before and what will follow – and helps children to relate to the natural and human world. Children's memories are strengthened by recurring experiences: daily, weekly and yearly events in kindergarten (e.g. festivals and celebrations) are remembered and often eagerly anticipated.

In Steiner settings, regular patterns of activities are repeated within the day, week and year to provide structure, routine and rhythm. Each day has its own rhythm that supports activities, and songs, poems and rhymes are used to enhance seasonal themes.

Emphasis on the rhythms of life promotes a feeling of security in children. Seasons come and go, birthdays are celebrated, festivals are noted and the sun rises and sets. The expressive movement art of 'eurhythmy' was developed by Rudolf Steiner and his wife Marie von Sivers. They developed an extensive set of exercises (starting with straight lines and curves and proceeding through successively more complicated geometric figures and choreographed forms) to develop coordination and concentration. Apparatus was also promoted in order to develop balance and precision in movement.

The purpose of eurhythmy is to 'awaken and strengthen the expressive capacities of children through movement'. Movements may be performed to classical music, poetry or stories, although silent pieces are also created. Steiner described eurhythmy as 'the art of the soul' and that it affects the very core of who we are. Only by engaging in productive rhythmic activities is it possible to communicate with others and the world on a meaningful level. 'In eurhythmy we present in the form and movement of the human organism a direct external proof of man's share in the life of the supersensible world.'[26]

Taking a rather more pragmatic approach, Phyllis Weikart developed her Rhythmic Competency Program on the basis of data collected by Kuhlman and Schweinhart (1992), whose evidence suggested that children's academic achievement was related to musical timing. Weikart's programme was based on the concept of 'movement key experiences' that included steady beat independence, coordination, aural-visual processing, attending and concentrating, 'space' awareness, language acquisition, creativity and problem-solving, planning and decision-making, and energy and vitality. The three-tiered structure of the sessions started with the child initially 'acting upon movement direction', then 'moving in non-locomotor ways and with objects', and finally 'expressing creativity in movement'.[27]

In one study, 189 young children experienced the Rhythmic Competency Program for approximately ten minutes a week for three months. The control group of 169 children continued with their usual music sessions. The practical sessions for the intervention group were delivered by the children's music teachers, who followed a very precise programme related to the 'movement key experiences'. The children were asked to follow movement directions, feel and express the beat and move with others to different genres of music. All the children in both groups were tested on the California Achievement Test pre- and post-intervention. Those in the intervention group not only improved their scores for rhythmic competency but also increased their rating on the standard test by a significant degree.[28]

In 2012, Susan Courey and Endre Balogh created their Academic Music Program to support children's awareness of fractions.[29] The programme involved clapping, chanting, drumming and using gestures and symbols 'to help children understand parts of a whole and learn the academic language of math'. In their study, 67 children aged 7 participated. Half the group joined a six-week movement-based program; the rest continued with regular maths lessons. Children completing the programme scored 50 per cent higher on the final fractions test than those in the corresponding group.

Adam Ockelford works with severely autistic children and uses music to enhance the communication skills of those who are nonverbal. For children on the autism spectrum (Autism Spectrum Condition or ASC), music provides a meaningful and productive way to communicate when language may be unavailable. His visionary practice demonstrates how adults supporting these children may 'use music before language takes hold to convey feelings and promote social bonding, and subsequently to scaffold and augment language through songs, chants and musical games'.[30] Francesca Happé also makes the point that 'music is an important common ground for people with ASC and neurotypicals' and music sessions offer a unique and secure framework through which many of the skills and disciplines of social interaction may be experienced and developed.[31]

Cross agrees:

Music's ambiguity allows for the exploration and rehearsal of skills in interacting with others, minimising the risks of engaging in conflict or misunderstanding, risks that would be more likely were the medium linguistic with unambiguous reference. Musical play can be a way to acquire social competence and confidence in cost-free and mutually rewarding interaction.[32]

Bowman adds an important physical dimension:

If listening and music-making activate and deploy the same neural circuitry as bodies in motion, we have the material basis for the claim that bodily action is an indelible and fundamental part of what music – Nkwa music – is. And if music requires bodily motion as a precondition of its being, so too may music shape and inform other possibilities for embodied being.[33]

Trevarthen makes a fundamental point here: 'We can agree in the shared embodied space of music and dance, whereas we may disagree in the shared objective space of verbal discussion, because our version of reality differs from that of another.'[34] It is the parity of status of all participants in movement, the shared spaces and rhythms, the sensitivity to others, the immediacy of response and the honesty and transparency of interactions that are all critical factors in supporting children's communication skills.

THE STUDY

It was noted that the children participating in the study experienced significant difficulty joining in any activity that depended on timing and rhythmic competency for success. Sitting in a circle and clapping, demonstrating the components of action songs and engaging in parachute games were all particularly challenging.

With Weikart's study in mind, and Steiner and Froebel's inclusion of rhythm as an aid to supporting group identity, each session of the movement programme began with a short sequence (see also Chapter 5):

- All stand in a circle – jump to the music, then stop – stand still and clap to the beat – then stamp to the beat.

- Hold hands and jump together – walk right and left in a circle – move in and out – stand very still – then change places.

- Sit in a circle – each child, in turn, runs around and back to their place – others clap or drum their feet.

The music chosen for each session had a strong, steady beat that did not include lyrics. The structure of the movement sequence remained the same. This was designed to give the children something to remember, anticipate and perform easily. Before starting each week, Nina asked them if they could remember how to begin and encouraged them to demonstrate the movements to each other. Verbal communication was not required – that removed any pressure or fear of failure. This was a simple but effective way of immediately binding the group together in a common task that was enjoyable and stress-free. The opening sequence became a very important part of the children's experience of the movement programme.

Nina also used rhythm and rhyme effectively throughout her independent delivery of the programme. In her first session, during which she used miniature teddies to explore the theme of prepositions, each child put their teddy in the box and waited while everyone knocked on the box and said together: 'Knock, knock, knock – who's in the box? Guess whose teddy?' This provoked language production as they manipulated the teddies and provided meaningful material for them to talk about. Because they so enjoyed this, she designed a new rhyme for each session, using the same rhythm but changing the words. The children subsequently used different body parts to make the rhythm, which provided an additional spur for vocabulary acquisition. The *context* for communication was relevant and a safe environment was created within which the usual precision and accuracy of word production did not feature and the children were free to use whatever interactive strategies they preferred.

Action songs

Their behaviour when exposed to action songs in the nursery was concerning. They found the language and vocabulary confusing (why is the spider 'incy wincy' – what is a bobbin – where is the bus with a conductor?) and the accompanying actions did not make much sense. So, was there any merit in encouraging them to participate more proactively?

Patricia Eckerdal and Bjorn Merker describe action songs thus:

Action songs combine melody, words and schematised sequences of obligatory bodily action into a narrative sequence that provides scope for the infant to participate in predictable ways in interaction with an adult.[35]

If the purpose of these songs is to be a 'hypothetical language device', then lyrics that contain idiosyncratic and marginally grammatical constructions and nonsense words are patently ill-suited to the task. Musically they are hardly challenging. It doesn't matter if they are sung out of tune or continually interrupted. So what is their point?

Eckerdal and Merker provide some answers: that the language and melody included are not particularly important because the 'integrity of communicative contact' takes precedence over any aesthetic aspect. It is not really about active participation either as this is often more effective in other scenarios, and the same goes for communicative exchanges as these happen more meaningfully elsewhere.

What they conclude in their study of infant–mother engagement in action songs is that it is fundamentally about 'the process of first introduction to active participation in human ritual'. The nonverbal communicative competence shared by parent and infant becomes a 'means of instruction for the infant's first participation in ritual interactions'. The purpose of action songs is 'mere participation in the arbitrary form itself', not a perfect performance of actions or remembrance of words, but 'exposure to the ritual form without requiring formal contributions by the infant'.

This is a useful way of approaching action songs, particularly if they are used with children who experience language difficulties or who are new to English. What is important is joining in, contributing, feeling comfortable in a group and having a mutually positive rhythmic experience that does not claim to be relevant or meaningful.

Timing ability

For young children, one of the most important implications of embedding music and rhythm in our practice is the development of their timing ability. This skill has fundamental links to many sports, particularly those that use bats/racquets/balls and gymnastics and dance – all disciplines that are heavily dependent on timing ability for success. Children need plenty of opportunities to engage in trial and error to develop their timing ability. Observing the children in the study struggle with parachute games, it was apparent they were physically quite able to join in but the correct timing of activities eluded them: when to let go, when to lift up and down and when to run underneath before it dropped down again.

Music and rhythm can play a vital role in supporting children's development, particularly their communication and language skills. They provide a social and unifying element in their lives, forming a bridge between home and settings and a critical link to the wider community.

Engaging in rhythmic activities provides a safe space for all children to join in and contribute, and it supports the 'older and alternative' ways of engaging with music that Cross writes about.

For many children, opportunities to actively contribute and feel part of a group are experienced infrequently, maybe due to language issues, physical ability or basic temperament. Working with music and rhythm offers them a supportive context in which they may acquire, rehearse and refine their communication skills. By using movement as a framework, all children may contribute using the skills they own already and are comfortable to employ.

In this poem, Gabrielle Roth beautifully captures why music and rhythm are so important in all our lives:[36]

> *Energy moves in waves,*
> *waves move in patterns,*
> *patterns move in rhythms.*
> *A human being is just that:*
> *energy, waves, patterns, rhythms.*
> *Nothing more. Nothing less.*
> *A dance.*

5

Group Work Supports Communication and Language

we are evolved to know, think, communicate, create new things
and care for one another in movement—through a sense of
being in rhythmic time with motives and in tune with feelings
to share the energy and harmony of meaning and of relating.

Stephen Malloch and Colwyn Trevarthen,
Communicative Musicality[1]

CONTEXT

In 2013, *Forbes* picked up on a small-scale study conducted in Bethlehem, Pennsylvania, in the USA, in which local employers were asked to list what attributes they prioritised when hiring staff, mainly college graduates. Top of the list was the ability to work effectively in a team, whatever speciality they had studied.[2] *Forbes* determined that, if this skill was not evidenced and embedded, the chances of employment would be compromised.

In 2017, Youth Employment UK published a report that identified the core skills most valued by employers: communication, teamwork, problem-solving, self-management and self-belief. This is despite the fact that 60 per cent of available jobs in ten years' time may not yet be evident and many of these will be technology-related, not a field that usually demands a high degree of interpersonal skills.[3]

Do twenty-first-century lifestyles, education and entertainment fail to provide children with the range of opportunities afforded previous generations to acquire and practise the skills that support effective communication and teamwork?

Sioban Boyce suggests that the prevalence of forward-facing buggies, changing models of mealtimes, shopping and play, the ubiquity of DT devices and day-long childcare have all conspired to affect the quality and quantity of organic opportunities that ensured children enjoyed and appreciated extended periods of time being, playing and working together.[4]

Sally Howard writes that 'the brain learns best when it is challenged in an atmosphere of relaxed alertness, thus creating the optimum emotional and physical environment in which to take risks and to explore new experiences'.[5] Creating this 'optimum emotional and physical environment' is highly dependent on well-developed interpersonal communication skills that are essentially preverbal, physical and movement-based.

Successfully moving, communicating and working in a group requires spatial awareness, the ability to turn-take, anticipate outcomes, maintain eye contact and correct posture, keep still and match gesture to intent, long before spoken language is added. How children manage themselves physically within a group has a profound effect on their ability to make and sustain friendships, how they are perceived by adults and how effectively they engage with the nursery day. Misinterpreting situations, interrupting or interfering in others' play, invading their space and talking over them, are all scenarios that have the potential to compromise relationships because the physical skills that form the basis for positive communication are not soundly established.

Returning to Locke and Rousseau: these thinkers held very different points of view regarding the way in which children should take their place in 'civilised society'. For Locke, 'citizenship' was critical, and this was to be gained by producing 'social beings' that could fit in and manage the demands of culture and community with ease. Becoming a 'man of action in society' was of paramount importance. In contrast, Rousseau determined that children should be removed from society to develop all-important personal moral standing. Only then would they be ready, willing and able to take their rightful place in society.[6]

So, for Locke, citizens are formed within a community and parental involvement is critical. For Rousseau, citizenship emerges only after an extended period apart from parental and community influence.

There are profound differences of opinion regarding the role of adults in children's development and in their expectations for children. These issues are reflected in the varying approaches taken by adults worldwide to embedding the social and communication skills deemed essential to assuring children's place in society.

PARENTING STYLES

The LeVines point out that[7] Western parents 'care a great deal about talking and hope to see their children talking as early as possible'. They conduct 'play dialogues', mock conversations (proto-conversations) in which they ask questions of their infants and provide relevant answers. Proactive verbal engagement between children and parents is considered a critical factor in ensuring smooth overall development. African parents, in contrast, tend not to engage in direct language instruction. It is assumed that children will learn to understand and speak without overt guidance, and that the environment will offer continual opportunities to participate in verbal interactions with a wide variety of people within the community.

As the LeVines determine:

the acquisition of the basic grammatical competence to make and understand sentences in a particular language during the early years (especially between eighteen and thirty-six months) is a robust universal development in humans that makes few demands on parents, particularly if the family's residence offers an environment full of opportunities for watching and participating in speech every day – even when most of it is not directed to the child.[8]

Chinese parents choose a third way: a form of 'didactic guidance' in which children are viewed as 'apprentices in an age-graded respect hierarchy'. They are not treated as equal conversational partners but must learn to understand the importance of 'submission to authority and life experience'. Western expectations for children's early verbal competence and independence do not feature in the childrearing goals of Chinese parents. They have minimal language performance expectations for young children, preferring the 'I talk and you will listen, for your own moral benefit' approach.

Japanese mothers believe that developing their children's sense of *omoiyari* – empathy – lies at the very heart of all successful relationships. They bring awareness of the potential feelings of others into all conversations with their children while teaching them how to express their own feelings within an empathetic framework. Japanese children become very sensitive to the possibility of hurting others verbally and attuned to their own capacity for provoking negative reactions. The philosophy of *kokoro* underpins all their relationships – that considers heart, mind and a sense of 'knowing in the world' to be inseparably linked. Japanese mothers therefore place significant value on the interpersonal aspects of babies' needs and much less on their cognitive interest in objects and events.[9]

Asian children are often described as *dŏngshì* or 'understanding'. This 'understanding' emerges through a significant period of apprenticeship with adults who imbue a sense of moral leadership and authority. Individuals are considered primarily as part of the greater whole of family and community in which harmony is all.

For Western children, the prevailing culture is a focus on the individual. Becoming a functioning, contained, independent unit is the desired state. Being unique, verbally confident and autonomous are all considered highly desirable. The LeVines write of American children that:

From infancy onwards the child is encouraged to characterise himself in terms of his favourite toys and foods and those he dislikes: his tastes, aversions and consumer preferences are viewed not only as legitimate but as essential aspects of his growing individuality – and a prized quality of an independent person.

Susan Cain also reminds us that 'a profound difference in cultural values has a powerful impact on the personality styles favoured by each culture'.[10] Western education prioritises individuality, democracy, equality, initiative, autonomy and self-reliance. The Asian approach values diligence, sincerity, perseverance, endurance, humility and respect.

What different cultures and communities prioritise in terms of children's development will have a significant effect on provision and practice in the learning and care environments they experience. Jerome Bruner writes that 'perhaps even more than with most cultural matters, childrearing practices and beliefs reflect local conceptions of how the world is and how the child should be readied for living it'.[11] In the West, a continual flow of advice is available on how to make children more social and communicative, when environments and lifestyles often fail to support the basic skills that would ensure this. To Asian ears, this focus on individuality and early verbal independence is quite strange when *their* emphasis is on fitting in, being respectful, empathetic and functioning effectively within a group.

This emphasis on the individual in childhood learning and development has a significant effect on children's relationships with adults, although as Helen Penn reminds us:

The nuclear family itself, which underscores so much of the literature on early childhood, is a recent historical invention, not a universal phenomenon. Parenting is not a given. Many societies are profoundly communal, and kinship and community counts far more than individual relationships.

We think it's important to respect individuality, but for others, being an individual, on your own and without the constant intimate presence of others, is the worst kind of punishment.[12]

Liz Brooker determines what an idealised picture of the 'early-childhood child' would consist of, one who is:[13]

- Full of potential, naturally curious and eager to learn.

- Active, outgoing and communicative.

- Independent, autonomous and able to show initiative.

- Capable of selecting and sustaining self-chosen games and activities.

- Able to learn through play and exploration.

They also 'need to be able to choose...make choices...maintain things independently, things that interest *them*, the sort of things that *they* will then learn from; and you have to have enough opportunity for them to develop their social skills, because that's one of the most important things'.[14] Often, these expectations can be demanding and exhausting for some young children.

The Early Years Foundation Stage Curriculum (EYFSC) states that:

Every child is a unique child who is constantly learning and can be resilient, capable, confident and self-assured.

Children learn to be strong and independent through positive relationships.[15]

With this focus on uniqueness, individuality, strength and independence, how may children develop the skills needed to work effectively in a group or as a team? There is little acknowledgement here of their importance. The Japanese approach of minimising competition and helping children develop the feeling that 'we're all in it together' – harmonising emotionally with others, being a kind, responsible member of the learning community – seems quite at odds with the ethos of mainstream Western early years practice and provision.

There are three approaches in which group work, cooperation, community and responsibility are fundamental to practice: Forest School, Steiner and Montessori.

FOREST SCHOOL/STEINER/MONTESSORI

Martin Pace suggests that one of the reasons the Forest School approach is so beneficial for children is that:

We take the same children in each group into the forest each week by design. The principal motives for this are that we find children bond better in a consistent group. Relationships forged in the woodland can be very strong.

> *Perhaps most significantly, children quickly recognise each other's competencies and call on those as required, an affirming experience for the individual.*[16]

The emphasis on engaging with projects that require a high degree of practical cooperation minimises the need for complex language use. Forest School is an active promoter of risky play and engaging with the outdoor environment, but much more interesting is how the children choose to communicate with each other. By removing the pressure to contribute verbally, children experience an unexpected level of freedom to employ a wide range of interactive skills that often remain unacknowledged and underused in mainstream settings. Solitary exploration in a forest setting will never be as much fun as collaborating to construct, build and investigate. As Pace writes, 'just the fact that there is nothing to break or damage, nothing to keep in order or to keep clean, will often immediately relax children and adults alike and give a sense of freedom to any endeavour'.[17]

The Steiner literature makes clear that: 'the kindergarten is a community of "doers", and through "work" the child learns not only social and domestic skills but is able to develop "good motor and practical skills"'.[18] In aligning Steiner principles with the 'learning goals' of the EYFSC, it clearly states that children are expected to 'interact with others, negotiating plans and activities and taking turns in conversation'.

The role of 'mood' in Steiner settings is important, promoting an almost Japanese sense of empathy and sensitivity to others. The creation of different moods for different activities encourages awareness of how 'invisible boundaries' often determine appropriate behaviour in various situations. Mealtimes are always sociable occasions, so, too, is the marking of festivals; but, equally, there are times for quietness and introspection. Caring for others and the environment is central; contributing to the group, feeling a sense of belonging and taking responsibility for personal welfare are all important elements of Steiner practice.

According to Montessori,[19] at around 3 years, children enter the 'social embryonic' stage, when they become aware of being part of a group and develop a sense of belonging to a cohesive social unit. The Montessori principle of learning in mixed age groups strengthens the formation of supportive units and the emergence of empathy so prized by the Japanese. Visiting a Montessori setting recently, I was frequently told, 'We're a community here.' The sense of cohesion across age groups and between children and adults was evident in practice.

DT has offered us new ways of viewing concepts of community, groups and teams. Helen Knauf[20] presents an inspiring case for using technology, particularly Twitter, so that 'the social world of the kindergarten is connected to other social worlds and becomes visible within and as part of them (e.g. to people in the USA or kindergarten-aged children around the world).' She writes that 'the space of the real world is extended into the virtual sphere'. The traditional model of education is replaced by a more open model: 'You are what you can share.'

The community is not just the school class or social community; it also refers to a virtual global community in which pupils have 'digital citizenship'. Use of Twitter in this study strengthened the children's concept of community, that they could be active participants in varying modes of communication and extend their knowledge of topics by linking up with other interested parties around the globe.

By about 9 months old, infants begin to feel that they are part of a wider group: that there are 'interested others' who care for, talk to and entertain them. What matters most of all at this stage is the consistency of interactions – the attachments they form, not just with people and peer groups but with objects and the environments they experience.

In the 1960s, Marjorie Boxall developed 'nurture groups' in order to ameliorate the negative effects on children's development of poor nurturing and insecure attachments. These groups were designed for parents to understand and respond to children's behaviour more effectively. As she writes: 'The emphasis within a nurture group is on emotional growth, focusing on broad-based experiences in an environment that promotes security, routines, clear boundaries and carefully planned, repetitive learning opportunities.'[21]

Practitioners ever since have taken the central tenets of Boxall's approach, and the emotional wellbeing of children has become an important part of the rationale for including 'circle time' in daily practice.

CIRCLE TIME

The American statistician William Deming (1900–93) promoted the concept of the 'Quality Circle' in the 1940s as a means of assuring quality throughout commercial organisations. Initially adopted by Japanese companies, the ideal circle would include eight to ten people who met regularly to discuss workplace productivity and motivation.[22] Jenny Mosley further developed the concept of quality circles in school environments in the 1990s. These were weekly 'listening times' during which staff, parents and children could discuss openly any issues that concerned them and engage in games and exercises that fostered community spirit.[23]

Kathryn Solly writes that 'children's thinking should be nurtured and enhanced by social, collaborative learning, a collective intelligence that forms the sound basis for learning how the world works within a community of learners'. But does the current emphasis on individuality and uniqueness actually support this approach?[24]

There is a definite consensus that circle time is an important element of daily practice and that this is one way in which a community of learners may be fostered. However, as Jennie Lindon warns, 'Like any potentially good idea, there has been a problem that circle time has been increasingly promoted as a vehicle to carry so many adult hopes for children's learning.' She adds, 'If children struggle with communication, they need a much more personal approach and must not be considered as posing problems for adults.'[25]

We have all witnessed circle times that, for various reasons, just don't work: too many children are participating, interruptions keep happening, planning is inflexible, the time is too long, some children do not wish to engage and are physically uncomfortable, adult expectations may be unreasonable and it takes place at an unsuitable time of day.

So, what are the skills that children need to manage this central part of a nursery day?

Although a successful circle time largely depends on fluent verbal interaction, it is actually the underpinning physical skills that determine the quality of children's engagement.

The ability to remain still is one of the most difficult skills for children to gain. Remaining alert and unmoving requires even tension in the muscles and the correct degree of strength and control to maintain a balanced posture. Because stillness involves balance, the vestibular system must be well-developed through continual movement experience in order for this to be achieved. It is extremely challenging for children's bodies to maintain the required physical position during circle time (usually cross-legged), let alone to consider forming individual and appropriate verbal contributions.

A well-developed proprioceptive sense is also necessary to accommodate the demands of sitting in close proximity to others. As Gill Connell points out,[26] children with poor spatial awareness 'may misread how much space there is to sit in and accidentally sit on another child. Visual estimation of space is an advanced ability in large part because the child is still mapping her body'.

The vestibular system, working alongside the auditory system, plays a critical role in the development and processing of language. As Anne O'Connor says, 'Being able to hear isn't the same as being able to process *what we hear.*' Understanding is linked to the way vestibular sensations become integrated through physical experiences within the environment. Vestibular development is critical for effective auditory processing and the production of speech that requires motor control and planning for the muscles in the throat, tongue, lips and jaw to work synchronously.[27] Jean Ayres also suggests that the urge to vocalise is linked to movement and vestibular stimulation. If children do not experience a level of vestibular stimulation in their earliest years through movements like rocking, swaying, rolling, sliding, swinging, running very fast, spinning and twirling that *provoke* vocalisations, their future speech and language development may be adversely affected.[28]

It has been suggested that Broca's area of the frontal lobe in the brain that is responsible for speech and formal reasoning may also affect motor skills involving the hand. If hand movements are closely related to the precise articulation of words, then being active and engaged is a much stronger stimulus for communication than simply sitting in a circle. Carla Hannaford reminds us that, 'There is a greater array of receptors for touch around the mouth and hands than any other area of the body.'[29]

Before young children can begin to contribute verbally within a group and manage the demands of team work, certain fundamental and primarily physical skills that inform and support effective communication need to be in place.

NONVERBAL COMMUNICATION

Boyce, in her Not Just Talking programme, advocates an emphasis on preverbal skills as an effective preparation for successful later verbal interaction. Although this programme does not include a significant movement element and is specifically aimed at children experiencing language difficulties, it is interesting that an experienced speech/language professional promotes the role of underlying physical skills that affect verbal communication.[30]

It is generally accepted that 60–90 per cent of communication is nonverbal. This includes the ability to read facial expressions and body language correctly, use appropriate gestures and body positions, determine the level of body tension required, understand boundaries and spatial norms, maintain eye contact, engage in turn-taking, timing, manage touch and silence without feeling anxious, and anticipate the beginning and ending of interactions.

Many of these skills come under the banner of 'social skills'. Deborah Plummer suggests that, in practice:

Helping children to build social skills will enable them to develop a balance between the formation of healthy relationships and personal autonomy. We are giving them the tools for social intelligence and personal fulfilment. We are promoting mutual respect and understanding while still recognising and celebrating the integrity of the individual.[31]

Balancing the need to form healthy peer group relationships, connecting with others and negotiating social situations – with fostering self-esteem, self-reliance, self-respect and self-efficacy will always be a challenge.

How may these essential social and communication skills be embedded in a movement context, and what does movement in particular add to the children's experience of their rehearsal and refinement?

Lindon has coined the term 'the invisible backpack', meaning what life experience, expectations, behaviours, habits, dispositions and values[32] children bring with them into their learning community. In terms of communication, an awareness of what constitutes this 'invisible backpack' is important because it affects directly the opportunities afforded children to work and play together and navigate circle time successfully. As stated previously, cultural expectations of children's verbal independence vary greatly, as does their social experience within communities and joining in group activities with those of a similar age. The whole agenda around sharing and turn-taking may therefore be confusing: sharing space and sharing 'stuff' require very different skills, so, too, does sharing adult attention and engagement.

THE STUDY

During the study, one of the issues Nina encountered in her therapeutic practice was teaching the children specific social and play skills out of any relevant or meaningful context. Focusing on particular skills that she had assessed previously as being immature ignored the wider context in which these skills needed to be used reliably and effectively.

As she clarified in conversation:

We focus on developing underlying skills, play skills, but we usually teach these in a very explicit way, by actually pulling out the rules: 'This situation requires this behaviour.' So, for example, how do you not interrupt a conversation? You have to wait.

But being able to wait requires a raft of physical skills: stillness, eye contact, timing, anticipation, correct body position, spatial awareness. These children found managing activities within the wider nursery group challenging and therefore spent a significant amount of time playing alone because it was much less demanding. The physical skills that anchor effective communication were not reliably embedded and they did not have enough in their 'invisible backpacks' to react and adapt easily to rapidly changing situations.

Forming their own, unified group was important, but it was *moving* in a group that made a significant difference to their social and communication skills. Circle time in the nursery always focused on two particularly challenging skills, sitting still and talking. *Moving* together in a circle to music and using reliable physical skills as a base provided a more positive and effective communicative experience.

Colwyn Trevarthen maintains that the way we appreciate mindfulness in others, how we share in 'each other's personal and coherent consciousness'[33], is through rhythm.

Working in a small group and using music and rhythm provided two positives. First, the children shared difficulties in the same developmental domain that immediately established a unique bond; and second, using music provided a rhythmic structure, a framework within which vital social and communication skills were identified and practised.

The short movement sequence that formed the first phase of each session provided a meaningful context within which the physical skills that inform social interaction were practised (see also Chapter 4):

- *Standing in a circle*: Focus on – spatial awareness/stillness/balance/anticipation/prediction/memory/eye contact.

- *Holding hands*: Focus on – spatial awareness/touch/sensitivity/matching the correct level of physical force to the task.

- *Moving in and out of the circle/left and right*: Focus on – steady beat competence/direction/spatial awareness and sensitivity/anticipating/predicting/memory.

- *Clapping/stamping*: Focus on – timing/anticipating/predicting/ memory/turn-taking.

- *Jumping and running*: Focus on – direction/timing/turn-taking/ anticipating/predicting/spatial awareness/sensitivity.

The two critical factors of this phase were: first, the sequence was simple to remember, and second, it was physically manageable. Achieving the perfect performance was not important; what mattered most was increasing the confidence of the children to engage with each other, within a framework that was based on the physical skills they had gained already and could use without difficulty.

Music and rhythm provided the supportive 'envelope' that unified the group as both adults and children moved *together*, performed the same movements, negotiated the space and navigated obstacles. Young children can often find themselves out of sync with adult rhythms, particularly in speech and movement: 'sympathetic coordination' can be an elusive state to experience when the prevailing culture is one of uniqueness and achievement and not Japanese empathetic communication. Moving together to music became a positive way for the participating adults to communicate with the children and to appreciate the skills they did have rather than focus on those that were so visibly absent in the wider nursery environment.

This group of children had very little in their 'invisible backpacks' regarding curricular materials. They were adept at avoiding activities that could publicise their fine-motor and manipulative difficulties: particularly anything that required using a pencil, pen or paintbrush, that involved threading or cutting (scissors in particular) or that needed a twisting action (e.g. taking tops off sticks of glue).

During the third phase of each session the children made their 'books' together on the floor; a way of recording their experiences and something they took home to share with their families. Preparing the group for this phase was carefully managed. The table and chairs were removed so they were not expected to sit and engage with the materials in the usual way. Physically, they were gradually prepared through their experience of the first two phases, the movement and hand-apparatus components. Moving together in the room supported spatial awareness and sensitivity so that when they shared the floor space and materials there was no tension evident as they reached over, stepped over and occasionally fell over one another. The hand-apparatus phase also supported their engagement with curricular resources. All the skills needed for making their books were practised previously with materials that had no obvious curricular agenda attached. When the time came to use paper, pens, Sellotape, glue and stickers, they were unafraid to try and happily showed each other their work.

Sharing resources was an unfamiliar experience for these children. Not only did they rarely seek to join in activities that required this, but also the verbal skills needed for successful negotiations were not reliably in place. Initially, enough paper, pens, felt-tips and stickers were provided for each child to have their own supply. The only material that *had* to be shared was the single glue stick. This was manageable. They didn't have to negotiate over *everything*, just one resource at a time.

Eventually they began to share more of the resources. *Graduating* these demands was a critical element in ensuring all the children worked within their range of abilities and accommodated the varying levels of challenge that sharing posed to individuals.

Touch

Touch is a critical component of communication for young children, and tactile experience is vital, not just for physical and emotional wellbeing but also for nerve growth and learning development.

As Guy Claxton writes:[34]

> *Skin is at once our most basic and sophisticated organ, and touch is our prototypical sense. We could not live without it, and the other senses are merely specialised forms of touch. One can live a rich life without vision, but without touch one is really in trouble.*

The tactile system is one of the earliest systems to develop *in utero* and is the most mature at birth. Tiffany Field, who founded the Touch Research Institute at Miami Medical School, says that, 'We know from the science of what goes on under the skin that when the skin is moved, pressure receptors are stimulated – this slows down heart rate, blood pressure and the release of cortisol.' Being touched increases the number of natural killer cells, 'the frontline of the immune system. Seratonin (the body's natural antidepressant) also increases, that enables deeper sleep'.[35] As Harry Harlow proved with his experiments on baby monkeys, touch is such a fundamental need that the monkeys in his laboratory chose to *feel* nourished rather than *be* nourished.

The act of being touched increases production of the vital Nerve Growth Factor (NGF) within the brain that helps maintain neuronal functioning. Hannaford writes that if touch is lacking in children's lives, they will exhibit depressed motor and mental functioning. Field also asks if 'kids are getting more and more aggressive because there is less and less touch'.

Being able to tolerate the close proximity of others does not come easily to all children, especially if they are unused to sharing their space with siblings and wider family members.

Graduating the level of physical contact throughout each session was very important and beneficial for the children. The first (movement) phase involved simple tasks such as holding hands and moving in a circle in a carefully controlled way. The possibility of individuals engaging in the 'wrong' or inappropriate level of touch was minimised as the movements were planned and known in advance. This removed any pressure for the children to make their own decisions regarding proximity and touch, which gave them greater confidence to repeat the sequence each week.

Silence

This element informed the third (recording) phase when they sat, lay and worked together on the floor while sharing resources to make their books. Interestingly, the more confident the children became in their ability to manage physical proximity, the quieter and calmer their bodies became, and silence emerged as a very positive addition to their learning experience.

Jonathan Silin writes that silence may be viewed as 'a communicative act, an essential component of human development, a moment to be savoured rather than papered over'. He asks, 'What if we considered the ability to remain still as a critical social skill and silence as an essential aspect of our humanity?'[36]

Working with children who experienced a range of language difficulties taught Nina and me a very important lesson. Silence had always been viewed by adults as a symptom of their difficulties and they experienced it in the nursery as a form of coercion and control. However, throughout the study, companionable rather than anxious silence became a valuable way by which the wellbeing of the group was assessed. As Silin suggests: 'Silence may be about presence as well as absence, care as well as neglect, thoughtfulness as well as mindlessness.' Maryanne Wolf agrees: 'In music, in poetry and in life, the rest, the pause, the slow movements are essential for comprehending the whole.'[37]

When Nina delivered the movement programme independently, she introduced a final 'reflective' component: a mini circle time at the end of each session in which the children could contribute verbally if they wished. She used this as a way to reinforce any vocabulary she had highlighted, communication skills she knew may be needed during the day, and to hear from them what they had enjoyed, how they felt, what they might repeat at home or with their friends.

It was important they had something relevant and meaningful to talk about, a shared, immediate experience that related to a two-dimensional record in the form of their books. How often do we ask children to talk about events that happened days ago, or about concepts of which they have minimal experience or knowledge? Giving these children manageable experiences in a group context afforded them maximum levels of opportunity to contribute verbally and use the communication skills they *did* have to work together effectively.

Ultimately, the experience of moving and working together as a group highlighted the importance of trust. Solly defines trust as a 'firm belief in the reliability, truth or ability of someone or something; and allied to that is respect: the feeling of deep admiration for someone or something elicited by their abilities, qualities or achievements'.[38]

First and foremost, children need to trust themselves and their bodies: that they *are* capable and confident to move in a group, that they *do* have the skills to communicate within defined and manageable moments, that practising essential underlying physical competencies in meaningful situations supports positive interactions.

Respect is threefold: for their own capabilities (that they can contribute in a meaningful way), for each other (being sensitive to individual needs and abilities) and for the environment in which they are moving and working (including resources).

Maybe this is connected to the philosophy of *Ubuntu*: 'the belief in a universal bond of sharing that connects all humanity'. In his book *No Future Without Forgiveness*, Desmond Tutu writes the following:

Ubuntu speaks particularly about the fact that you can't exist as a human being in isolation. It speaks about our interconnectedness. You can't be human all by yourself. And when you have this quality – Ubuntu – you are known for your generosity.

We think of ourselves far too frequently as just individuals, separated from one another, whereas you are connected and what you do affects the whole World. When you do well, it spreads out; it is for the whole of humanity.[39]

6

Apparatus Extends Opportunities for Learning and Development

One of the main problems with product-oriented activities, no matter how well they have been prepared, is that very young children are just not interested in the product the adult has in mind.

Pre-school Learning Alliance (PSLA), *Patterns of Care* (2013)[1]

Learning requires enquiring and experimentation into possibilities, and this requires materials that are open-ended and have the potential for being used in different ways.

Ibid.[2]

Guy Claxton suggests we were *Homo fabricans* long before *Homo sapiens* emerged, 'or rather the *sapiens* grew out of the *fabricans* and still relies deeply upon it'; that 'Without the hand we would not be able to make or use even the simplest tools, and without tools we would demonstrably be a whole lot less smart than we are.' He asks, 'Would the human race be quite different if Adam and Eve had possessed paws instead of hands?'[3]

Frank Wilson also writes that human toolmaking is the centrepiece of our survival strategy, that: 'Humans are behaviourally defined by their uniquely elaborated and refined use of tools and language, lacking either of which human society (and, for all practical purposes, individual human life) would not continue.'[4]

CONTEXT

Mankind has always created tools, utensils, weapons, jewellery, toys and religious artefacts. Our relationship with 'things' is as old as life itself. They are useful, entertaining, comforting and profoundly meaningful. Exploring the properties of natural materials drove innovation: 'In any skilled activity there is a vital role for messing about, trying new tricks, seeing what happens when you force the material to behave differently.'[5]

Hands have played a central role in the emergence of civilisations throughout history. In communication, gesture plays a significant role. Membership, rank and duty are reinforced through use of special signs, salutes and hand postures. Adornment of fingers and hands through gloves, rings, tattoos or varnish conveys complex messages about identity, status and attachments. In religious rituals, highly choreographed hand movements are central to worship, and many social customs surround the use of the left and right hands.[6]

With our uniquely opposing thumbs, nails instead of claws, handedness and fingerprints (established at four months' gestation and unchanging throughout the lifespan), hands speak a 'primary language' and play a critical role in establishing successful relationships, supporting learning and determining occupations.

The advent and universal use of DT has profiled a range of issues relating to hand use. Many activities taken for granted in previous generations have almost disappeared (e.g. tying shoelaces, playing card games, mending clothes, pickling foodstuffs) in favour of tablets and mobiles that require quite different manipulative skills not immediately related to the handedness and dexterity fundamental to many curricular activities, including handwriting.

The bones in young girls' hands develop at approximately 4 years 2 months. For boys, this is established at 5 years 6 months.[7] Add these facts to changes in play opportunities and the daily use of technology, we should be mindful that expecting young children to engage successfully with writing, painting and craft materials may now challenge their capabilities unless much more careful and sensitive preparation is assured.

The relationship between domestic chores and nursery provision was highlighted by the early pedagogues because children engaged in and observed these actions daily. They made meaningful links independently as washing, sweeping, polishing, scrubbing and brushing already played a significant role in family life.

What part can apparatus now play in children's lives that is relevant and meaningful? How can we preserve this link between home and settings that is so critical in supporting overall learning and development when computers may be the only similar resource? Reviewing the different approaches taken by Pestalozzi, Froebel, Montessori, Pikler and Elinor Goldschmied may provide some pointers.

Foreshadowing Froebel, Pestalozzi[8] emphasised the importance of children engaging with *real* materials through *real* experiences; that children learn by doing; that education is about interdependent action and fitness for life. In his school, spelling and reading were practised with pebbles and beans, and fractions were introduced by using apples and cakes.

Froebel

Froebel[9] spent time teaching at Pestalozzi's school in Yverdon in Switzerland, eventually setting up his own school in Griesheim, Thuringia, in Germany. Consciously building on Pestalozzi's work but with a much clearer emphasis on children's physical involvement in learning, Froebel created a set of 'gifts': six beautifully handcrafted small wooden cubes, spheres and cylinders. Using only natural materials, including yarn for the spheres, these 'gifts' were designed to be introduced sequentially to young children, who were initially encouraged to play freely with them alongside a supportive adult. 'Freedom with guidance' was his mantra.

Although there was no prescribed, linear order in the way these gifts were introduced to children, they were carefully seriated and became increasingly complex and challenging to manipulate. Froebel expected the gifts to encourage children to use their environment as a learning aid, to explore possible connections between human and natural life and to establish a firm bond between children and the adults who played alongside them.

Although these classic Froebelian resources are not in widespread use today (they might possibly be in more use in Korea and Japan), the hollow unit blocks and wooden bricks that most children encounter are their legacy. What is most interesting is Froebel's insistence on making visible, meaningful links between the gifts and real life, e.g. that spheres may be realised in peas, berries and oranges. As he said, 'Link. Always link.'

The 3D gifts were designed to underpin and support the 2D 'occupations' of painting, drawing, parquetry and felt-boards in which (unlike the gifts) materials may be transformed, either permanently or later returned to their original form. Clay and sand may move from dry to wet and back to dry again, whereas paint once dry cannot return to its initial state. Ultimately the gifts and occupations were considered to be a child's 'work', that engaging with these materials would embed positive habits, behaviours and dispositions toward work that would later be necessary in the adult world.[10]

Montessori

Montessori also developed a range of didactic materials, or 'materials for development', that were linked to her 'exercises in practical life'. Montessori 'sensorial resources' are particular to this approach: 'The purpose and aim of sensorial work is for the child to acquire clear, conscious information and to be able to then make classifications in his environment.'[11]

These materials are only used by children in the 'prepared' Montessori environment – they are not encountered in other environments they experience daily. Through engagement with the pink tower or cylinders, and by continual repetition of a narrow range of movements performed in a specified pattern and manner, children acquire the skills to 'organise their own intelligence and adapt to the environment'.

There is a defined, correct way of interacting with materials. These are kept limited to ensure that children must wait and be patient for their turn to use. Each material is designed to highlight a very specific skill: 'not so much to give the child new impressions as to give order to the impressions already received'.

As E. Mortimer Standing writes (who worked closely with Maria Montessori for over thirty years): 'There is a right use for everything. The child must respect the principle of order which is inherent in each of the materials. By doing so, the principle of order in the child, which is the intellect, is strengthened.'[12]

The insistence on order in engagement with materials within the prepared environment is linked to Montessori's claim that one of the 'sensitive periods' in children's lives is 'order', that emerges at around two years and continues until four years.

Although each of the materials contains an intrinsic rationale for use, it also 'foreshadows and prepares the way for what will follow later'. For example, use of the seriated cylinders is designed to support specific skills needed for later handwriting.

In contrast to the sensorial materials that are designed quite deliberately to bear no immediate relation to daily life, the 'practical life' exercises that Montessori created mirror historical everyday activities and include materials that are real, breakable and functional – though possibly not as familiar to children in the twenty-first century.[13]

Again, there are graduated activities, that begin with pouring, folding and carrying, progress to handwashing, dusting, sweeping and watering plants and culminate in exercises of 'grace and courtesy and control of movement'. There is a right way of fulfilling these tasks that children perform individually, at their own pace in an uncompetitive and supportive environment. All tasks must be completed before moving on to another activity or resource.

Inevitably, Froebelians and Montessorians have significant differences in their rationale and use of apparatus. For the former, children should have the freedom and liberty to make their own decisions about resources: to explore their properties, play and have fun. For Montessorians, this 'making everything out of everything' is not encouraged or valued.

Pikler

Another approach to apparatus was created by Emmi Pikler. In Pikler practice, hands play a central role. Adults will always approach children with palms facing upwards: a peaceful, inviting and trusting gesture. They will never either place an object in a child's hand deliberately or remove something without mutual agreement.[14]

For Pikler, independent experimentation is the most profound source of learning. Surrounding infants with oceans of stimulating stuff simply blocks their innate ability to explore, enquire and experiment. As Eva Kallo writes: 'It is an exciting moment when the infant first discovers his hand and later becomes engrossed in observing it.'[15]

Play materials, or playthings, are not introduced to infants until they are observed to play regularly with their hands and begin to notice their immediate surroundings. Hanging mobiles do not feature in Pikler settings as these have little merit and only provide an unnecessary distraction from the valuable experience of exploring their bodies. If we think back to the 'enabling' and 'immediate' environments of Chapter 3, this is how it all begins: investigation of a small body part before relating to a 'first plaything'; in the Pikler approach this is a soft, colourful cloth 35 x 35 cm that is carefully placed next to infants of around 3 months old when lying on their backs.

As Pikler wrote, 'He may ignore it for weeks, but he ordinarily notices it quite readily, crumples it up, twists it this way and that, puts it in his mouth. Often, the infant draws it over his eyes and is then startled when he suddenly finds himself in the dark.'[16]

Infants are never overstimulated but afforded ample time, space and opportunity to explore *all* the properties of the apparatus. Agency and ownership are important because even very small children are considered perfectly capable of making their own decisions and acting accordingly.

Between 3 and 6 months, a small selection of objects that may be held easily in one hand are introduced and must be accessible from a supine position. These objects are often made of natural materials – wood, wool, cloth, rubber – and may increase in complexity and weight as children grow and develop.

Between 6 and 12 months, the range and number of objects slowly increase (to 3–4), although infants are never discouraged from playing with the same objects for extended periods. The emphasis on exploring all the properties of each piece of apparatus is important and something that should be seriously considered. Just because we *can* give children so many choices and so much 'stuff' is available to us doesn't mean we have to use all of it all the time. An interesting nugget: balls are not introduced to infants in Pikler settings unless and until they can be retrieved independently, either by crawling on tummies or hands and knees.

The Pikler approach requires highly developed observation skills 'to figure out which and how many toys a particular group of children needs so that each child has an adequate assortment keyed to his interests and developmental stage to choose from.'[17] As Pikler said, 'A child who achieves things through independent experimentation acquires an entirely different kind of knowledge than does a child who has readymade solutions offered to him.'[18]

The Pikler insistence on valuing and respecting even the youngest child's ability to act and interact independently without overt or intrusive stimulation from adults is refreshing. Affording infants the time and space to first become familiar with their bodies, particularly their hands, before creating relationships with objects and investigating their properties is unique.

Elinor Goldschmied and Sue Gascoyne

Elinor Goldschmied (1910–2009) introduced the concept of treasure baskets to teachers in the 1950s, and they soon became an accepted component of the Italian nursery system. However, it was not until the 1980s that this innovative approach to play with very young children between 7 months (when they are usually sitting without support) and 15 months (when many are on their feet and on the move) gained wider acceptance.[19]

Treasure baskets consist of a range of natural and everyday objects that 'promote relaxed exploratory play that enable babies to discover for themselves'. Goldschmied stressed the importance of including materials that support all the senses: hearing, vision, touch, smell, taste. Commercially produced plastic toys are not included in a treasure basket; everything must be 'safe, interesting and provide open-ended outcomes'.[20]

There are, however, very precise instructions that inform planning for use of the basket, its dimensions, content and the adult role. Goldschmied determined that only by complying with these instructions would the experience for children be of the highest quality.

Engagement with the treasure baskets (proposed as a daily experience) developed into the concept of heuristic play for children in the second year of life. As Sonia Jackson writes: 'Put simply, it consists of offering a group of children for a defined period in a controlled environment a large number of different types of objects and receptacles to play with without adult intervention.'[21] Again, the materials are (mostly) familiar, abundant and very carefully selected. Heuristic play is certainly not random: in its pure form, there is a defined space (clear and carpeted), a designated time (30–40 minutes) and a highly ritualised presentation and clearing away of the chosen resources.[22]

The rationale for treasure baskets and heuristic play is to give children time and space to explore materials and opportunities to extend their personal schemas in a safe, supportive environment, 'to develop independence of thought, explore the senses and develop social behaviours including sharing'.[23]

Sue Gascoyne has further developed these ideas to work with older children in 'sensory-rich play'. She observed how older children used the sensory objects 'less in an exploratory way and more in a symbolic or representational way. Objects can be combined with other resources such as sand and water or used in adult-led ways to categorise or explore properties such as whether they will float or sink'. She firmly believes further research is needed to identify the developmental transition between exploratory play – 'what does it do?' – to pretend play – 'what can I do with it?' This may have a positive effect on the opportunities afforded older children to engage in sensory-rich play and identify further resources that may be incorporated.[24]

The Japanese have a very different approach to resources. Thomas Weaver, in his discussion of early years' provision there, cites Japanese children creating *dorodango* – mud balls as an example. To construct these, children carefully take lumps of clay and patiently roll them in their hands, creating identical smooth spherical shapes.[25]

For Western practitioners and teachers, the purpose of this activity would be to explore size, shape and texture. In Japan, the purpose is to evoke mental balance and peace of mind. Mental preparation, attitude, perseverance and self-motivation are of paramount importance as the repetitive nature of the task and the creation of perfect objects leads to a 'calm and beautiful mind'.

Engagement with materials has historically played a critical role in the development of pedagogical thinking. Approaches differ. Both Froebel and Montessori created specific seriated resources, but Froebel insisted on the inclusion of a play element that Montessori omitted. Pikler takes a minimalist approach: one resource at a time is to be intimately explored; in contrast, the treasure baskets include a wide range of articles for infants to engage with simultaneously.

These approaches have the following principles in common: the degree of respect that children are expected to show towards resources; mainly natural materials should be used; and *how* children engage with apparatus is considered more significant than the rehearsal and refinement of specific manipulative/curricular skills.

APPARATUS IN A MOVEMENT CONTEXT

The use of apparatus in a *movement* context differs from the approaches mentioned previously in the following ways:

- Any apparatus should be cost-free (if possible) and available in all the environments children experience. For this reason, mainly familiar, household materials are used.

- No specific agenda is attached to any resource. The outcomes are always open-ended.

- The contributions made by children when engaging with materials is valued. Their ideas should not be compromised by predetermined adult expectations.

- A wide and varied range of physical skills is practised. The focus is not only on small manipulative skills that have obvious links to curricular learning, but engagement is extended to include gross motor and locomotor skills that relate to other physical disciplines and support overall health and wellbeing.

- Apparatus is carefully chosen to illuminate and extend the understanding of concepts. These may be abstract (e.g. speed, time), social (e.g. sharing, turn-taking), emotional (e.g. persevering, supporting) or mathematical (e.g. pattern, shape).

- Apparatus is not mixed. One type of material is chosen at a time: either one piece for all to share (e.g. a large box/sports bag) or many of the same (e.g. paper bags, plastic bottle tops, socks). This is applicable to infants and older children.

- The adult role varies throughout. This may include direct instruction or demonstration, gentle support and free play. Adults are capable of adapting and reacting according to children's responses.

'Conversations with a paper bag'

This demonstrates the breadth and depth of learning possibilities offered by a simple, easily accessible resource (Table 6.1). Paper bags may be sourced easily and are available in a range of sizes and colours, with writing or clear sides. This type of material is often called 'vanilla', 'asensory', 'neutral', 'a relief from the sensory world'.

Table 6.1 Conversations with a paper bag

Actions	Concepts	Skills
Place bag flat on knees. *Pat* bag with both hands – keeping wrists on the bag.	Size, shape. Loud, quiet, soft, hard. Changes in movement dynamic/force.	Processing instructions. Sitting still. Core strength, Balance. Coordination.
Scratch bag with *all* fingers – very slowly – then as fast as possible. Isolate each finger and scratch the bag – fast and slow. *Rub* bag with both hands – along thighs – down to knees and back. *Smooth* bag with both hands.	Perimeter, edge, corners, length. Part/whole. Speed. Serrated/smooth.	Manipulative skills/ isolating fingers. Vocabulary.
With one finger – trace around the perimeter of bag. Change hands.	Rough and smooth sides. Corners, angles.	Isolating fingers. Vocabulary.
Pick up bag at two corners with thumbs and forefingers.	Corners. Body parts.	Pincer grip. Language/ vocabulary.
Move bag up the body to cover tummy/chest/chin/nose.	Area, shape, size – bigger/ smaller than.	Pincer grip – core strength, balance.
Hold bag tightly at nose level – deep breath and – *blow* – repeat – then *roar.*	Breathing. Force.	Oral motor – lips pursed and mouth wide.
Keep bag covering mouth and head *still* – look right and left/up and down.	Right and left/direction. Up and down/direction.	Core strength/balance. Keep head *still*. Eyes crossing the midline – left to right – up and down.
Fold bag in half to make a triangle (pizza slice, hanky, boat, sandwich, bib, sail, beak, hat?).	Shape. Fractions. Precision.	Manipulative. Imaginative. Foveal (close focus) vision – accommodation (changing focus near/far). Mathematical vocabulary – half/whole.
Now fold into a rectangle.	Shape, fractions.	Manipulative/eye skills.
Try a smaller square – keep folding to…	Shape, fractions, conservation of volume.	Manipulative/eye skills.
…make the smallest square possible.	Shape. Conservation of volume.	Manipulative/eye skills.

Actions	Concepts	Skills
Now place this shape on different body parts – on my head/under my chin or arm/next to my leg/between my feet. Using *one* hand (own choice), unfold the bag on knees. Now use both hands to smooth out all wrinkles.	Prepositions. Using the 'immediate environment' of the body. Conservation of volume, size, shape.	Information processing. Memory. Balance. Coordination. Core strength. Agility. Manipulative. Observation.
Find the *centre* of the bag – balance on tip of one finger and lift as high as possible. Change hands.	Centre.	Trial and error. Balance – hand and core strength.
In a small group (lie/sit/kneel or stand): copy a linear pattern made with the bags on the floor –a combination of all shapes made previously – triangle, rectangle, square.	Patterning, Sequencing: 1. □ △□ □ △□ □ △□ 2. □□□ △ △□□ □ □△△□□ 3. □ ▽△□ ▽ △□ □□	Mirroring. Memory. Precision. Cooperating/negotiating/decision-making/teamwork.
Put one hand inside the bag.	Inside/outside. Size, shape, area, volume.	Manipulative. Timing. Treating bag with care.
Rustle hand inside the bag –try different speeds. Use the bag as a 'flannel' to 'wash' all over.	Sound. Speed.	Core strength. Body position. Manipulative. Vocabulary.
Change bag to other hand – repeat – rustling and 'washing'.	Parallel. Equal and opposite.	Timing. Crossing the midline. Body parts/vocabulary.
Swap own bag with someone else – hand to hand.	Sharing, turn-taking.	Eye contact. Timing. Spatial awareness. Treating bags with care.
Scrumple the bag with one hand to make a small ball.	Conservation of volume Shape.	Manipulative.
Open palm and balance 'ball' on the palm with fingers together – change hands.	Balance.	Timing. Hand strength. Speed.
Throw 'ball' upwards – either allow to drop – or catch. Two hands. Then right and left. Catch on palms and backs of hands.	Height. Speed. Direction. Force.	Throwing action. Timing. Body position. Eye-tracking.
Now try a range of throwing/kicking skills – forward/backward/sideways.	Direction, force, distance. Target/goal, aiming.	Coordination. Strength. Concentration. Focus.

cont.

Actions	Concepts	Skills
Blow 'balls' across the floor. Flick balls using one finger at a time. Lie on tummies/walk on knees and pat the paper balls around (use both hands). Make a 'goal' to aim at.	Direction. Force, distance.	Timing. Oral motor. Body position. Core/ hand strength. Spatial awareness. Aiming. Manipulative.
Unfold the paper ball and now fold/twist into a pencil shape.	Conservation of volume. Shape.	Manipulative. Eye skills.
Close eyes – put tip of 'pencil' on different body parts: ear, nose, tummy, knee – same side and opposite.	Body parts.	Proprioception. Body position. Vocabulary. Crossing the midline.
Close eyes – draw different shapes/ letters in the air.	Shapes – letters, numbers, size.	Crossing the midline. Memory. Pattern – spelling.
Open eyes – use 'pencil' to tap out different rhythms – on other hand/ knees/chairs/table, etc.	Rhythm. Timing. Rhyme may be added.	Memory. Anticipating. Predicting. Cooperation. Turn-taking. Creativity.
Unfold bag and place on floor. Place one foot on bag – 'skate' around. Change feet.	Direction. Speed. Timing. Spatial awareness.	Balance. Core strength. Spatial awareness.
Put both hands on the bag – *push* around the floor – start on knees then graduate to feet.	Direction. Speed.	Strength. Coordination. Balance.
The following activities are suitable for individual children, and small groups		
Ask children to scatter their bags anywhere on the floor – retreat.	Scatter. Pattern. Shape and space.	Teamwork, decision-making, cooperation.
Everyone find their *own* bag again. Stand on it with two feet – keep very still with arms raised above heads – then by sides – lift one foot then the other for a few seconds. Retreat. Approach bags in different ways – on tummies/crawling/ walking on knees/walking/ jumping – fast and slow.	Spatial memory.	Balance. Strength. Spatial awareness.
Change positions – put elbows/ knees/hands/bottom on the bag.	Body parts. Positions, space and shape.	Agility. Strength. Balance. Coordination. Vocabulary.
Keep bags in a *scatter* formation.		

Actions	Concepts	Skills
Make the following shapes in small groups/teams: *Tower*: Stack bags precisely on one spot *Winding path*: All bags touching/ then make small gaps then wider *Plants*: Different types e.g. sunflower, cactus, poppy *Home*: Various possibilities e.g. tent, caravan, house, flat *Transport*: Bus, car, tractor, bicycle, canoe.	Shape. Conservation of volume. Precision, symmetry, pattern.	Cooperation. Timing. Decision-making. Vocabulary.
Number bonds. Use 10 or 20 bags. Put bags into different groups, e.g. twos, fives, tens.	Number bonds. Add, subtract, divide, multiply.	Decision-making. Memory.
Arrange the bags in a long straight line – with no gaps.	Space. Shape.	Cooperation. Precision.
Walk forward carefully with feet on either side of the bags without moving them – with arms raised – out to the side. Try backwards. Fast and slow.	Direction. Speed. Start and stop – beginning and end.	Balance. Coordination. Heel-to-toe walking.
Jump forward along the 'road' with one foot on either side – on toes and flat feet. Small and big jumps.	Direction. Speed. Force.	Balance. Coordination. Strength. Different parts of feet.
All step *over* – then leap over the road. Try with all holding hands.	Force, direction, speed.	Balance, Strength. Agility. Cooperation.
Make a *zig-zag* shape with the bags on the floor – wide gaps to start – then narrow.	Pattern shape, space, direction, force, speed.	Balance. Strength. Agility.
Walk and then run in and out – a wide gap makes it easier to run *fast*.	Speed, direction.	Balance. Coordination. Strength.
Shorten the gap – more challenging.	Speed, direction.	Balance. Strength. Agility.
Run all the way *around* the 'road'. *Both* directions.	Speed, direction. Start, stop.	Balance. Strength. Agility.
Note: A range of materials for these activities may be used, e.g. magazines, dishcloths, video boxes.		
Further possibilities for using apparatus are explored in Chapters 9–10 and 11.		

Children should always be afforded time and opportunities to contribute their own ideas. By using their bodies as the primary reference point for the apparatus, all the properties of the materials may be investigated and a range of learning possibilities explored. The health element is also important as the movement possibilities are extended to support a wide range of motor skills.

THE STUDY

Each of the ten sessions experienced by the participating children in the study was designed around a particular theme. Specific vocabulary related to the theme was introduced during the initial movement phase – e.g. 'feeling *strong*', 'we are *stretching*', 'what is this *sound*', 'how *long* can we jump for'. The apparatus introduced in the second phase reinforced this vocabulary and supported children's understanding of the themes in an immediate and visual way. During the third phase, the children made paper-based records ('books') of their experiences: these included representations of each theme in photographic or sticker form, e.g. for the 'stretch' session, the children chose pictures of snakes.

Number was the theme for my eighth session and we used paper plates to explore a range of mathematical concepts. Nina spoke to me afterwards:

> *It's very obvious that their concept of number is limited. But using apparatus that they weren't threatened by made it more meaningful and gave them really vital visual clues. I think the way these things are presented is crucial. It wasn't like the usual 'Come to the maths table now'; it was just an instant and easy way to expose them to concepts they were previously resistant to. It was also great that they added their own ideas, when the plates became steering wheels of tractors and they sat on them to shuffle around the room and laughed. This way of working has been particularly useful for Ant, who would be worksheet king given half a chance! Working like this makes him confront the underlying meaning of concepts, and it doesn't concentrate so much on the outcomes or an end product.*

Using apparatus that is familiar and easily accessible has many advantages. Unlike sports equipment (e.g. footballs) or materials that are created specifically for creative movement (e.g. sheets of stretchy coloured Lycra), socks, tights, paper bags, water bottles and balloons do not have prescribed agendas attached. In practice, this means that anything is possible. Language may be anchored in relevant and meaningful contexts that is particularly useful for children experiencing language issues or who are new to English. Specific skills may be highlighted and rehearsed in an incidental way, slotted in underneath whatever practical activity the children are enjoying. This approach gives them the confidence to extend the ways in which apparatus is used and to know their ideas are valued.

Using only one material at a time provides clarity of focus, eliminates the issue of choice and creates a unifying experience that is the basis for later teamwork and many sports. Jennie Lindon[26] writes of the importance of using 'scrap materials': 'Scrap's lack of determinedness and specificity provides the agents who work with it the conceptual space to make decisions about it and to determine its character and identity, rather than being confronted with a predetermined identity.' Affording children opportunities to appreciate materials that are mostly taken for granted, and often binned, abandoned and underused is also important. As she writes: 'The discarded can offer a starting point for an alternative rhetoric of creativity based on the preservation and conservation of human development.'

As an unsustainable financial outlay is often attached to many mainstream materials, it may be time to acknowledge the possibilities inherent in a wider range of resources (often considered 'unworthy') that offer children a wealth of learning opportunities which not only extend their learning but also support their overall health and wellbeing.

7

The Transfer of Skills between Environments Is Actively Supported

*A weed is a plant that has mastered every survival
skill – except for learning how to grow in rows.*

Doug Larson (1926–2017)[1]

In the App Generation (2013), Howard Gardner talks of the current tension between educational means and goals and the skills that business leaders demand of their workforce. He describes the 'constrained curriculum and traditional standard tests of a bygone era' as being antithetical to the 'Four Cs' of critical thinking, creative thinking, collaboration and community.[2]

Scaled down to the Early Years, we see these competing agendas reflected in the evident disparity of status between the skill set required for curricular engagement and assessment and the life skills necessary for children to navigate successfully the demands of different environments and continual transitions throughout the day.

CONTEXT

Physical skills may provide a particularly useful bridge between agendas, being equally relevant and essential in all environments children experience. They offer a meaningful conduit for a range of behaviours, competencies and dispositions that support smooth overall development throughout early childhood.

Reflecting on the introduction to this book, there is a significant difference in design, delivery, expectations and assessment of children engaging in physical activity programmes linked to specific disciplines (e.g. ballet, football, gymnastics) and those for whom physical play provides their most significant daily physical experience.

Gill Connell talks of 'splinter skills' that are 'isolated, unrelated and often unrelatable skills that may give the *appearance* of full physical competency but actually mask deficiencies. Often they involve muscle memory for specialised, high-performance tasks'.[3]

We may have noticed children who are gifted footballers but cannot climb a tree; wonderful dancers who find riding a bike really difficult; confident tennis players who struggle with group activities; excellent swimmers who cannot catch a ball.

Many physical disciplines demand a very specific skill set, and these skill sets are often divorced from the daily reality of children's lives. No one is going to practise pliés in the park or karate in the kitchen; these skills are rehearsed and refined in particular environments, wearing particular clothes, following prescribed lesson plans and linked to continual assessment of performance.

Of course, children love the uniforms, the badges, the camaraderie, and their inspirational teachers but, for those not naturally motivated or gifted, many of these opportunities are neither enjoyable nor accessible.

What all young children need is a 'transferable portfolio' of abilities, a broad range of physical skills that they may apply, adapt and use whenever and wherever required in all areas of their lives. Essentially, what they learn in a movement context should not be situation-specific. Skills must be taken out and forward into daily life. Only then can they move seamlessly between environments, managing the demands of curricula, peer groups and the cultures and communities within which they grow, learn and develop.

In a Harvard paper, 'Building Core Capabilities for Life' (2016), the writer determines that as adults we:[4]

> *must be able to focus, plan ahead, avoid distractions, and shift our behavior according to the differing demands and rules of work and family. We need to remember important information and follow multiple-step processes or instructions. We need to be able to stop ourselves from acting impulsively and persist in tedious tasks in order to achieve long-term goals.*

If we substitute school for work, this is a fairly realistic picture of what we expect of young children generally, not just when they start school. The demands placed on them are immense. Within a relatively short time, they are expected to manage their behaviours, their bodies, their language and their emotional states in a wide variety of environments; what are often described as 'transitions'.

TRANSITIONS

A typical dictionary definition of 'transition' is: 'A change or passage from one state or stage to another; the period of time during which something changes from one state or stage to another; a linking passage between two divisions in a composition; a bridge.'

Two types of transitions have been identified: vertical and horizontal. *Vertical* transitions are those that mark significant changes at specific times in a child's life, e.g. moving from nursery to school, or up a year at school. *Horizontal* transitions may be experienced by children on an hourly, daily or weekly basis, e.g. moving from home to setting, from room to room within a setting, inside to outside, home to other family residences or to places of worship, entertainment or sport.

Physically, their bodies are in an almost continuous state of transition as they grow and develop. They become taller and heavier and increasingly independent as their strength, speed, agility, balance and coordination improve.

Do we too often assume that children have enough in their 'invisible backpacks' to manage the continual transitions of daily life? The relentless narrowing down of the curriculum to 'the basics' of literacy and numeracy will inevitably compromise the provision for children to not only fully understand and appreciate their personal bodily transitions, but also how physical skills provide an essential support mechanism to manage the wider variety of transitions they experience.

Young children need to understand their physical selves and how their bodies change over time, allied to the creation of a transferable portfolio of physical abilities that can be safely stored in their 'invisible backpacks' and used whenever and wherever necessary.

Deciding what should be included in this transferable portfolio will be dependent on a wide range of factors that may include: the environment (e.g. Finnish and Canadian children must learn to skate and ski, and Australians to swim), the different definitions and terminology used within curricula (e.g. in England and Wales 'Physical Development' is used; in Scotland, 'Health and Wellbeing'; in Northern Ireland, 'Health, Wellbeing and Movement') and available funding for initiatives (e.g. training for practitioners, resources and equipment).

Priorities will vary, but there are core physical abilities that are generally considered to impact on children's level of engagement with the learning opportunities they experience.

Penny Tassoni writes of 'specific physical skills that children need to acquire':[5] core strength (in the trunk area to ensure sitting and standing still are achieved); bilateral coordination (both sides of the body working synchronously); symmetrical bilateral movements (clapping, drumming, catching a ball); alternate bilateral movements (walking, running, cycling); balance (for proprioception and core strength); crossing the midline (for coordination); hand strength (for all curricular activities).

Sally Goddard Blythe talks of the 'ABC of learning': *attention* (linked to visual and auditory processing), *balance* (dependent on core strength and important for stillness and movement) and *coordination* (required for a wide range of tasks).[6]

Although these skills form a valid and useful list, they should be placed in a wider context.

LEARNING DISPOSITIONS

Lilian Katz[7] believes that children's dispositions and feelings towards learning matter as much as knowledge and goals; that if children's disposition towards applying skills is disrupted, the knowledge gained will be less useful.

Margaret Carr[8] (a member of the team that developed the bicultural Te Whāriki curriculum in New Zealand) built on Katz's work to describe five distinct domains of learning dispositions: *taking an interest*; *being involved*; *persisting with difficulty and uncertainty*; *communicating with others*; and *taking responsibility*. Aligning children's physical development with these 'dispositions' places this area of development within a wider and more meaningful framework.

Taking an interest

All young children are acutely interested in their bodies: what different parts can and can't do, how they change over time, what small parts are for, how their bodies compare to others'. Using their bodies as the primary reference point for learning provides vital material for children throughout all developmental stages.

Children's bodies are often undervalued as a source of learning because quantitative evidence of progress can be elusive and challenging to collect.

Progress in physical development involves stops, starts, regressions and plateaus. It very rarely follows a data-friendly, linear path. Skills-based programmes offer ample opportunities to assess, grade and award, but acknowledging that the foundations for learning across all developmental domains are primarily physical requires a more subtle and trusting approach.

One of the most difficult and frustrating aspects for adults to resolve is aligning the extraordinarily mercurial nature of children's physical development with the demands of assessment procedures. Often, we are despondent at their perceived lack of engagement or progress – that they are doing nothing or nothing is happening. Nothing, in fact, could be further from the truth. Something is always happening. It may not be visible, quantifiable or assessable, but never was the aphorism 'absence of evidence is not evidence of absence' more true. We need to trust that children know themselves pretty well. They are extremely adept at gauging their own capabilities and should always be afforded the time and space to just watch, to listen, to absorb the atmosphere and become familiar with the properties of apparatus or the environment.

Progress often emerges in unexpected ways: in different play patterns, in extended use of language, in new interests, in different spaces. We should be more aware and sensitive to the significant differences in timescale for children to acquire new skills and how, when and where they choose to use them. Jonathan Silin[9] asks us to consider the following statement: 'What about the value of letting go, of allowing experiences to come to an end without trying to capture and preserve them?'

In our determination to take an interest, add to observations and support assessments – do we sometimes completely miss the point?

Being involved

Mihály Csíkszentmihályi[10] is a founder of positive psychology and the modern interpretation of the 'flow state'. This describes the feeling of 'unique insight and clarity, when motivation, task, skill, opportunity and environment are perfectly aligned to produce the optimum product or performance'. Flow state is never passive or static. To achieve this requires active engagement with, and focus on, a given task. Effortlessness is not gained lightly. Patience, tenacity, resilience and perseverance are all necessary to reach the point at which control is exercised over consciousness and we are not being passively influenced by external forces. It thus denotes quite the opposite of the term 'going with the flow'.

From a wealth of data, Csíkszentmihályi determined certain conditions in which a 'flow state' may be experienced by learners:

- They must know *what* to do for any given task – goals should be clear and unambiguous – progress is assured.

- They must know *how* to do it – the perceived skill and perceived challenge are aligned.

- Distractions must be minimised and uninterrupted – concentration supported.

- Any sense of failure must be minimised.

- Self-consciousness must be minimised.

- Time restrictions and issues must be minimised – or absent.

- Activities become intrinsically valuable – learners are 'doing it for themselves'.

Ferre Laevers[11] cites Csíkszentmihályi as one of the seminal influences on his creation of the 'Leuven Involvement Scale for Young Children'. Laevers specifically identifies wellbeing and involvement as being 'fundamental underpinnings to a child's successful development'. For Laevers, 'wellbeing' describes an emotional state 'in which a child's basic physical, social and emotional needs are met'. Comfortable, confident, eager, relaxed – children in a state of 'wellbeing' have a high chance of learning and achieving.

How may the concepts of 'wellbeing' and 'involvement' be aligned with children's physical development?

Wellbeing

- Children feel physically safe and secure in their environment.

- They are well fed and rested.

- A range of opportunities are provided to rehearse and refine their physical skills – both individually and communally.

- Inside and outside environments are valued equally as support for active/physical/movement play.

- A wide variety of hand apparatus is available to practise skills.

- Adult presence is muted but supportive.

- Consideration is given to the physical factors that may affect engagement – vaccinations/teething/latent illness/growth spurts/ nutrition/sleep/clothing and footwear.

- Easy physical contact between peer groups and adults is supported – spatial awareness and sensitivity is continually practised through movement opportunities.

- Children's ideas and contributions during physical activities/play are valued and respected – they may give and receive feedback to/from their peer group and adults without fear of failure or retribution.

Involvement/flow

Emerging from this state of 'wellbeing' is a sense of 'involvement' – or 'flow' – a 'deep cognitive immersion in an activity and/or thinking':

- Children's physical response to stimuli (verbal, physical, musical) is immediate and positive.

- An extended period of engagement in physical activity/movement is experienced (time flies).

- There is intense interest in the individual properties of the body – what can I do now – what I can't do yet – and why?

- Time is afforded for children's physical skills to emerge in their natural order – they are not forced or over-rehearsed.

- There is an openness to positive suggestions from peer groups and adults.

- Engagement in positive verbal and nonverbal communication with adults and peer groups is promoted during physical activity/play.

- Reflection is encouraged about physical activities that are enjoyed or disliked – what may be the reasons for this?

In order to achieve this state of 'involvement', children need experience of both 'surface' and 'deep-level' learning.

The Swedish academic Roger Saljo[12] identified *three* types of *surface-level* learning. How may they be aligned to children's physical development?

A quantitative increase in knowledge

- In physical development terms, this relates to the underpinning knowledge of body parts: visible – e.g. head/arms/body/legs/hands/feet – and invisible – e.g. muscles/bones/blood/brain/organs and systems: what body parts can do and why – they include a wide range of physical skills – gross motor/locomotor/manipulative – and may be applied to different terrains (and water).

- Self-knowledge and awareness as the body develops naturally over time: bodies get taller/heavier and more skilled. Evidence of change may include: replacing car seats/buggies, and swimming aids and bike stabilisers becoming redundant.

- Boundaries and routines relating to self-care change. Independence is encouraged around feeding and dressing and through making choices based on knowledge of the environment, e.g. wearing wellies on rainy days and hats in the sun.

- Knowledge of movement language increases – the ability to explain ideas coherently, organise and delegate effectively and process instructions of increasing complexity.

Memorising

This will include the following:

- Being able to use physical skills in the appropriate context – matching skills to tasks.

- Responding appropriately to verbal and nonverbal cues.

- Remembering sequences of movements/steps/drills.

- Passing on knowledge, experience and expertise to others when appropriate.

- Retaining awareness of space and shape – e.g. dance formations/lining up/circle time – and where/how equipment and resources are stored.

Acquiring facts, skills and methods that may be retained and used as necessary

- Approaching physical tasks well-prepared – knowing what is needed and why – choosing appropriate equipment and asking for assistance when/if needed.

- Decision-making and delegating – what works/doesn't – am I tall enough/strong enough/competent enough?

Saljo also identified two aspects of deep-level learning. Both types of learning are considered 'wholly interdependent' and equally important.

How may 'deep-level learning' be aligned to children's physical development:

- Making sense of/abstracting meaning: making connections between newly learned facts and skills with current experiences and understanding:

- Making connections between surface knowledge of 'what I can do' with 'why can I do it/how can I do it better/how or where else can I use these skills?'

- Physical relationship to others and the environment: Knowing how/when to 'fit in'. In a very fundamental way this is linked to rhythm – how children begin to align their personal rhythms (in communication/play/sleeping/eating) with the rituals and demands of others.

- The value of physical skills in the environments children experience: Are their physical 'firsts' acknowledged and encouraged? What messages are they receiving if they feel no one has noticed or cares?

- Transfer of skills: The ability to use appropriate physical skills in all environments experienced.

- Interpreting and understanding reality in a different way; the application of knowledge:

  - First experience of concepts (e.g. strength/time/shape/number/ speed/up-down) is physical, what it feels like, looks like and linked to relevant and meaningful language.

  - Knowledge gained from this initial exposure may be transferred/ retrieved to enhance understanding of the concept as presented in other media: e.g. literature/art/music/poetry, in everyday life, on the street/at home/at nursery/on TV.

  - 3D and 2D representations of physical experiences will deepen understanding and creativity: e.g. moulding/constructing and writing/drawing/painting.

  - Use of DT to record physical experiences; collect and collate material to share with others, review and reflect.

Persisting with difficulty and uncertainty

A possible disconnect is emerging in young children's lives between their digital and daily physical experiences. Technology provides instant gratification, a world in which progress is reliably linear and mercifully free from the demands of other people, where contention rarely arises, disputes may be avoided, and the possibility of accidents is minimal. If something proves difficult or unmanageable, the programme may be changed immediately to another less challenging.

Contrast this with the world of physical development. I am not talking here of gymnastics, dance or sports disciplines that require a significant degree of persistence to attain any degree of success, but the experience of most children acquiring the skills necessary to engage in accessible, physical, everyday activities – e.g. climbing a tree, bicycling, somersaulting, building sandcastles, skimming stones or walking along a wall.

Relative to rapid changes in the digital programs they experience, children's bodies grow slowly, and learning new skills requires patience, practice and often painful episodes over a significant period of time. There are no cups or medals awarded for catching a ball, yet even this basic skill may now be ignored if it is not easily accomplished.

What physical skills highlight and digital technology does not is the value of persistence. Technology can only ever offer one solution, yet bodies offer many. It is the one area of development that guarantees a high degree of agency and autonomy as children may choose to rehearse and refine physical skills in a range of environments.

The quality known to have the greatest impact on children's lives, and very important in terms of physical development, is resilience – from the Latin verb *resalire*, to jump back. In social, behavioural and biological sciences the term 'resilience' is used in a variety of ways and contexts, as an individual characteristic, as a process or as an outcome.

However the term is considered, 'the essence of resilience is a positive, adaptive response in the face of significant adversity'. Jennie Lindon[13] has a more Early Years-friendly definition: 'An outlook for children characterised by the willingness to confront challenges with a sense of confidence, that it is possible to deal with setbacks and a backdrop of emotional security that familiar adults will help.'

In terms of physical development, resilience includes the following characteristics:

- The ability to gauge accurately if a task is manageable with or without help.

- To understand that some skills are easier to acquire and practise than others – e.g. running fast is usually less challenging than catching a ball.

- To accept that competency requires practice and persistence over time.

- To accept that accidents do happen sometimes – they are a generic experience.

- To appreciate the strengths, weaknesses and ability of self and others.

- To have the courage to give it a go: not to be defeated and have a positive attitude.

- To develop the ability to determine what is the best way to achieve the desired individual outcome: e.g. if you want to climb higher, you may need to source a step, get adult help or support from a peer group.

- To remain unaffected by negative peer pressure or adult assumptions of ability level.

- To develop a belief in personal ability: to engage positively in whatever physical activity is offered at an appropriate level.

- To appreciate the freedom to make mistakes and learn to adapt and react.

- To take risks that are manageable.

Physical experiences provide children with a range of opportunities to build resilience that will transfer into other developmental domains. The gains are significant, as children learn to trust themselves, their own judgement and abilities. Being confident and competent physically brings a host of rewards in terms of wider friendship groups, opportunities to engage in a broad array of physical disciplines, and the forging of closer family ties.

Communicating with others

Working in a group or team is a highly prized ability, and moving together provides the perfect opportunity to rehearse the essential preverbal communication skills that underpin and support effective verbal interactions.

Physical/active/movement play is very evident in the early years and by 4–5 years forms around 20 per cent of children's behaviour.

It provides a wealth of opportunities for children to communicate, negotiate and delegate. The beauty of this type of play is that it is ever-evolving and there is no pressure to achieve, perform or provide concrete evidence of progress or learning. Opportunities to link up with different individuals and groups continually present themselves as children observe and determine the best way to try new activities.

Risky play has become something of a hot topic, maybe in response to questionable Health and Safety regulations and parental reluctance to allow children to engage in perceived risky play. Children themselves deem the following activities to be risky: climbing high; hiding; running fast; rough-and-tumble play; playing with banned materials; and jumping down from a height. Extensive collaboration and discussion is needed to make these opportunities work. Practice runs have to be sorted; deciding who goes first must be negotiated; determining what could go wrong is very important; and strong community bonds are formed through doing things they shouldn't.

Taking responsibility

Children's health and wellbeing has increasingly become a government concern and centralised edicts are disseminated via devolved local authorities who are now responsible for health budgets regarding children and healthcare staff. The muted response to the original UK Chief Medical Officer (CMO) Early Years Physical Activity Guidelines (2011)[14] highlighted the difficulties in implementing centrally created initiatives. Parents have been sceptical as to their need and, overall, guidance for this initiative remains patchy. Opportunities for parents to engage physically with their children are not nationally available and are often linked to obesity initiatives that may be inappropriate.

An Australian initiative may offer an alternative approach.[15] The 'Australian 24-Hour Movement Guidelines for Children of the Early Years' (2015) says: 'To promote healthy growth and development, infants, toddlers and pre-schoolers should achieve the recommended balance of physical activity, high-quality sedentary behaviour and sufficient sleep.' What is innovative about this framework is that, by making the guidelines '24-hour', responsibility for children's health and wellbeing may be shared between the different environments they experience: that everyone – children, parents, carers, teachers, grandparents and babysitters – can play a positive role in supporting them. The Canadians have followed suit by launching their own 24-Hour Movement Guidelines for the Early Years (0–4 years) in 2017.[16] The message is equally simple, accessible and sustainable – 'Move more – Sleep well – Sit less.' The tone is supportive, positive and, above all, aspirational. A 'progressive adjustment' towards the recommendations is encouraged whilst acknowledging that adherence may prove challenging at times. It is expected the UK will broadly follow the Canadian model in due course. In 2018 the Laureus Sport for Good Foundation in South Africa created a model of 'A Healthy 24 hr Day' for young children – that integrates physical activity, sitting behaviour, screentime and sleep. 'These guidelines take into account the natural and instinctual integration of these behaviours across a 24 hr period, and are intended to provide a more cohesive message for parents, caregivers, teachers and practitioners.'[17]

MENTAL HEALTH

The mental health of young children is causing increasing concern. Engaging in physical activity offers a wealth of opportunities to support the following four areas that the Mental Health Foundation (1999) have determined contribute to the positive mental health of young children:[18]

1. *Learning to enjoy solitude. To be able to live quietly and enjoy peace.* Childhood can be demanding and sometimes overwhelming as the varying agendas of adults, peer groups and environments are accommodated and aligned with personal growth and development. The ability to enjoy being alone and to know when time is needed to rest, recuperate and revive are valuable skills to acquire, particularly in terms of physical development when opportunities for solitary practice may be unavailable and deciding to take time out may be considered disruptive.

2. *Initiating, developing and sustaining mutually satisfying personal relationships.* Engaging in physical activity offers the breadth and depth of interactive experience that children need to ensure ease of communication with adults, peers and siblings. They may initiate and develop relationships through active play and choose to sustain them by revisiting and refining activities over time.

3. *Playing and learning.* All play is a learning experience for children, but physically active play offers unique opportunities to engage with wider friendship groups, initiate and develop projects, experience abstract concepts in relevant and meaningful contexts and determine personal and group boundaries.

4. *Resolving problems and learning from setbacks.* Being physical is the perfect way to support children's problem-solving abilities, not just

interpersonally but in working out how, when or where physical skills can be improved and developed. Learning through setbacks, having another go or trying a different way to resolve difficulties may all be enhanced.

Starting school

Being physically active offers huge untapped potential to support children's mental health. The first major vertical transition they experience, and possibly one of the most stressful for all parties concerned, is starting school, a critical time when a reliable portfolio of transferable abilities is needed to ensure children, parents and teachers manage this period positively and effectively.

'School readiness': was there ever a more contentious term? How children should be prepared, what they are being prepared for, why they should be prepared, remains a source of friction and debate with no consensus in sight.

In England, this term has usually covered competencies connected to: the process of learning; approaches to understanding; taking responsibility for personal learning and development; and the fulfilling of school tasks – e.g. reading, writing, independent activity and the passing of tests.

There has been some progress over the years to break away from a skills approach to school readiness and encompass a broader range of dispositions and abilities.

The Home-Start Evaluation Report *Big Hopes, Big Future* (2015) states that: 'Nursery school readiness depends upon much more than early literacy and numeracy. In particular, social competencies, self-regulatory skills, practical or daily living skills are all pivotal for success in the first few years of nursery leading to school.'[19]

The National Association for the Education of Young Children (NAEYC, 1995) states that:[20]

School readiness involves more than just children. School readiness in the broadest sense is about children, families, early environments, schools and communities. Children are not innately ready or not ready for school. Their skills and development are strongly influenced by their families and through their interactions with other people and environments before coming to school.

They call for:

A broad definition that embraces the home and cultural environment within which children are growing and developing: an equal access to positive opportunities for all children, recognising and supporting children's individual differences and establishing reasonable and appropriate expectations for what children should be able to do when they enter school.

But what are 'reasonable and appropriate expectations'? Who decides, and what happens if the views of parents, children and teachers do not align?

In May 2006, the State of New Mexico, USA, in their 'High Horizons' framework determined school readiness to be 'rich, multifaceted and multidimensional. Any readiness framework has to reflect not only the biological, cognitive, emotional, motivational, social and cultural domains but also their interaction'.[21]

They propose a 'ready states approach': that state systems and infrastructure must be ready for policy and programmatic innovation, not just parents, teachers and children who are intimately involved in the implementation of policies.

Ultimately, 'Readiness must be conceptualised as a broad construct that incorporates all aspects of a child's life that contribute directly to that child's ability to learn. Ready families plus ready communities plus ready services plus ready schools equal children ready for school.'

Recognising the importance of culture and community, that a child 'does not merely grow into readiness but must be exposed to situations and carefully assisted by others to develop the necessary skills and ways of functioning', is promising.

But, again, the specifics remain elusive. What constitutes 'necessary skills' and what is meant by 'ways of functioning'? Confidence, curiosity and self-control are mentioned in this document, but do they fit comfortably into either category?

Kathryn Peckham[22] extends school readiness to offer 'features of a lifelong learner': intrinsic qualities (self-motivated, confident, courageous), behavioural qualities (intuitive, curious, imaginative), modes of thought (thinking logically, widely, simultaneously, creatively) and approaches to learning (playful, sociable, independent, practical, adaptable, reflective).

This encapsulates the conundrum. If school readiness is not about skills and more about qualities and dispositions, then the 'ready' element of school readiness becomes redundant – if by 'ready' we mean 'fit for immediate use' and 'with preparations complete'?

In February 2005, the Getting Ready report prepared by the Rhode Island KIDS COUNT organisation was launched.[23] Whilst this 17-state initiative fully acknowledges the importance of families and communities, it also attempts to create a set of national school-readiness indicators: 'a set of measurable indicators related to and defining school readiness that can be tracked regularly over time at the state and local levels'. Five domains of school readiness are listed: physical wellbeing and motor development (interesting that this is first on the list), social and emotional approaches to learning, language development, cognition and general knowledge. The authors write: 'The need for children to develop across all five domains is supported by kindergarten teachers.' They agree that physical wellbeing, social development and curiosity are very important for 'kindergarten readiness' but also that 'Teachers also place significant importance on skills such as the ability to follow directions, not being disruptive in class and being sensitive to other children's feelings.'

Curiously, the link between physical wellbeing and 'not being disruptive' is not made, and under the section 'Ready Children – physical wellbeing and motor development', it simply states: 'Percentage of children with age-appropriate fine motor skills'. No mention is made of any other physical competencies or reasons given for their omission.

For Public Health England (PHE) (2015),[24] school-ready children should have the following skills in place. This is much more specific, but again, there is no rationale for their inclusion:

- Recognise numbers and quantities in the everyday environment.

- Participate in music activities such as singing.

- Have good oral health.

- Are able to communicate their needs and have a good vocabulary.

- Are well-nourished and within normal weight for height.

- Have received all childhood immunisations.

The following skills included in the list are highly dependent on underpinning physical competencies – that I have added in italics:

- Are able to sit still, take turns and play – *core strength, spatial awareness, rhythm and timing*.

- Are independent in getting dressed – *coordination, proprioception, timing, sequencing, fine motor skills*.

- Going to the toilet – *core strength, balance, body awareness, sequencing, timing, fine motor skills, hygiene*.

- Are independent in eating – *homolateral coordination, eye–hand coordination, timing, core strength.*

Finally:

- Are able to socialise with peers and form friendships – *the high status afforded to physical skills by children will provide support.*

- Develop motor control and balance for a range of activities – *both are essential for positive physical play.*

PACEY, in their 2013 report *What Does 'School Ready' Really Mean?*[25] state that:

For parents, the term 'school ready' is not about how proficient their child's handwriting is or what stage reading book they are on – it is more the practical aspects such as whether they can do up their own coat, open their lunchbox easily or simply have the maturity to be able to listen and understand instructions from teaching staff. When questioned about specific skills: 16% of parents and 24% of teachers rated the ability to be away from parents or carers and make themselves understood clearly as the most important skill for school ready children to possess.

In the PACEY 'Ready for School: Advice for Parents' document (2015),[26] it states that: 'It will make life easier for your child (and school staff!) if your child can master these self-care skills before they start school: going to the toilet, washing their hands, dressing and undressing, feeding themselves, using a tissue, tidying up.' Again, all the skills cited as being important to prepare children for school are fundamentally physical, yet this is never made explicit.

The Government's Early Years policy statement, 'Supporting Families in the Foundation Years' (2011),[27] says that: 'Growth and physical development are as important to education as they are to developmental medicine, but have been largely overlooked by the educational system since the phasing-out of routine developmental tests for all children.' This isn't entirely true. There is a clear acknowledgement that physical skills matter, but no real understanding of why they are so important or how they may be supported effectively.

In the Ofsted report *Are You Ready? Good Practice in School Readiness* (2014),[28] the practitioners quoted focus on children's 'care for themselves in toileting, dressing and drinking from a cup' but acknowledged the difficulties children experienced in riding a bike, throwing, catching and kicking a ball.

The relationship between the two skill sets is ignored – that if the latter were acquired, the former should be gained without difficulty.

The Australian Early Development Census (AEDC):[29]

> *provides a national measurement to monitor Australian children's development. The AEDC provides evidence to support policy, planning and action for health, education and community support. It is an assessment that all children undertake within the first two weeks of starting school, and highlights what is working well and what needs to be improved or developed to support children and their families.*

As the documentation states, 'By providing a common ground on which people can work together, the AEDC results can enable communities to form partnerships, to plan and implement activities, programs and services to help shape the future and wellbeing of Australian children.'

Five domains are included: physical health and wellbeing (again top of the list), social competence, emotional maturity, language and cognitive skills, communication skills and general knowledge. Each domain may be assessed as 'children on track' or 'children developmentally vulnerable'. As it is a nationally implemented assessment procedure, future intervention measures may be tailored to suit the demographic in question based on localised data. The physical health and wellbeing domain has three parts, as shown in Table 7.1.

Table 7.1 Physical health and wellbeing domain

Theme	Children on track	Children developmentally vulnerable
1. Physical readiness for school day.	Never or almost never experience being dressed inappropriately for school activities, and do not come to school late, hungry or tired.	Have at least sometimes experienced coming unprepared for school by being dressed inappropriately, coming to school late, hungry or tired.
2. Physical independence.	Are independent regarding their own needs, have an established hand preference and are well-coordinated.	Range from those who have developed independence, handedness or coordination, to those who have not developed any of these skills.
3. Gross and fine motor skills.	Have an excellent ability to physically tackle the school day and have excellent or good gross and fine motor skills.	Range from those who have an average ability to perform skills requiring gross and fine motor competence and good or average overall energy levels, to those who have poor fine and gross motor skills, poor overall energy levels and physical skills.

Source: Australian Educational Census.

This provides a holistic approach in which the importance of physical health and wellbeing to other developmental domains is fully comprehended: that unless children are physically well and functioning reasonably independently, emotionally and physically, the demands of the school day will be a formidable challenge.

Researchers in the Netherlands have recently developed a new school-readiness tool – the 'Adjustment Scales for Early Transition in Schooling: ASETS'.[30] They ask the question: 'when can a child be said to have attained a sufficient level of behavioural adaptation to be able to take part in structured learning processes; in other words: When is a child ready for school?' For this group, it is the behavioural and socioemotional requirements of structured, formal education that are most important, 'the social and self-regulatory skills which ensure a child is able to focus adequately and is able to deal with his or her emotions with other children and teachers'. The three areas of focus are: the right attitude to learning tasks, sufficient regulation of aggression, and teamwork skills. They also reiterate that it is not enough just to note behaviours on a checklist – there should be information provided as to where issues may occur, how they impact on the learning process and when they become apparent.

The ASETS framework aims to provide practitioners with an assessment tool that may determine how the demands of the curriculum relate to children's behaviours; how interactions with teachers are experienced; what adjustment issues emerge with a more structured learning approach; and whether issues with classmates become more apparent during this transition. On the basis of information gathered, any problems may be determined and addressed in a positive and supportive manner, as 'problems children in kindergarten experience during the process of adapting to first grade do not always spontaneously disappear as they get older'.

The research group write that 'it is important to develop a clear definition of school readiness that goes beyond the predominantly cognitive conceptualisation of the term'. The range of approaches to school readiness cited here have different priorities, but informing them all is the fundamental presence of physical skills. Whether parents, teachers or researchers are providing data and information, it is clear that, for young children to manage successfully their first experience of school, their invisible backpacks must be brimful of transferable physical skills that provide the support necessary to navigate the demands of the day.

REFLEXES

The role of primitive sensory motor reflexes in children's learning has received significant attention over the last twenty years. Goddard Blythe describes them thus:[31]

> *Primitive reflexes are a group of reflexes which develop during life in the womb, are fully developed at birth in a full-term baby (forty weeks) and are gradually inhibited and transformed into more matured patterns and postural abilities during the first six months of postnatal life... Reflex integration takes place as a result of a combination of maturation in the central nervous system and physical interaction with the environment.*

Primitive reflexes assist the baby's survival (grasping, rooting, withdrawing, startled) but, if a wide range of movement experiences are afforded, integration, inhibition and release of these reflexes is assured.

Postural reflexes emerge after birth and ideally will be fully developed by school-starting age. They begin with control of the head and are linked to the unconscious control of posture: 'the reflex anti-gravitational adaptation of a living body to the environment in which he or she lives'.[32]

Issues may emerge if traces of these primitive reflexes remain present in a normally developing child and the 'development of certain motor functions necessary to support learning fail to remain commensurate with chronological age'.

A longitudinal study of nearly 15,000 children that tracked their motor development from 9 months to 5 years (study conducted 2000/2001, findings released in February 2010) provided evidence to suggest that:

> *Children who failed at nine months to reach four key milestones in gross motor development – sitting unaided, crawling, standing and taking first steps – were found to be five points behind on average cognitive ability tests taken at five years compared to those who passed the milestones.*[33]

Although taking first steps at 9 months may seem ambitious (for most children this happens much later), the link made here between delay in motor functioning and cognitive development is informative.

For Goddard Blythe, the concept of school readiness must accommodate the following skills to:

> *sit still, focus on one task without being distracted by irrelevant environmental stimuli, hold and manipulate a writing instrument, and*

to control the eye movements necessary to maintain a stable image on a page, follow a line of print without the eyes jumping or losing their place, and adjust visual focus between different distances at speed.

Physical health and wellbeing are not specifically mentioned but there is a fundamental belief evident here in the importance of movement experience to ensuring the smooth maturation and development of curricular skills.

Goddard Blythe believes a significant number of children may be underachieving at school because a range of essential physical skills are not embedded early enough, thus preventing them from engaging successfully with formal curricular activities.

The Institute for Neuro-Physiological Psychology (INPP) has developed a range of screening tests for retained reflexes and accompanying movement intervention programmes to afford children of 4–7 years a 'second chance'. By inhibiting these reflexes in a therapeutic context, the 'right state' may be achieved and the 'gates of learning opened'.

The INPP screening tests have been created to narrow the gap which exists between the professions of medicine, education and psychology in identifying children who may experience physical barriers to learning.

A team at Loughborough University, UK, have created a Movement for Learning programme informed by the INPP approach and linked to a longitudinal research study.[34] The baseline, pre-intervention data gained from 120 reception-age children is of interest – considering the 50th percentile is 'advisable', the 100th is 'desirable' and any measure below the 16th percentile is 'cause for concern':

- For balance 9.5 per cent of the group scored below the 16th percentile.

- For manual dexterity 36.4 per cent scored below the 16th percentile.

- For aiming and catching 51.5 per cent scored below the 16th percentile.

- For overall physical development 28.9 per cent scored below the 16th percentile.

The group subsequently participated in the movement programme that includes specific exercises performed daily before the start of classes. Each session lasts for 15–20 minutes and the children are barefoot. There is a warm-up phase followed by activities using equipment and then a cool-down that includes listening to classical music. The movements are simple and repetitive. The programme is divided into six units of 4 weeks, delivered over 24 weeks in an academic year.

Pre-intervention data suggests that at the start of the reception year around 30 per cent of children who participated in the study experienced movement difficulties that would have a negative effect on their learning. Post-intervention data gained from school staff suggests a positive improvement in their fine and gross motor skills, behaviour and concentration. This study highlights the relationship between specific physical skills and children's success in a range of school activities.

Evidence of neurological delay and the possible physical basis for children's learning issues should be properly explored. It is estimated that 18.4 per cent of children within the school population generally have some form of diagnosed developmental delay or neurodevelopmental disorder, so it is important that this approach may be considered as an effective support.

NEW ZEALAND

Children in New Zealand typically start school on their fifth birthday, although school is not compulsory until age six. Transitions from kindergarten to school are therefore a highly individual and ongoing process throughout the year.

In their book *Crossing the Border: A Community Negotiates the Transition from Early Childhood to Primary School*, the authors describe the concept of 'border crossings' and what successful negotiations entail.[35] They propose that a 'shared space' between early childhood and school may be considered as an important entity in its own right – a borderland:

> It is a valid space, a site of connection, intersection and overlap. The borderland is a space not only of existence but of coexistence... As children move from an early childhood setting into school, this involves crossing both a physical and cultural 'border'. There is both a symbolic as well as literal change of environments.

How this space is perceived and managed by all parties became the focus of a project at one setting in Auckland. How does a child become a pupil? What does this entail? Does it mean learning the *culture* of the school (i.e. 'doing school'), before the *content* of schooling may be managed successfully?

This approach does not focus on the specifics of skill acquisition but on ensuring that the relationships children experience, their established and emerging interests, their family practices and previous learning are fully acknowledged and accounted for prior to formal schooling.

This is achieved through the use of portfolios, a well-organised buddy system and focus on the five 'key competencies' of: thinking (exploration), using language symbols and texts (communication), managing self (wellbeing), relating to others (contributing) and participating and contributing (being actively involved in communities).

The portfolios are critical. Created with family support as the children start in kindergarten, they are a continual record of 'all about me': added to, carried around and taken home, full of stories and observations of family life, celebrations, holidays and friendships that build a comprehensive portrait of each child. Crucially, these portfolios belong to the children, 'promoting an environment in which the children could engage with others and convey a sense of their own self-worth'. The portfolios acted as a 'virtual schoolbag', to be opened and shared between the different environments children experienced. Their physical identity was very significant in the photos that were taken and in the accompanying text that acknowledged their growth and development.

The 'buddy system', in which older children befriended and mentored those moving from kindergarten to school, supported the concept of a learning community. *Being* a buddy conveys responsibility and sensitivity. *Having* a buddy ensures a familiar face in a new situation and a source of encouragement and support.

The five key competencies are designed to afford children the maximum degree of authority or agency in their learning. As the authors conclude, quoting James Greeno:

Authoritative and accountable positioning characterises aspects of learning processes that are crucial for understanding transfer. The reason is that transfer, except in the simplest of cases, is an inherently authoritative action. By definition, transfer involves doing something that one has not been taught explicitly to do.[36]

It is assumed here that children will be physically ready for school. The role of professionals, working closely with parents, is to ensure that positive learning dispositions are in place; that children are emotionally secure, confident and competent in their use of language and can work independently on individual projects.

The authors agree that transitions are always multifaceted, dynamic and complex but, when boundaries are actively blurred, children 'begin to see opportunities for applying their knowledge and skills in the new setting, adding to their perception of themselves as capable and confident learners'. Teachers should therefore offer *complementary* activities so that children recognise that strategies acquired in their early childhood setting can be applied to school.

This is the critical element: that children themselves recognise that not only strategies but also skills, behaviours and dispositions may be transferred – both vertically to formal schooling and horizontally across new and varied situations and environments.

The concepts of transition and transfer were central to the study. A majority of the children were heading for mainstream reception classes and there was huge concern from parents, teachers and children themselves as to how this would be managed.

THE STUDY

Transitions and the transfer of skills were two themes that emerged very clearly. The children were navigating the competing demands of home and nursery alongside the third therapeutic environment.

Evidence to support the seamless transfer of a portfolio of abilities was difficult to find. The nursery and therapeutic environments had carefully defined remits and responsibilities that frequently affected the quality of information-sharing between the adults involved in the children's learning and care.

The transfer of skills was supported through the three-phase structure of the sessions, that covered a wide range of competencies. First, basic movement patterns with and without music (communication and language); second, hand apparatus (curricular skills); and third, recording and reflecting (school readiness).

Halfway through the initial program, Nina noted the following:

Jim wants to do jumping before each therapy session, and Ned in his friend's group wants to hold hands, walk round, change direction and stop. Leo has completely retained the first ten minutes and is insisting that we do it together every time. Generally they're all remembering the experiences of the sessions and are using them to help communicate with their peer group in a very positive way. I also think they're starting to build other friendships in the nursery, and more notice is being taken of them by everyone because of this. The staff have told me that, outside, Ned and Leo hold hands and move around together in a circle.

Using the movements and language included during the first phase provided the children with practical skills to build friendships and rehearse the communication skills they knew would work in specific situations, both indoor and outdoor.

During the fourth session, we used paper bags to explore the theme of shape. A member of the nursery staff, who assisted throughout, noted how the children subsequently transferred ideas from this session to the indoor nursery environment:

> *This week, when they were finally sitting and working with playdo with the other children and making triangle shapes, Ant said: 'Mine's a pizza.' Leo said: 'A sandwich.' Ned put his under his chin and said: 'It's a bib.' What they said was exactly the same as when we folded the paper bags into the same shapes last week, and it made the other children make up their own ideas as to what their playdo shapes could be.*

Throughout the study, Nina kept extensive notes. These revealed the extent to which the parents became more positively and proactively engaged through the books children made and took home each week:

> *They love being able to know what's going on, and they're really trying to talk to the children about what they did in the sessions. It's sort of giving them something concrete to talk about and make the transfer of skills to the home situation more explicit. It's not something I'd been able to do before with their daily diaries, but I can now see ways to integrate your approach with the ongoing language support the children really need from their parents at home.*

The children's evident lack of engagement with curricular materials in the nursery was of concern, and this issue was considered important to address as it would impact on their future school experience.

Three aspects of the third phase of the programme made a difference. First, the children chose which materials they brought from the nursery into the therapy room. Second, they were free to use the materials as they wished within the given framework of their books. Third, they worked together as a group to encourage and support each other. As Nina wrote towards the end of the programme:

> *The recording part of the sessions is really, really important for them. It makes them feel they can do what their friends spend a lot of time doing: like using pencils and paper. It's given them the chance to do it on their*

145

own terms, without anyone telling them 'That's rubbish!' all the time. Generally I think at this time their concentration span is increasing and they are now able to finish their books with much less adult help. They're doing what they like with their books now, which is really good, and enjoy making their own decisions regarding the stickers and colours.

As the year progressed, Nina became increasingly concerned at the prospect of the children entering a mainstream school environment. She began to scope out the terrain of the 'borderland' by introducing specific elements that the children would be expected to engage with.

When she delivered the programme independently, she gradually introduced selected books from the nursery library during her final reflecting phase. This was designed to clarify and reiterate the purpose of books and extend the children's ability to make links between their physical experiences, print and pictures. An unthreatening engagement with books ensured they gained enough confidence to use the library independently later on. As she said after her first session when small teddies were used to illuminate prepositional language:

Getting a book out of the library corner was a real challenge for all of us today. I know they never look at books unless they're forced to, and they usually hate it if I bring books out during their individual time with me. But I was really surprised that they responded so well. I don't think they would have been ready last term, but being around schooly things during the programme with you has obviously rubbed off. I was especially pleased with Leo, who usually just stares at me if we do anything paper-based. Did you notice how he thought the teddy sitting under the bed was so funny?

Nina also adapted the manner of her interactions with the children to replicate that which they would encounter in mainstream school. She asked for a higher level of cooperation from the children in setting out the room, sourcing materials and tidying up. They were all given specific tasks that she expected to be completed. As she said:

Initially I was really uncomfortable pitching my voice like that. Usually I'm very quiet and supportive, and I thought they might react badly if I talked to them like the others do in the nursery. I was surprised that they didn't really notice any change – which is a good thing, because that's what they'll be faced with very soon. I also realised I got in lots of vocabulary practice, which went well, I thought. It doesn't come naturally to me to interact with them so forcefully, but it's important that they are comfortable with it, as it's going to be a vital part of their preparation for the next stage.

Here are some of the parents' comments. They noticed in their children's behaviour how the movement programme had provided a manageable and relevant way to acquire and practise essential skills. They were well aware that 'crossing the border' to school was going to be a challenge; but by finding a positive role for themselves to support their children, being aware of *their* part in navigating the borderland, using the children's books as a conduit for ideas and information, the borders began to seem a little less threatening and more manageable:

She's doing a lot of balancing and concentrating on different positions at home. She has really enjoyed bringing her books home and showing her dad and her sister. Her concentration is much better, and she's finally found some friends. Her social skills are better now, and she doesn't get so close to people. She's much more sensitive, I think, and she's going to try gym lessons soon. She makes friends more easily now because she's more confident.

He really enjoyed the programme. He joined in and seemed to look forward to telling me about what he'd done. I think it's given him a lot of confidence, and he's enjoyed being accepted by the group. He keeps wanting to put my tights on my head! The programme really helped him prepare for school. He still doesn't like going to his language classes, but he can now do most of the things he's asked to in school.

He really enjoyed running and jumping. He enjoyed the programme and can still remember a lot of what he did, like going round in a circle and stopping. He still has some problems relating to other children, but the programme has definitely started to help him.

He told me a lot of what he did, and he especially remembered the tights. He keeps rootling through my drawers and making them long. He's doing a lot more of relating concepts to himself. He told me today his hair was short, like his dad's. The programme is an ideal framework for him, because language concepts are the crux of his difficulty, and using physical or visual cues are a tremendous help. He's much more accommodating now with other people, and he's obviously learnt how to negotiate in situations.

*I think he really enjoyed the physical aspect of it. He liked showing
me his book, and he seems much more organised and focused. He has
started to try harder in his swimming lessons, and he can finally pedal
his bike. He thinks he's a very good jumper. He's definitely getting more
confident, because he said hello to the builder who was at the door
yesterday, and he would never have done that before.*

The parents' feedback demonstrates how the children transferred the skills
they acquired in a movement context to support their friendships in the
nursery, engage positively with curricular materials and ease transitions
between the inside, outside and therapeutic environments.

The first (movement) phase ensured the key physical skills that inform
communication were highlighted. The second (apparatus) phase ensured
vital manipulative skills were practised that led directly to their calm and
positive engagement with curricular materials in the third (recording) phase.
Language was introduced in a relevant and meaningful way, ensuring the
children remembered and used phrases and vocabulary in a range of contexts,
secure in the knowledge that their contributions would be received positively.

Transitions are a continual source of learning. Skills acquired in a
movement context may be transferred to support seamless transitions in all
contexts. The portfolio of physical abilities that inform children's invisible
backpacks may be enhanced, pruned, curated and amended over time. The
transfer of skills between and through environments is to be encouraged
and supported. The borderland as a distinct entity should be understood
as having its own rationale, demands and expectations. Being school-ready
remains undefined, but the physical element, whether through general health
and wellbeing or the acquisition of skills linked to learning, should be fully
acknowledged in any approach. 'School preparedness' may be a more useful
term, as this supports the definition of 'ready' as being 'in an appropriate
state'. Finally, ask the children themselves what they think 'school readiness'
means – you may be very surprised by their answers.

8

A 'Canopy' Approach to Movement Provision Is Created and Implemented

canopy – awning – ceiling – cover – roof – tent – dome
– marquee – pavilion – arbor – bower – pergola –
shade – shelter – shield – sunshade – umbrella

'Canopy' is a useful concept as it implies enveloping, embracing, structure, support, simplicity, parameters that are movable and flexible, beginnings and endings, and particular times, places and occasions when things happen; it also suggests certain behaviours and rituals.

Applied to children's movement experience, what should be included under the canopy:

- A wide range of opportunities to engage in movement experience across different timespans – hourly, daily, weekly, termly.

- Opportunities to rehearse and refine movement skills in a variety of inside/outside environments.

- Opportunities to move with and without apparatus, with and without music, with others or alone and always supporting inclusivity.

- Different types of movement opportunities – e.g. dance, yoga, gymnastics, swimming, sport.

- Free physical play in both inside and outside environments for extended periods of time.

- Semi-structured opportunities for movement during which adults may facilitate and support.

- Structured opportunities when appropriate.

- Frequent incidental opportunities to move when appropriate.

CONTEXT

There is a general consensus that physical activity is good for young children for a range of *health* reasons. As Richard Weiler and colleagues write:[1]

Childhood physical inactivity has been linked to cholesterol and fatty streaks appearing in the aorta in the first decade of life and in the arteries of the heart, brain and peripheral arteries in the second and third decades. Furthermore, obesity, insulin resistance and inflammation (i.e. paediatric metabolic syndrome), Type 2 diabetes, mellitus and other risk factors for cardiovascular disease have been found to be common in inactive children, following a similar distribution in adults.

Also, that 'higher levels of sedentary behaviour are associated with worse mental health and lower cognitive function'.[2]

The British Heart Foundation (BHF) cite a range of positive outcomes for children engaging in physical activity: 'Physical activity is good for blood cholesterol levels. It has a protective effect against weight gain and general bone health.'[3]

Data from the Centre for Diet and Activity Research (CEDAR) study (2015) also suggests that children who engage in high levels of screen-viewing are likely to have poor diets, including insufficient consumption of fruits and vegetables.[4]

Evidence linking physical activity to *cognitive* functioning in young children is available but not yet of sufficient quality or quantity to merit a confident addition to policy initiatives. A paper produced by the Education Endowment Foundation (EEF) in 2015 states the following:[5]

Existing studies suggest that physical development approaches (that aim to improve young children's physical growth, skills and health) are associated with a small improvement in cognitive outcomes equivalent to approximately two additional months' progress.

However, though the overall picture is positive, the evidence base is not well-developed and findings are inconsistent. It is not possible to provide a clear account of the reasons why some physical development approaches are effective, and very few individual interventions have been evaluated to a high standard. In several cases, claims are made about the positive impact on learning of specific physical development approaches that are not supported by rigorous evaluation. There is some evidence that programmes that combine physical activity with strategies to promote self-regulation can improve executive function and have a positive impact on learning.

Evidence relating to the general positive impact of physical activity on cognitive outcomes is currently stronger than that related to specific programmes, and provides some indications that physical activity, including outdoor play, can support children's learning.

No high-quality evaluations have assessed the long-term impact of physical development approaches on learning.

The evidence base related to physical development approaches is currently limited. Two recent systematic reviews have been conducted, but the reviews did not identify high-quality evidence related to learning outcomes for young children.

No high-quality studies appear to have been conducted in early years settings in England.

Given the weak evidence in this area, it is important to evaluate the impact of any new physical development approaches and it would be valuable for early years professionals to be cautious about the claims of new interventions that do not appear to have been evaluated.

Having established that physical activity is generally positive for children for a wide range of reasons, determining exactly what they do, when they do it and with whom becomes a significant challenge. As a Master's student writes:[6]

To date there is no agreed, reliable and valid method of measuring physical activity levels in children participating in free play.

Measuring physical activity levels in young children offers unique challenges as their movement patterns are highly variable, non-structured and generally comprise short and frequent bursts of moderate to vigorous activity.

Another confounding factor is the differing rates of maturation and development among same-aged children.

Relating to research methodology, the lack of consistency of agreed, valid methods makes the results difficult to compare.

The author cites known issues regarding the following: self-report recall methods (not appropriate for very young children), proxy reports by parents and teachers (not always reliable), questionnaires (it cannot be assumed that accurate information will be provided) and direct observation (often time-consuming). Accelerometers (particularly uniaxial accelerometers) are often used by researchers and, although pedometers are easily used to measure the volume of physical activity, they cannot measure intensity very accurately or accommodate activities like cycling, skateboarding, swinging, hanging or spinning).

Researchers tend to use either the Children's Activity Rating Scale (CARS) in a modified version for young children[7] or the Observational System for Recording Physical Activity in Children – Preschool (OSRAC–P) developed in 2002.[8] There are acknowledged limitations to the use of both systems, but work is ongoing to mitigate the difficulties that have undoubtedly delayed progress in terms of research.

Physical activity is included in internationally accepted policy documents and, on many levels, is considered beneficial for young children. However, as Greet Cardon points out:

> While there is evidence that physical activity is important for infants and toddlers, it can be concluded that very little is known about their (in)activity levels. The limited evidence shows that very young children spend a large proportion of time sedentary, that TV-viewing is already common in infants and toddlers and that time spent in moderate to vigorous physical activity is limited.[9]

According to the Canadian, National Longitudinal Study of Children and Youth (NLSCY) (2011), only 36 per cent of 2–3-year-olds and 44 per cent of 4–5-year-olds engage in unorganised sport and physical activity each week.[10] PHE data for 2015 suggests only 9 per cent of boys and 10 per cent of girls experience a level of physical activity that would effectively support their health. Overall, 84 per cent of children aged 2–4 engaged in low levels of physical activity for less than one hour a day.[11] The BHF Evidence Briefing, *Physical Activity in the Early Years* (2015), includes the following statement:

> Physical activity levels in childcare appear generally to be very low; the majority of studies suggest that children accumulate less than 60 minutes of moderate to vigorous physical activity over an eight-hour day.[12]

This is where things start to get complicated. What is meant by 'physical activity – light, moderate/vigorous'? What do we do about the disconnect between the *perceived* levels of children's activity as being high ('they are supercharged dynamos – they never sit still') and *evidence* that 'gives cause for concern that levels of physical activity in early childhood are typically much less than optimal'?[13]

The New South Wales (NSW) Centre for Physical Activity and Health defines physical activity as 'any bodily movements produced by skeletal muscle that results in a substantial increase over the resting energy expenditure' (2011).[14]

Physical activity is typically categorised into different intensities and is measured in metabolic equivalents (METs). Hence, 1 MET is equivalent to rest and 1.5–2.9 METs align with *very light activity*. Children's physical activity is very light, almost physically passive, when they 'sit in one place, draw, look at pictures and read, make sand-cakes at the sandbox, watch television or use a computer, build structures using building blocks, solve a jigsaw puzzle, play with small objects or eat'. *Light intensity* for young children is when they 'walk slowly, play games involving a low level of physical activity, throw and catch a ball, swing on a swing and maintain a balance, dance or move to slow and peaceful music, engage in role-play or perform normal daily tasks such as putting clothes on, taking clothes off, or organising their toys and things'. *Moderate physical activity* is equivalent to 3–8 METS. This is when children 'walk briskly, use a scooter, ride a bike, skate, dance to fast and rhythmical music, play with a ball or use a large shovel'. *Vigorous physical activity* is when children 'run fast, play games in which participants need to be chased, jump on the trampoline, push a large truck, climb up a hill, wrestle, swim, ski or walk up the stairs'.[15]

Australian research data (2007) indicates that 3–5-year-olds spend approximately 60 minutes daily in moderate to vigorous physical activity (MVPA), which is around 8 per cent of waking hours. A substantial amount of light-intensity physical activity is accumulated: around 80–150 minutes daily: around 11–20 per cent of waking hours. Current estimates suggest that preschool-aged children spend a total of approximately 2–3½ hours per day in some sort of physical activity.[16]

However, significant variations and inconsistencies arise between the studies that inform this data: 'Methodological issues such as application of different measurement instruments, the use of different definitions for physical activity intensities, and differences in the interpretation of guidelines have clearly influenced our understanding of physical activities patterns in the early years'.[17]

PHYSICAL ACTIVITY GUIDELINES

A range of physical activity guidelines has been created to enhance the physical activity levels of young children to support their overall health and wellbeing, although Australian academics caution that (2011):

> *Overall, mixed evidence for the association of physical activity with health benefits in preschool-aged children was found. The difficulty in accurately measuring physical activity within this age group, the small and underpowered samples in many studies and the fact that children are generally healthy and free from risk factors for chronic disease (as such, one would not expect to see variations in many of the health*

outcomes, certainly not enough to be influenced by behaviours such as physical activity) are possible explanations for the mixed evidence. Although the evidence for younger children is limited, there is strong evidence showing associations between physical activity and health outcomes in older children and adults. Therefore physical activity habits established within the early years are likely to promote later physical activity and health.[18]

Empirical evidence does not support the prescription of a *level of intensity* for children's physical activity but is more reflective of the typical amount of *time* children typically spend moving: around 2 hours in a 12-hour day. The Australian and Canadian 24-Hour Movement Guidelines (see Chapter 7) and the current UK CMO/EY/PA (Chief Medical Office Early Years Physical Activity) guidelines refrain from specifying the intensity of physical activity children should experience, 'which aligns with young children's natural intermittent and sporadic physical activity patterns', but all models support the daily physical activity recommendation of 180 minutes (3 hours). This is an aspirational timeframe and allows for a possible decline in physical activity levels when children start school. The UK guidelines state that:[19]

1. Physical activity should be encouraged from birth, particularly through floor-based play and water-based activities in safe environments.

2. Children of preschool age who are capable of walking unaided should be physically active for 180 minutes (3 hours) spread throughout the day.

3. All under-5s should minimise the amount of time being sedentary (being restrained or sitting) for extended periods of time except while sleeping.

4. The UK will publish its own EY Movement Guidelines in the near future.

New Zealand takes a slightly different approach: Sport New Zealand's 'Physical Literacy Framework' suggests that under-5s require 'physical movement in everyday life environments, including nature, to encourage creativity, imagination and exploration'. These guidelines promote 'regular physical activity, limited time spent sitting for prolonged periods (in front of or independent of screen-based entertainment) and an adequate amount of good-quality sleep'. Interestingly, they also include spiritual growth as a reason to encourage children to be more active.[20] In April 2019 the WHO published 'Guidelines on physical activity, sedentary behaviour and sleep for children under 5 years of age', a comprehensive and useful resource that is accessible and manageable for both practitioners and parents.[21]

In 2016, the Finnish Ministry of Education and Culture published their framework, *Joy, Play and Doing Together: Recommendations for Physical Activity in Early Childhood*.[22] In Finland, initiatives in this field are primarily research-based. This document was created in response to data that suggested the rapidly changing lifestyle of Finnish children and their families was having a negative impact on the level and quality of physical activity they all experienced.

Children's physical activity in Finland is monitored nationally and includes random sampling. As mentioned previously in Chapter 3, from 60,454 observations taken in 2015, data suggests that:

Young children are highly physically active for an average 47.5 minutes between 8 a.m. and 4 p.m.

The least active group manage 4.8 minutes, the most active 163 minutes.

68.6 per cent of children's high physical activity occurs during outdoor activities (Finnish children spend 91 minutes daily outdoors on average).

In sessions taught by a teacher, e.g. sports, only 8 per cent of children manage a high level of physical activity.

Peer activities are 'dense' with high physical activity. 75 per cent of high-level physical activity is connected with other children.

This evidence led to the development and implementation of initiatives that supported children's outdoor play with their peer groups – the two factors identified as being the most supportive of high activity levels.

Trina Hinkley adds the following observations:[23]

Young children are more active if they are boys, their parents participate in physical activity and are active with their child, and they spend more time outside… Fewer children per square metre of outdoor space, shorter recess time, active opportunities, fixed and portable play equipment, and staff trained in physical activity for young children have also been found to promote physical activity.

The research gaps are significant, but work is ongoing to fill them as the concept of primordial prevention for children's health receives increasing attention.

A FRAMEWORK FOR PRACTICE

The following framework for practice supports a canopy approach to movement experience for all young children. Essential factors to consider:

- Time. Enough time is allocated for all children to enjoy being physical, both inside and outside throughout the day.

- Space is available at all times for children to rehearse and refine their skills.

- Being physical is actively supported and valued by all children and adults.

- A range of resources and materials is easily available to increase children's level of engagement in physical activities and active/ movement play.

- Interest is encouraged in the language of movement – songs, rhymes, games, poetry and drama from different cultures.

- Children contribute ideas for shaping their environment to support and extend their movement skills. They develop and revisit physical activity projects over time.

- Adults find a proactive role to support children's physical activity: e.g. practical delivery, sourcing music and resources, liaising with parents, and making posters.

THE FOUR COMPONENTS OF A 'MOVEMENT CANOPY'

There are *four essential components* that form a comprehensive canopy movement experience. These four components may each be broken down into *four modes of delivery*. Not all components may be experienced daily, but should be adequately provided for over a week. This provides a manage-able, sustainable and flexible framework that accommodates a wide range of ages, abilities, environments and the specific skills required by a range of physical disciplines.

Movement experience

This includes all the 'foundation'/functional gross motor and locomotor skills: rolling, crawling ('commando' and all-fours), walking, running, jumping, climbing, hopping, skipping:

Structured

Recommended 15 per cent of available time:

- A range of mainstream resources and materials are provided to increase children's level of engagement in physical activities and active play.
- Specific timeframe (often timetabled).
- Designated environment (hall, specified space, inside, outside).
- Specific skills (outside activity providers may be involved).
- Uniform kit (change from home clothes).

Adult presence is very visible. Children do not make a significant contribution and tend to engage in organised group activities. As they get older, they increasingly appreciate this element and respond positively. Very young children may enjoy an occasional 'taster' experience of this approach.

Semi-structured

The usual approach taken with children aged 3–5 years. Recommended 25 per cent of available time:

- Allows for wide variations in competency, ability, size, strength and speed.
- Sessions may be based on a particular theme, new vocabulary, an event or novel resource.
- Children's contributions are actively acknowledged and valued.

Free play

Children rehearse and refine their skills with minimal adult input, although the environment may be prepared and available resources determined by adults. Recommended 60 per cent of available time.

Incidental

Opportunities emerge spontaneously – as and when:

- A period of time becomes available, the weather changes, an unexpected resource appears.

- Involves transitions from inside to outside or to different areas.

- Maximising incidental movement experiences is an effective way of supporting the CMO/EY Physical Activity Guidelines.

Hand apparatus

This includes mainly apparatus that fits easily into one hand (not mainstream sports equipment), writing and printing materials. A range of hand and manipulative skills are highlighted, including: grasp, grip, shake, squeeze, poke, squirt, hold, fold, flick, smooth, press, pat, beat, punch, pull, roll, sweep, brush, wipe, lift, carry, turn, catch and throw.

Structured

- Works best for older children who can process more complex instructions.

- May focus on specific skills for therapeutic or sporting purposes.

- Specific vocabulary may be introduced.

- Group work/teamwork is encouraged.

- Goals, targets and scores may be introduced when appropriate.

Semi-structured

- Apparatus may be used to: illuminate a theme, reinforce specific vocabulary or focus on a particular skill.

- All properties of the chosen apparatus are explored, either in groups or individually.

Free play

This should be included in any provision for hand apparatus. It is a very important element within which children investigate the properties of the apparatus, exchange ideas, negotiate and delegate.

Incidental

This may be a significant source of broadening experiences with hand apparatus. Something new and interesting is discovered on site or unexpectedly presented by staff/parents.

Large apparatus

Includes: Transportable materials – tunnels, boxes, cushions, big beanbags, duvets, mattresses, sheets, throws, benches, chairs, tables. Skills include: climbing, pushing, pulling, constructing, carrying, swinging.

Structured

Obstacle courses for different aims (speed, strength, agility, balance). Making dens. A specific skill may be highlighted that is relevant to older children.

Semi-structured

A useful approach for younger children. A particular physical skill (e.g. carrying, constructing), communication skill (e.g. sharing, supporting, negotiating) or vocabulary (e.g. positional) may be the focus.

Free play

This is a very important element to include when engaging with large apparatus. Adequate provision is necessary and may happen largely outside.

Incidental

Something is discovered that interests them (a big box, a hole in the ground) inside or outside, a space becomes available or time is freed up suddenly.

R & R (Rest & Relaxation)

Includes: Rest, sleep, withdrawal (from people, noise, overstimulation): downtime (being quiet and physically calm), restoration (recover energy levels); relaxation (time to have a clear mind, absorb the atmosphere and the environment); regeneration (regain energy, focus and impetus); reflection on what has been experienced: change in feelings; sharing of experiences through different media (poetry, paint, stories, drawing); linking to other genres: poetry, music, literature, art, sculpture.

Structured

- Daytime sleeps should be factored into your movement canopy: 12 months approximately (2.5 hours). 2 years (1.5 hours). 3 years (45 minutes).

- You could create a project around sleep. Explore how other species sleep, where they sleep, when they sleep.

- Time may be allocated to being quiet, reflective and mindful each day. Focus on breathing, being calm and centred.

Semi-structured

Children are afforded specific times and spaces to be restful and quiet. They know what behaviours are expected (choose a book, listen to music, be calm). Reflection time may include a group discussion or time at the end of a more structured session to talk about what they have experienced.

Free play

Children are able to be quiet and reflective at any time. Spaces and resources are available to support this inside and outside.

Incidental

There is a sudden, overwhelming need for a quiet moment. This may occur during a more structured session or in response to something, e.g. a change in temperature (usually heat). Reflection may often occur in response to an event or a new skill that has been observed or acquired.

OBSERVATION AND ASSESSMENT

Observing children moving is a wonderful privilege. You can tell an enormous amount about where children are by simply hovering: what they do, how they do it, where they do it, who they do it with and why they do it.

Jan White talks of 'noticing and recognising' children's physical play in order to plan effectively 'for movement and physicality'.[24] Noticing and recognising are two very different processes. As she says, they are the 'what and so what' of the planning cycle and should both be critical components of any meaningful observation:

- *Noticing* implies an initial moment of, 'Hmm, that's interesting!' – something that informs a previous niggle or may be completely random. In terms of physical development, this may involve a new interest (e.g. climbing), a recently acquired skill (e.g. catching, skipping), a different area in which physical activity is experienced (e.g. in a movement corner or outside) or a change in collaborators and friendships. Noticing, as Jan says, is the *what* of the observation process. It is not really suggestive of action.

- *Recognising*, in contrast, is definitely full of actionable possibilities. It involves making connections between previous 'noticing moments' and an understanding of precisely what may be useful or helpful to support and extend movement experience. Recognising also includes an element of where links may be made between physical activity and other developmental domains including communication, language and emotional wellbeing.[25]

For physical development, two of the most effective observation mechanisms are visual and audio recordings. Visual materials provide not only snapshots of individual children but also how they operate physically within a group. Comparing and contrasting footage over time is very useful. Parents and children may contribute their own material, and all parties may benefit from reviewing film together. It gives you time to reflect and share observations with fellow professionals if this is deemed appropriate or necessary. It also minimises subjective bias as your interpretation may not always be the most useful or valid.

Audio recordings of children discussing their experiences often provide a welcome addition to observational data: how they remember an activity, what it felt like, who did what, how they could do it better. Again, their views may not align with your reflections at all.

So, notice all the time and recognise when some form of action is warranted. Both feed into effective observation that in turn is an important factor in the assessment of children's physical development. Remember that, although the EYFS requires practitioners to make observations, their frequency and type are unspecified.

In 2014, researchers at Loughborough University studied the provision for physical activity in Early Years settings in a Northern county of the UK.[26]

The issue of assessing children's physical development emerged as a source of considerable debate between practitioners, parents and health professionals: 'There was a strong feeling among some participants that care should be taken when referring to measuring or assessing development, with one respondent arguing that we need to problematise the notion.' Some respondents felt that the concept of measurement against some fixed standard (e.g. developmental milestones) was too rigid and ran the risk of labelling children unfairly. Some individuals favoured alternative terms such as 'monitoring' or 'tracking', while others suggested that more thought needed to be given to the consequences of assessment.

There was consensus from all parties included in this study that assessment regarding physical development was valid. The health check at age 2 was considered useful in that it flagged up potential problems around physical development, but concerns were raised that basing physical development assessment around developmental milestones may be somewhat inflexible, and linking expectations of physical development too closely to chronological age may erroneously identify problems.

The Loughborough study proposes that parents could also be asked to identify the physical activities their children enjoy – e.g. water-based activities, bikes, scooters, sport or dance – and include the estimated time that their children are active per day.

It also makes clear that a more collaborative approach to the evaluation, monitoring and assessment of children's physical development is sorely needed. A coherent approach for sharing responsibility would ease the pressure on health services (the number of health visitors has fallen from 10,039 in 2015 to 8,275 in 2018)[27] and give proper regard for data gained from parents and teachers.

There is obviously a real need to ensure that consistent measures, standards and terminology are used but, as one contributor noted, 'I don't think it matters who does the measurements; what is more important is that everyone is trained and using the same standards.'

Generally, there is a need for a better coordinated continuous assessment process that allows for physical development issues to be identified at any age, and much more use should be made of parental and practitioner input. As one of the participating practitioners commented, 'Would it be more helpful (and kind) to have a framework that ensures that each child is receiving the kind of movement opportunities that they need by a particular stage?' Standard training opportunities should also be provided for all those involved in the monitoring and assessment of physical development to ensure a holistic, realistic, relevant, valued and authentic picture of each child is gained.

In 2014, researchers at the University of Minnesota created the Early Movement Monitoring Assessment (EMMA) tool. As they write:[28]

Monitoring functional movement skills of infants and toddlers frequently (3 week intervals) and quickly (minutes) produces information on whether development is on track or in need of intervention.

Monitoring development can identify which skills are happening at a given time, what environment is appropriate for practicing those skills, and what support is needed for the next developmental steps.

Frequent assessment captures skills on a near monthly basis and accommodates the variability expected by producing a trend line across multiple sessions closely linked in time.

The procedure includes the functional movement skills of sit, stand and crawl, considered 'potent to development' and 'readily observed by the non-movement expert'. The chosen resources were 'two balls, a pushcart and a toy car', that 'quickly engaged the infants and toddlers in moving'. Parents were closely involved in the process at all times.

Once the children who participated in the study were walking and running, the researchers write that 'a ceiling effect occurred with our tool' and the frequency of change slowed down. They also became less interested in the toys and preferred to play with other children rather than with their parents.

In future, the EMMA may be adapted to accommodate a range of disability areas, premature babies and to provide support for very young mothers.

TOWARDS A POLICY

Creating a specific policy for physical activity may provide additional impetus for supporting practice in physical development. This policy would set out the agreed ethos, values and intentions towards physical activity in your setting and provide clear documentation as to expectations and the possible future development of initiatives.

Common understandings

These will emerge through ongoing discussion and debate and may include the following:

- That physical activity plays a vital role in supporting all developmental domains.

- All adults may find a proactive role that supports effective physical development practice both inside and outside.

- Children should be given appropriate opportunities, time and space to be physical in their own way and to explore personal interests and abilities.

- A positive attitude towards physical activity, health and wellbeing should be shared with parents and the wider community, including the promotion of active travel by walking, bikes and scooters.

- A collaborative culture in which children's contributions are valued is promoted.

- Visible support for physical activity is promoted through the use of posters, photo montages and visual material.

Priorities

These will be informed by your common understandings and may include the following:

- Review the use of outdoor space, free flow and the adult role.

- Children's clothing, footwear – is it appropriate and manageable?

- Possible overuse of bikes and trikes – is there provision for those less competent?

- Not enough water/sand resources?

- Indoor space – can it be adapted to support more physical activity?

- Time spent sitting – monitor.

- Clutter – does this prevent physical activity?

- Staff training attitude – who is interested?

- Involve parents in any initiatives.

- Review observation, assessment and recording procedures.

Targets

These may now be determined on the basis of your common understandings and priorities. Try not to be too ambitious or intimidated by what others are doing. They may have completely different budgets, environments and levels of support from parents and the wider community.

By keeping your intentions transparent, simple and achievable, you will encourage support from children, parents, fellow professionals and your community.

RISK ASSESSMENT

What is it? It is a careful examination of what, in your school setting or learning environment, could cause harm to people, both children and adults. It is a process that allows you to weigh up all the factors which could result in potential harm to individuals.

Kathryn Solly is right when she says: 'Children technically speaking present a hazard in themselves' and that they 'are biologically programmed to take risks, and what they need is a vibrant, flexible and open-ended environment to look, feel and explore within'.[29]

She suggests that children's own involvement in risk assessment should be encouraged. As the Royal Society for the Prevention of Accidents (RoSPA) advises, 'We must try to make life as safe as necessary, not as safe as possible.'[30] Any effective risk assessment should therefore include not just the physical environment (the obvious one) but the enabling environment of their growing and developing bodies.

Anything that prevents, affects, compromises or negatively influences children's physical development and opportunities for physical activity should be included in all risk assessments, particularly during the first 18 months of life. Continually placing children in car seats and baby-walkers affects the time and space needed to practise the movement skills that impact on safety and minimise risk. Around 35,000 children every year are injured by falling downstairs[31] – and, in Sweden, between 1998–2007, there was a 13 per cent increase in fractures to the distal forearm due to falling.[32] There has been a steady rise in playground injuries in the USA – A&E admissions for children have increased from 156,000 in 1980 to 271,475 in 2013,[33] and a 150 per cent increase in PE-related injuries has been noted from 1997–2007.[34]

If opportunities are not provided for bones to be strengthened through continual movement, they will become weaker, and more porous: a reduction in load-bearing capacity leads to the breakdown of calcium that is reabsorbed by the body and leads to bones becoming more brittle and prone to fractures. If children have strong, reliable bodies that may confidently and competently engage in physical activities, they are more likely to make appropriate decisions for themselves and successfully conduct their own risk assessments.

As children emerge from infancy, arrive at nursery and then enter reception, our role in supporting their physical development changes: from supporting parents to make the right decisions, to affording maximum opportunities to rehearse and refine a range of movement skills, and ultimately to ensure that all children are physically able to manage the inevitable challenges of life at home and school.

Part Two

INTO PRACTICE

9

The 'Foundation' Year

Foundations have to be broad and deep; they have to be flexible; they must compensate for buildings that are under stress. Most important of all, foundations take longer to create than buildings, so it is vital that we resist the temptation to move children on too soon and attempt to build too high, before the foundations of learning are securely in place.

Julie Fisher, *Interacting or Interfering?*[1]

WHAT YOU WILL LEARN

- How to provide the optimum movement experiences during the first year that support the smooth overall development, health and wellbeing of babies (up to 4 months) and infants (4 months to 1 year inclusive).

- How hand apparatus and movable large apparatus may be used to extend and support movement experience.

- How the eight principles apply to practice and provision.

Back in 1999, BBC Radio 4 produced a series entitled *Tuning into Children: Understanding a Child's Development from Birth to Five Years*. In the accompanying booklet, Libby Purves wrote the following:

The daily tasks and terrors can come to obscure simplicities. We are bullied by circumstances and superstitions and rivalries and fears and fashions. Sometimes we forget that the most important task of any parent, or substitute parent, is to relate directly and receptively and with loving attention to the individual child. To have such attention is not a luxury; it is a necessity and a right.[2]

This was written before the advent of social media or websites devoted entirely to providing an endless stream of information, guidance, resources and support.

She also wondered if:

We may be too rushed and impatient to catch their pace, too full of our own ideas to grasp the importance of what they are trying to tell us. We may be looking out too anxiously for the next prescribed developmental stage to notice they have leapfrogged it, side-lined it, in favour of a quirky individual talent that is all their own. Forests of knowledge, rivers of preoccupation, carapaces of worldly wisdom are no substitutes for tuning in and really understanding the small beings with whom you engage.

This chapter is written with these thoughts in mind. All babies are unique. They learn, grow and develop within eras, environments and cultures that offer particular opportunities and experiences that inform their physical development.

Parenting approaches, cultural norms, expectations and priorities relating to physical development vary widely and are often influenced by the advent of new resources, scientific breakthroughs and academic research. Other factors may include the changing economic and working climate for women, the frequent fragmentation of family life and increasingly fluid family constructs.

THE FOUR COMPONENTS OF A 'MOVEMENT CANOPY'
Component 1: Movement experience

In physical terms, what is really needed during the first year when we know that if left to their own devices, babies would probably spend 40 per cent of their waking time kicking, waving, wriggling and generally moving?

Two issues have had a dramatic impact on the quality and quantity of babies' and infants' physical experience. First, the 'Back to Sleep' campaign and, second, the prevalence of containers and sitting devices.

In 1992, the American Academy of Pediatrics (AAP) began to recommend that infants sleep on their backs.[3] In 1994, the AAP and partners (including the National Institute for Child Health and Human Development) launched the Back to Sleep (now Safe to Sleep) campaign. Prone sleeping has decreased in babies from over 70 per cent to 20 per cent. As a result, the incidence of Sudden Infant Death Syndrome (SIDS) has reduced by 50 per cent.

As babies and infants can spend up to 18 hours asleep, this initiative has had unforeseen effects on their physical development. Doctors have noted an increase in instances of:

- Plagiocephaly: Flattened areas on the back of the head. Although 20 per cent of babies will have this naturally, a 2004 study of 343 infants found that 15.2 per cent had significant cranial deformities affecting the skull base and face.

- Torticollis: A twisted neck condition in which the head tilts to one side while the chin tilts towards the other.

- Decreased strength and stability of the trunk, neck and upper body, and difficulty bearing weight on palms of the hands.

- Late rolling-over (later than observed in infants who sleep on their side or tummy).

- Significantly later acquisition of gross motor skills, e.g. not yet crawling at 9 months. A 2006 Canadian study suggests that 22 per cent of babies who slept on their backs experienced some delay in motor skills, that included rolling over, sitting up and climbing stairs.[4]

- Children are more likely to fall behind in their cognitive development, particularly in reasoning and language skills.

It is estimated that babies and infants have now 'lost' around 600 hours of 'tummy time' or 'prone play' in their first year. With this significant decrease, it is worth revisiting the benefits of this physical experience.

'Tummy time'

- Control of overall balance and coordination begins with the head. If babies want to change position, they must lift up their heads – by 4 months they can reach up to 45 degrees. Centring the head on the neck and shoulders affects the balance needed for later standing and walking.

- Spontaneous large movements of arms and legs stimulates and supports whole body strength – particularly in the *outer* core muscles of the abdomen that are used for pushing and pulling actions, and the *inner* core muscles around the pelvic floor, diaphragm and spine that inform postural stability and control.

- Beginning of 'body-mapping' supports proprioceptive development: 'How long am I, where are my hands?'

- Lengthens the spine and encourages the development of the mature S curve (from the immature C curve *in utero*) that is essential for later postural control and balanced locomotion.

- Expands the chest cavity – very beneficial for breathing generally.

- Encourages weight-bearing on the hands as the palms flatten and bodies are pushed up.

- Eyes are supported to focus and track at close range in this position – the distance from hands to eyes is the same as experienced later when reading printed material. There will be 2–3 babies in every 10,000 who will have eye problems requiring treatment.[5]

- Bowel and bladder control is supported through increased awareness of the soft organs in the body – this has a positive effect on later 'on-time' toilet training.

- The arches (that run along and across both feet and start to develop properly in the second year) are strengthened by pushing forwards – in preparation for later heel-to-toe walking.

- Pushing forward also helps to stabilise the hip sockets: from lying at 180 degrees at birth, they must align at 90 degrees for walking to be accomplished successfully. There will be 1–2 babies in every 1000 who will have hip problems that require treatment.[6]

'Back time'

This is equally important. Why:

- Spontaneous large movements using arms and legs promote overall body strength and coordination.

- It enhances communication between adults and babies as they can maintain eye contact more easily and extend opportunities to interact.

- It promotes control of eye movements as babies interact with their carers. At around 3–4 months their visual acuity improves dramatically: from being able to see things around 22–30 cm away, it quickly becomes nearly the same as adults.

- It supports rhythmic awareness as they kick and wave – rhythmic movements are energy-efficient and give a good indication of levels of strength and stamina.

- Back time encourages the crossing of midlines from left to right as they reach across the body to retrieve objects – and between the upper and lower body as they grasp their feet.

- *Rolling over* can happen very suddenly and unexpectedly. First from front to back, between 5–6 months, and back to front a little later, between 6–7 months.

- Once this is achieved, the movement repertoire expands significantly – it is the beginning of self-determination and making personal choices: 'What position do I like – how long do I like being in it – how can I change position?'

When should babies and infants experience 'tummy time' and 'back time'?

For newborns this may include 'skin time': chest-to-chest or tummy-to-tummy with carers. For the first few months, they need to spend a significant period of time in the prone position in physical contact with their carers. Between 10 weeks and 7 months, babies should spend time independently on the floor, variously described as the 'baby's first playground', 'the athletic field of the child' and 'a natural playground'. Ideally, infants up to 10 months should experience around 30 minutes to one hour per day on the floor on their tummies in 5–10 minute bursts. 'Side time' is a good alternative to tummy time. You can support babies' backs with a rolled-up towel and a small folded cloth under their head if needed, both arms in front and legs forward with knees bent.

As for surfaces, the harder the surface, the harder babies' muscles have to work (remember that Pikler babies are exclusively placed on a covered wooden floor as mentioned in Chapter 6). A range of surface materials may be explored, including furry throws, sponge, bubble wrap, grass, Lycra, velvet, towelling, carpet or corrugated cardboard – these surfaces should not be too slippery as their feet need to gain enough traction to push forward.

Anne O'Connor[7] has a wonderful range of ideas for tummy time:

- *Body tummies*: Tummy-to-tummy for eye contact and warmth.

- *Towel tummies*: After bath with no nappies or clothes on – freedom.

- *Tipping tummies*: On a Swiss ball or propped up on the arm of a chair, tiger in the tree hold or on knees.

- *Flying tummies*: On one arm (about 3 months), on legs (6–9 months).

- *Sliding tummies*: Being pulled around on the floor on a blanket (beloved of older siblings).

Ensure that babies experience a range of different tummy positions throughout the day with you and independently. Try not to keep them in one position for longer than 15 minutes. Check that babygros are not too tight on their feet and take all clothes and nappies off if warm, comfortable and the environment is appropriate.

Back time can also be enjoyed during nappy changing, bathtime and bedtime – and if you have a pram in which they are lying flat.

Containers

If the Safe to Sleep campaign has had a significant impact on the quality and quantity of babies' and infants' experience of tummy time, the prevalence of 'infant sitting/positioning devices' and containers has had an equally detrimental effect on their physical development.

Babies and infants not only spend a significant amount of time asleep on their backs but may also experience 2–5 hours daily being supported in sitting devices that include car seats, carriers, high chairs, Bumbos, baby-bouncers and baby-walkers. In the USA, it is not unusual for babies to spend at least 60 hours per week being restrained or 'contained'.

Twenty years ago, an American study concluded that:

Car seats that double as infant carriers and infant seats likely are being used extensively outside of automobiles. Prolonged use of infant seating devices with infants who are too young to sit unsupported may have several potential adverse consequences.[8]

What the evidence highlighted was that no longer having to move infants from car seats to buggies to cots was predicted to have an adverse effect on their physical development. Placing infants in a supine semi-reclined position ensures the trunk, head and neck are completely supported for extended periods of time. Thus, the daily 'incidental' opportunities to strengthen postural muscles and promote vital vestibular and ocular input that happened previously (as they were continually moved around, carried and held) are minimised. The expression 'Container Baby Syndrome' (CBS) was used to describe children with 'flattened heads, coordination difficulties, muscle weakness and abnormalities and altered walking and movement patterns'.[9] During 1992–2008, there was a 600 per cent increase in diagnoses of CBS – in 2008 alone, 1 in 7 young children were diagnosed.

The Baby Be Well campaign[10] recognised these issues and advocated that babies spend no longer than 90 minutes in a car seat at any one time. The creators highlight that the quantity of oxygen to babies' lungs decreases when strapped in a reclining position. The lungs also work less efficiently and oxygen desaturation (a decrease in blood oxygen levels) may occur. They also reiterate the possibility of flat-head syndrome, poor spinal alignment and diminished opportunities to enjoy close physical contact and practise a range of visual skills.

The New Zealand (2017) initiative, 'Sit Less, Move More, Sleep Well'[11] includes the following statement from the Ministry of Health:

Some equipment that restricts a child's free movement is necessary for safety, especially in uncontrolled environments. Child restraints (baby capsules and car seats) are legally required to be used in New Zealand when travelling in a vehicle. Long car trips should be broken up with regular stops. During the stops, under-fives should be removed from their child restraints so their movement is not restricted for too long. Capsules and car seats should only be used for transportation, and under-fives should not be left to sleep in them.

This same document also makes crystal clear that:

Seating equipment such as high chairs, seat swings, activity gyms and baby-jumpers should be used in moderation and only once a child is developmentally ready. Using seating equipment for a child who is not developmentally ready can delay the development of their natural sitting abilities since the equipment supports the child and negates the need for the child to use their own core muscles. If a child is developmentally ready and can sit up on their own, this equipment can be useful for containing them, for example during mealtimes.

Considering sitting emerges naturally at 7–9 months, we should be more proactive in raising awareness of the developmental issues related to overuse of 'containers'. What are some of these issues?[12]

Baby-walkers

- Compromise the level of muscle development required to ensure independent, fluent walking.

- Legs are placed wide apart and the muscles that stabilise the hip joints cannot ensure they align at the necessary 90 degrees.

- Postural/back muscles are completely supported in a 'neutral' position, so they are not gaining the level of strength needed to maintain children's independent upright stance.

- Feet are hidden, that compromises proprioceptive development – this may lead to issues with sleeping in the dark and an increase in accidents and falls.

- The development of walking skills is compromised – for every 24 hours of use, walking is delayed by 3.4 days.

- Baby walkers are the cause of 24,000 reported accidents per year.

Baby-jumpers

- The body is completely supported (as with the baby-walkers) – the postural muscles are not gaining the strength needed for future movement skills.

- Feet are not placed flat on the floor – tendons and calf muscles tighten, that compromises an efficient heel-to-toe walking action.

- Legs are again placed in a wide position that prevents the muscles surrounding the hip joints from strengthening and supporting alignment.

High chairs

- The 'baby-led weaning' approach to infant nutrition may have inadvertently affected the natural accomplishment of sitting independently.

- In this approach parents are encouraged to sit children up (usually in some sort of high chair) so they can make their own decisions about food when progression to solid foods begins, usually around 6 months.

- Perhaps much earlier than may have happened naturally, infants are propped up and become reluctant to be on their tummies or backs and get into the optimum position to crawl. On average, 92 per cent of infants spend two hours a day in high chairs.

An interesting new approach, 'baby-wearing', is slowly becoming established in UK nursery practice.[13] It involves carrying a baby upright in a sling carrier – close to the carer's body and facing outwards – leaving legs and arms free to move and the trunk properly supported.

In a recent project, the participating babies were observed to be much more settled, spent more time in a quiet, alert state and instances of crying were reduced by 40 per cent. Slings support physical development as babies can keep moving while they engage with others and the environment. Emotionally they feel protected, safe and secure. The neck and trunk are correctly positioned and the postural muscles are working hard to maintain stasis.

If babies and infants were simply left to enjoy self-initiated motor exploration – with minimal input or interference from adults – what may be the outcome? Probably the following. This evidence was gained from a study of 591 normal infants whose birth weight was over 2.49 kg (in the study, 5.5 pounds):[14]

- 17 weeks: Turned onto side.

- 24 weeks: Turned back onto tummy.

- 29 weeks: Turned tummy onto back.

- 39 weeks: Started to commando crawl on tummy.

- 44 weeks: Crawled on hands and knees.

- 49 weeks: Sitting unaided, stood up in the same week.

- 66 weeks (15 months): Took first steps.

- 72 weeks (17 months): Walked with ease.

The data was averaged, but significant variations between children were noted. Generally, motor milestones were reached later than would be expected. Evidence that reaching these milestones early is of any long-term benefit is not forthcoming, and spending an extended period of time experiencing and enjoying the pre-walking movement stages may have a more positive effect on overall development.

We have looked at tummy time and back time. Now for the skills that inform 'being on the move'.

Commando crawling on tummies

The grunting and snuffling that happens when infants begin pulling themselves along on their tummies can be quite alarming. It 'requires the ability to turn the head, stretch out the arm on the same side, place it on the floor and then bend the arm to pull the body forward while pushing off with the opposite leg'. For small bodies this is very hard work. Although many babies ignore this stage, despite being happy on their tummies, it is a useful precursor to hands-and-knees crawling. Possible difficulties may occur later in swimming front-crawl or marching with opposite arms and legs if this stage is missed.[15]

Crawling proper – on hands and knees

This will happen sometime during the first year, at 6–8 months onwards. It is the first time that infants are independently and purposefully mobile. It forms the initial experience of concepts including force, weight, direction and speed. Resilience and self-regulation are supported as they manage the emotional curves of feeling determined, strong and in control or thwarted, furious and despondent. The emergence of crawling as a generic movement pattern is interesting. Infants don't learn this movement skill by imitation, so it must be an intrinsically important skill to master before walking independently. After a fair amount of rocking and possibly going backwards or sideways, it happens. As with tummy time and back time, it is worth revisiting the benefits of this stage:

- The crawling action stabilises and coordinates eye movements. The change from peripheral (wide) to foveal (close) focus as they look forwards then down is a very important skill to acquire for later curricular activities.

- It also trains the eyes to cross the midline of the body – a critical skill linked to later reading and handwriting.

- Crawling promotes the hand–eye coordination that is essential for later curricular and sporting activities.

- Shoulders and hips are rotated into alignment – shoulder stability is essential for later writing, hip stability for walking.

- Hands open out as bodyweight is supported – an essential precursor to isolating the thumb and forefinger for a successful pencil grip. Valuable tactile and sensory input is gained as hands press on different surfaces.

- Overall muscle strength is stimulated by holding this challenging position for extended periods of time. The crawling action is an effective preparation for later vertical climbing.

- On a neurological level, crawling supports the development of the corpus callosum, the major 'interhemispheric communicator': it knits everything together to ensure the synchronicity of particular specialisations.

- It is a very complex movement pattern: the ability to move one side of the body independently of the other is refined and the arms are also moving independently of the head.

- The vestibular, proprioceptive and visual systems are connected for the first time.

- Crawling supports practice in coordinating the left and right and the upper and lower body through cross-lateral movements: this is a complex task and impacts on later ordering skills including numbering.

- It aligns the top and sacral sections of the spine to prepare for standing and walking.

If you notice a baby actively avoiding crawling on all fours, preferring to bottom-shuffle or scoot, it is worth considering the following reasons:

- Sinus pressure: This would make holding the head in a horizontal position painful and uncomfortable and may be linked to food allergies.

- Ear infections would affect balance and make the position uncomfortable and painful.

- Inability to flatten out the hand to take body weight successfully.

Does it really matter if babies miss out this stage? Possibly, and for the following reasons:

- The ability to cross the midline of the body may be compromised. This may have an impact on later sporting ability and skills that include dressing independently and writing clearly from left to right.

- Motor planning (organising sequences into fluid coordinated movements) may be affected – efficient bilateral integration is positively affected by the quality and quantity of children's early movement experience.

- Visual development may be compromised as they experience fewer opportunities to rehearse the visual skills needed for later successful engagement with curricular materials. Evidence from a 1999 study suggests that children who miss out on the crawling stage scored lower on the Bayley Scales of mental and motor development.[16]

It is worth remembering that some children only crawl after they can walk, and there is plenty of time and opportunities (as we will see in the following chapters) to revisit this movement pattern very successfully. Four-week Crawling Programmes for adults have now been created 'to regain and build your original strength through crawling: a developmental movement pattern that is rehabilitative, restorative and even performance-enhancing – the pattern that was designed to keep you healthy, strong and resilient throughout your entire life.' It is obviously never too late to start again![17]

Walking

After a period of pulling themselves up, bouncing, cruising the furniture and climbing – all excellent means of supporting overall strength (particularly in the upper body) – at some point walking will commence.

Some important points to remember:

- Holding children's hands above their heads for support puts them in a very difficult position to walk fluently. It raises their shoulders, limits the range of movement and prevents use of their arms for balance. Try to leave well alone or hold them gently under their armpits.

- Walking trolleys are not really helpful because they give a false measure of strength and balance and possibly delay independent walking.

- Plonking back on bottoms and falling over are essential elements of the walking process. Working out for themselves how to get up again supports agility and the management of bodyweight.

- Mums of boys frequently overestimate their physical skills; those of girls will typically underestimate and 'swoop and scoop' much more quickly as they transition from crawling to walking.

- Walking probably has the widest age range for any physical skill: between 10 and 20 months, average age 12–14 months. As Usha Goswami writes:

Even though an expert crawler can move more quickly and efficiently than a novice walker, babies persevere in learning to walk. Newly walking infants take over 2,000 steps an hour, covering the length of approximately seven football pitches. The average distance travelled of 700 metres each hour means that during an average waking day, and allowing for meals, bathtime etc., most infants are travelling over 5 kilometres![18]

Tummy time and back time provide the essential movement experiences that support acquisition of the foundation movement skills: rolling, crawling, sitting, standing, walking. All later skills are built on the strength, balance, coordination and agility that are gained by continual practice of these movements throughout the first year. It is vital that time, space and support are available for babies and infants to rehearse and refine these skills in as unhurried and natural a way as possible.

Conclusions: Movement experience in the foundation year

- Must include plenty of tummy time and back time – on different surfaces and terrains – mainly through incidental opportunities – although there may be times when a semi-structured approach is appropriate, e.g. in baby classes or in a setting.

- The least time babies and infants are contained/restrained the better – safety issues must be addressed – but being in a 'neurologically neutral' state does not properly support their physical development.

- Review the movement possibilities for supporting vestibular development in the first year – rocking, swinging, tipping, sliding, bouncing, moving fast, falling, rolling.

- Review the movement possibilities for supporting proprioceptive development: pushing, pulling, stretching, 'rough-and-tumble' – carrying infants in different positions so they can feel and push against adult bodies.

- Try not to intrude or interfere too much. Whenever possible let them practise in their own time, under their own steam – 'swooping and scooping' is not always necessary.

- Keep opportunities to move calm and simple – you will quickly discover what they enjoy or dislike. Observe and record if appropriate and necessary.

Component 2: Hand apparatus

The apparatus a new baby engages with most often (after their own hands and mouth) is the physical body of their primary carer as they root, nuzzle, cling, push and squeeze. For the first month or so, babies simply need to get used to being themselves, a newly separate entity who is experiencing different sounds, textures, temperatures, rhythms and faces daily. Do they really need things being rattled in their faces, pictures to stimulate their eyes, Mozart for their brains or mobiles waving randomly overhead?

In practice, the Pikler principle of only introducing hand apparatus once infants have enjoyed a thorough exploration of their hands and immediate environment (usually around 3 months) may seem a little purist, but a serious point is being made here: that overstimulating and overloading infants' sensitive systems with endless things to interact with demonstrates how easily we are influenced by advertising campaigns and shiny brochures and how quickly we forget that they have the perfect apparatus available anyway – in themselves and their carers.

Sue Gascoyne's research into the hand movements of infants and young children produced some fascinating findings.[19] During 2013–14, in Early Years and school settings, 82 observations were conducted. Each child was observed for an average of 10–30 minutes:

- From 0–8 months infants mainly gripped, turned and twisted and banged and hit when engaging with objects. To a much lesser extent they squeezed, pinched, rolled and prodded.

- Between 9–16 months there was a significant increase in instances of squeezing and pinching and a decrease in turning and twisting. They also became more engaged in prodding and poking.

The findings emerged from engagement with a wide range of materials including treasure baskets, sand, water and playdo.

Gripping/grasping and holding

- Babies and infants spend a significant amount of time repeating these movements, starting with themselves (hands and feet) and their carer (e.g. hair, glasses, necklace, clothes, bottle). From around 4 months onwards they will begin to grasp and grip objects efficiently and independently – opening up a range of new physical experiences and learning possibilities.

- Use a variety of manageable and familiar apparatus that is easily accessible.

- Sponges in various colours, sizes, shapes and textures are useful – they may be gripped in one or two hands – spring back into shape – may be used when lying on back/side or tummy – damp sponges add different weights and textures.

- Muscles in the hands will be challenged and strengthened as other movements are added, e.g. prodding and twisting.

- Balls that you make yourself are also effective, e.g. rolled-up socks, tights, scrunched-up paper bags and rolled-up jumpers in a range of sizes, colours, weights and textures. They can be held, carried, squeezed, patted and squashed.

- Gripping, grasping and holding are particularly important components in later emergent schemas of transporting, enveloping, enclosing and rotating.

Experience of different forces – feeling the difference between gripping (a strong movement) and holding (a lighter movement) and familiarity with different textures, weights, colours, shapes and sizes underpin successful engagement with a wider range of apparatus and the emergence of trajectory schema.

Banging and hitting

- Infants need significant experience of first using just their hands (e.g. clapping) and feet (e.g. drumming and stamping).

- It is important to feel and understand the difference between patting (e.g. a pet, baby), banging (e.g. a drum, bucket) and hitting (e.g. a balloon, water, the table).

- Appreciating the different contexts in which the physical *action* is the same – but the *force* required for each action varies – is a vital skill to learn.

- Add an implement that is easy to hold, e.g. wooden spoon or teaspoon, materials that they know well and see in daily use.

- Experience of the different sounds that varying degrees of force produce, e.g. tapping, banging, knocking, hitting, supports listening skills.

- Different rhythms can be created by using the surfaces of the immediate physical environment, e.g. floor, walls, furniture. Rhyme may be added if relevant and appropriate.

Dropping and throwing

- These are important movements to experience as they open the hands in preparation for isolating the thumb and forefinger – a basic skill needed for later writing activities.

- Eye-tracking skills are encouraged as apparatus is dropped and thrown – aiming may also be introduced.

- These actions support the understanding of forces: how much or little force is needed to reach a target/goal/container – or create an effect (e.g. ripples in water).

- Use the sponges and balls as before – the more familiar the apparatus the more resourceful and creative infants will become.

Consider the following:

- Where to find the apparatus – place under a mat, behind a chair, in a cupboard.

- Move it further away so it is a challenge to retrieve – they can slither, crawl, walk, climb, shuffle to do so.

- Place apparatus higher up so they need to climb, lean or stretch to reach it.

- Negotiate an obstacle to retrieve apparatus, e.g. crawl under a chair, walk over a cushion, climb onto the sofa.

Component 3: Movable large apparatus

You don't need to source specialist equipment. Just have a good browse – you will probably have some of the following readily available:

- Cushions (large and small, different shapes, weights, colours, textures): Good for carrying, pushing, pulling, stacking, standing, sitting, lying on, collapsing onto, stamping and jumping on.

- Large beanbags (different textures, colours): Good for pushing, pulling, wriggling into, pummelling, stamping on.

- Pillows (different sizes, shapes, textures): Good for carrying, lifting, pummelling, pulling, pushing, stamping on.

- Fluffy throws: Good for rolling/'swimming' on, being enveloped in, rolling up – all tummy time and back play.

- Carpet (soft, different colours and textures): Good for all tummy time and back play.

- Boxes (not too big): Good for pushing, pulling, sitting in, stacking, carrying.

- Sports Direct/laundry bag (large): Good for sitting in, being pulled around in, carried.

- Camping mattresses: Good for bouncing on, rolling/crawling over.

- Small fabric dog-beds: Good for crawling into and out of, curling up in, pulling, pushing, carrying.

- Empty small plastic paddling pools: Good for crawling and stepping into and out of, sitting and lying in.

Combining hand apparatus and movable large apparatus

As children start to walk and become stronger, faster, better coordinated and more agile, possibilities are presented in which large and small apparatus may be combined. Choose a specific area to work in, e.g. a corner or middle of your space:

- Place the sponges or balls under, on top of, into and around the beanbags, boxes, pillows, fluffy throws, dog-bed or paddling pool.

- Pile up the cushions and make 'sandwiches' – with the sponges or balls forming the 'filling'.

- Throw or drop the sponges or balls into the sports bag, big box or onto the beanbags.

Conclusions: Apparatus in the foundation year

- You really don't need very much apparatus, either hand or large movable apparatus at this stage of development.

- Choose carefully. Natural materials are always best and try to use resources that are familiar and easily accessible.

- Provide ample time for inspection, investigation and exploration of the apparatus: manipulate, nuzzle, pat, wallow in, walk around, gently engage.

- There will be significant differences in interest, levels of competency and engagement with apparatus during this phase of development, but solid foundations for the next stage should be laid through sensitive adult support and encouragement.

Component 4: R&R – Rest and relaxation

All of us – and the babies and infants we care for – need time, space and opportunities for rest and relaxation. Life can be noisy, stressful and demanding – finding pockets of time, a suitable space and chances to regroup can often seem elusive. The first few months of life are often called the 'fourth trimester' – a time of 'settling' that follows its own timetable, in which sleeping and feeding need sensitive management and carers may need much support:

- Melatonin levels do not stabilise in babies until around 12 weeks – so, night and day will not be defined before then. Usually, once they reach the magical 5 kg mark, they may sleep through the night.[20]

- Crying peaks at 46 weeks gestational – regardless of due date – e.g. for a baby born at 40 weeks, this will be 6 weeks post-birth.

- Some babies will develop colic within the first 12 weeks – it is very painful and probably connected to an immature gut and inability to process food efficiently.

- Lack of sleep and rest is debilitating – mothers may need to simply sit quietly for a time; don't expect too much in terms of energy level or contributions to a group.

- You need to be very flexible and adaptable during this year if working with parents and carers – some days and weeks will be better than others – so, always offer an option if joining in is too much to ask. Sometimes, just getting out and being with other people for a while is enough.

- As babies develop into infants it becomes clearer how much rest, relaxation and quiet time they need – it varies greatly but they need to know that there is a special place they can go to if necessary where they feel comforted, protected, safe and secure.

HOW THE EIGHT PRINCIPLES APPLY TO PRACTICE
Principle 1: The body is the primary source of learning and development

The foundation year builds on the concept of an initial 'proprioceptive self' and sees the emergence of embodiment and 'bodyfulness' as babies' and infants' movement repertoire expands:

- Independent movement supports the concept of identity and selfhood – particularly through crawling when decisions are made as to when, where and how to move.

- Body-mapping is supported: Where parts are – particularly the hands, mouth and feet.

- Body design is supported: How parts relate to each other and what they can do.

- Forces: Determining the appropriate level of force and speed for a specific action and understanding the requirements of different contexts.

- Strength: Overall strength determines a range of options – particularly crawling and climbing – and supports self-determination and self-efficacy.

- Balance: Develops with strength and through continual movement practice – managing falling over independently supports resilience and self-regulation.

- Agility (managing weight): 'What can I do now – and how am I going to do it?'

Principle 2: Start where they are

- Every baby is different and may take time to settle depending on environment, circumstance, birth experience, feeding and level of successful attachment.

- Physical development is affected by a range of variables. There is no rush to reach each designated milestone and certainly no need to encourage early walking by using baby-walkers and trolleys.

- Containers and sitting devices compromise the continual, incidental practice of movement skills. Essential for safety reasons, otherwise check if/when they are really necessary – explore the use of baby slings.

- Babies and infants need plenty of time on their tummies and backs – with clothes off if/when appropriate. Observe and tune in: what surface or element do they enjoy most? What position are they most comfortable in?

- All movement experience during this year supports the strength, skill, agility, speed, balance and coordination needed for the next phase of development.

Principle 3: The 'enabling' and 'immediate' environments support learning and development

- The primary 'enabling' environment is a reliably strong, coordinated, agile, balanced body. This will determine how babies and infants enjoy, engage with and experience the 'immediate environment' of other people and the physical environment in which they are growing and developing.

- The adult role in ensuring positive and enjoyable opportunities for movement are provided is critical.

- The first 'baby gym' is the body of the primary carer – it is important to be positive and supportive as they will sense immediately if you are reluctant to engage with them in this way.

- Offer a range of different elements for babies and infants to explore: water, sand, snow, earth, grass and different textures to touch, sounds to make, shapes to handle.

Principle 4: Music and rhythm extend opportunities for movement and learning

- Try to engage rhythmically in all interactions with babies and infants: when feeding, changing, moving from one position to another, getting dressed and undressed.

- Use your voice rhythmically, linking actions to sounds and speech – always try to describe what you are doing and why. Create rhymes or silly songs for specific routines that they can join in and contribute to in their own way.

- Most babies and infants love to dance with you. This can be very calming and healing, especially rocking and swaying if distressed. Curiously, we are one of the few species – apart from parrots – that are able to dance.

- Daily life can be very noisy. Enjoying silent time is important also, just to breathe, commune and be together.

- Notice how rhythmical their movements are, especially when playing on their backs. The more rhythmical the movement, the more economical it is and the less energy is wasted.

- Sing to babies and infants whenever possible – even if you don't think you can. It is the rhythm and cadence and the matching of words to actions that is more important than achieving perfect pitch and harmony.

- What sort of music to use: 'world' music, lullabies, personal preferences. Try to make your choices as rhythmical as possible and ensure the lyrics are appropriate.

Principle 5: Group work supports communication and language

- The recommended number for groups of any age is the age of the child plus one or two.

- Group work is not really necessary during this year, but mums and carers often enjoy being together and it is important for *them* to feel positive, supported and energised.

- There is no need for babies or infants to join in; they can just soak up the atmosphere, observe and listen.

- Towards the end of the first year most infants will enjoy being in a group (sometimes), but it is important to take it gently as everyone is finding their feet – literally, in many cases.

- Remember the ITERS Right to Choose:

Children feel empowered if they are allowed to make choices and decisions about their daily activities. This is the only way to enhance children's self-confidence and active participation in a democratic society. Early education is democratic and empowering where children have the opportunity to decide what, where, when and with whom they are acting (Hendrick 1992).[21]

Principle 6: Apparatus extends opportunities to move and learn

- Allow ample time for independent investigation and exploration.

- The physical skills acquired during this year as a variety of materials are introduced should provide effective preparation for all later engagement.

Principle 7: The transfer of skills between environments is actively supported

- Every physical experience at this age is relevant and meaningful and supports development across all domains and environments.

- Physical *opportunities* support the acquisition, rehearsal and refinement of physical *skills* that inform and underpin language acquisition, communication, positive attachment, confidence and self-image.

- Through movement opportunities, infants learn to trust themselves, others and the environment in which they are growing, developing and learning.

Principle 8: A canopy approach to movement provision is created and implemented

- You don't need many resources to provide this for babies and infants – you, the floor and what's around you will be enough.

- Minimise time spent in containers or sitting devices.

- Provide plenty of combined tummy time and back time – at least 30 minutes spread throughout the day – remember to change position every 15 minutes if possible.

- Provide a range of opportunities to move with and without you, with and without music, with and without apparatus.

- Maximise the *incidental* opportunities for babies and infants to move – whenever and wherever possible.

CONCLUSIONS

- Value and invest in movement experience for babies and infants during their first year.

- This will ensure that solid physical, emotional and cognitive foundations are laid for the next stage of development.

- Trust in yourself and your instincts. It is not a race or competition. They will all get to where they should be in a time and manner that suits them.

- They don't need too much stimulation or intrusion – remember: 'Let me be but be with me.'

- Observe, notice and recognise – know the difference and act accordingly.

10

The 'Enabling' Environment

…babies and young children firstly come to understand who they are through their physical selves. This means they also understand a lot of what others think of them and how much they are loved and valued through physical interactions.

Julia Manning-Morton, *Foundations of Being*[1]

Our body image is something precious and entirely personal to each one of us and our attitude towards ourselves is deeply bound up with our early experiences at the hands of adults.

Julie Fisher, *Interacting or Interfering?*[2]

WHAT YOU WILL LEARN

- How to provide the optimum movement experiences for children aged 1–3 years that support their overall learning and development, health and wellbeing.

- How hand apparatus and movable large apparatus may be used to extend and support movement experience.

- How the eight principles apply to practice and provision.

It is critically important that the physical competencies acquired during the initial foundation year are now further rehearsed and refined throughout the next two years.

Having a strong, agile, balanced and coordinated body ensures children are competent and confident enough to embrace whatever physical opportunities emerge in their daily lives. Ensuring a 'primary enabling environment' means feeling secure in the knowledge that the physical skills required for a task or activity are reliably in place for successful and enjoyable engagement.

The old adage, 'Give a man a fish and he eats for a day; teach a man to fish and he eats for life,' rings very true here. If we can get the fundamentals right, all children should be ready, willing and able to actively participate in movement experiences in ways that are right for them and that further strengthen the competencies needed for the following developmental stages.

We can no longer assume that children will naturally experience the level of physical activity and movement experience that ensures smooth physical development and that adequately supports their overall health and wellbeing. We also know that many 2-year-olds starting nursery will have spent more than 1450 hours in care and education by the time they leave at 4.6 years.[3]

As professionals, we are therefore in a prime position to make a significant contribution to children's physical development and ensure their long-term enjoyment and engagement in physical activity. Understanding, appreciating and valuing the enormous untapped learning potential that movement experience provides will have a positive effect on provision and practice in this field.

The years between 1 and 3 are possibly the most interesting, illuminating, rewarding and often exasperating period of children's development. The sheer volume of learning that happens during this time, the frequent 'firsts', the daily new experiences, are a huge challenge for young bodies and minds to process.

Life at this stage involves continual physical sensations and experiences that are acutely and often painfully felt. Being too hot or cold, feeling hungry or full, being tired, coughing, sneezing, vomiting, hiccoughing, crying, laughing, filling nappies, coping with the inevitable bumps and scrapes, experiencing different elements – water, sand, snow, earth; feeling free and contained, dressed and undressed; being in the rain, sun and wind – the list is a long one.

Meanwhile, hair grows, teeth appear and sourcing different sized shoes, clothes, car seats and buggies becomes essential.

So much is physically done *to* them – bathing, nappy-changing, carrying, nose-wiping, feeding, dressing and undressing, vaccinations, being picked up, rocked, hugged and comforted.

Emotions are registered in an obviously physical way: joy, fury, amusement, excitement, embarrassment, frustration and disappointment provoke visible reactions that often require careful and sensitive management.

What must be established in young children, even at this very early stage, is a profound belief that their physical *selves* are respected and understood, and that the physical *skills* they gain have significant value. How we react when they push boundaries, engage in messy play or suddenly acquire a new physical skill has a very profound impact on their attitudes toward participation in physical activity as they mature. Julia Manning-Morton reminds us that:

Practitioners must think very carefully about their non-verbal responses, such as looking shocked or bored, their gestures such as pointing or crouching down and their voice tone and volume. Children will be reading your body language and trying to make sense of your reactions, making inferences about what you think and feel about events and about them.[4]

Being infuriated by their speed, determination and waywardness, and giving pole position and praise to those easily able to sit still and listen, sends entirely negative messages to children, who, at 3 years, will be more active than at any other point in their lives.

TWO PRINCIPLES OF PHYSICAL DEVELOPMENT

These two principles of physical development were mentioned previously in Chapter 2. To recap: first, children's bodies develop from head to toe, known as 'cephalocaudal' development. We determined in Chapter 9 that tummy time supported head-lifting, that in turn informed the ability to get into the correct crawling position, strengthening relevant muscles and ensuring joints are aligned and stable. Eventually, the bones in their feet and ankles stabilise, the surrounding muscles strengthen and walking may begin.

Second, control of movement emerges from the centre of the body, the trunk, and extends outwards to fingers and toes, known as 'proximodistal' development. Essentially, this means that the large muscles of the body need to properly support the joints to ensure that the manipulative skills required later for successful curricular activities may be seamlessly acquired. For example, sitting still requires a stable spine supported by strong core muscles. Writing requires stability in the shoulder, elbow and wrist joints that is dependent on the level of strength present in the surrounding muscles.

So, this is the time for *big* movements to be practised, whenever and wherever possible: rolling, crawling, walking, running, climbing, throwing and kicking.

These movements will establish the essential strength, agility, balance and coordination needed that will ensure the smooth distal development on which many later manipulative tasks depend.

MOVEMENT, LANGUAGE AND COMMUNICATION

The close relationship between movement, language development and communication is important to acknowledge (review Chapter 5). Not until we stood upright as a species, thereby changing the shape of the larynx, were we able to talk – curiously this 'lowered larynx' is shared only by koala bears and Mongolian gazelles.

- The vestibular system requires continual refreshment through movement experience. It works closely with the auditory system in the ear to play a vital role in the development and processing of language. There may be a link between early trauma to the vestibular system and the later emergence of dyslexia.

- Differentiating between sounds and discriminating between foreground and background sounds are both critical factors in the understanding of spoken language and are intimately related to vestibular functioning.

- Stimulating the vestibular system through movement also provokes the production of sound – which explains why children love to shout when running fast, rolling down a slope or spinning around.[5] Being active is therefore a strong stimulus for communicating.

- Through the motor cortex area of the brain there is a strong link between the muscles in the fingers and mouth – manipulating and speaking are therefore intimately related.

- Speaking fluently requires the smooth coordination of muscles in the jaw, throat, lips and tongue.

- In communication, 93 per cent of meaning relies on the understanding of gesture, facial expression, body language and intonation.

- At 2–6 years children will be learning up to sixty new words per week. Initial exposure to new vocabulary in a movement context supports understanding and ensures further use is relevant and meaningful. This approach anchors the experience of language so it may be remembered and retrieved to later describe, review and discuss events.

- Acquiring vocabulary in a movement context also deepens the understanding of concepts (e.g. high/low. fast/slow. near/far) that may appear in a range of 2D forms – poems, stories and film. It also provides opportunities to introduce and play with unusual and interesting words.

- Ultimately, successful engagement with written language is informed by an acceptance of pictures disappearing. Once this stage is reached, understanding depends on the experiences individuals bring to the text, so it is critical that children enjoy a wide range of early movement experience that is linked to language that makes sense to them.

- They will gain a wide range of vocabulary that may be used when writing creatively later on.

The prevalent use of DT affects both time and opportunities to move and compromises the physical skills that inform later successful access to a language-based curriculum. In a 2014 survey,[6] data suggests that 42 per cent of children aged 0–4 used DT regularly, particularly tablets, with 25 per cent enjoying personal ownership. One fifth of 1–2-year-olds engage with devices independently. By age 3, many are downloading apps, playing games or streaming online programs. This report also highlights that under-5s watch around 2.4 hours of television daily, an increase of 12 minutes since 2012.

There are three points to consider: *first*, English is written in a linear, alphabetic script that demands the ability to maintain foveal (close) focus and employ eye-tracking skills (across the horizontal midline) to access successfully. Use of tablets and other handheld devices cannot adequately support foveal focus or eye-tracking skills. Engaging with DT demands that eyes mainly scroll up and down and use peripheral vision, skills that are much less physically demanding to gain and use.

Second, the swiping, poking and flat-hand movements required for DT use cannot properly support the highly complex hand skills required for clear, fluent handwriting. Although this may well become an obsolete skill in the near future, and we introduce it at a very young age, an appropriate level of muscle strength around the shoulder, elbow and wrist joints must be gained to hold a pen or pencil in the correct position for an extended period.

Typing with both hands also does not support the 'handedness' required for fluent handwriting.

Third, Pat Preedy writes that:

> *In a study of 894 children between age 6 months and 2 years from 2011 to 2015, researchers found that the more handheld screentime a child's parent reported, the more likely the child was to have delays in expressive speech. For each 30-minute increase in handheld screentime, researchers found a 49% increased risk of expressive speech delay.*[7]

The second significant issue that impacts on the quality and quantity of essential movement experience at this age is obesity. Globally in 1990, 32 million children aged 0–5 years were obese. By 2014, this figure had risen to 41 million. The predicted figure for 2025 is 75 million. Recent statistics for the UK show that 13 per cent of 2–4-year-olds are obese and a further 16 per cent are overweight. In the USA, 7.1 per cent of children under 2 years are obese.[8]

Although the link between obesity prevention and physical activity is currently considered 'tenuous and unproven' in the early years, the impact on overall wellbeing and development for children whose weight status compromises their enjoyment and engagement in physical activity is profound.

If we agree that the primary enabling environment for young children is a physically competent, able, reliable body, it cannot be acceptable that their lives are so badly affected by a condition that is, in the majority of cases, completely preventable.

Considering there is no physiological reason to carry excess weight during these early years – indeed, BMI should be highest at 14 months at 17.5 and lowest at rising 6 years at 15.5; and we are well aware of the main determinants of childhood obesity – nutrition, physical activity, sleep and sedentary behaviour – as professionals, we can play a more proactive and effective role in ensuring children are physically able to engage fully in whatever opportunities are afforded them.

The consequences of not being able to join in, keep up and contribute are lifelong. Most of the excess weight gained during these years will remain; 91 per cent of girls and 70 per cent of boys considered overweight or obese at age 9 have gained their excess weight by age 5. A final statistic: by 2050, 25 per cent of all children in the UK may be clinically obese.

TOWARDS PRACTICE AND PROVISION

During the years 1–3, it often becomes evident that the developmental milestones we have become so familiar with are in fact only a moderately useful construct. As Gill Connell points out, 'a child's age is perhaps the most misleading variable to consider in assessing a child's movement needs'.[9] Interestingly, the football community has begun to implement the concept of 'biobanding' – when young players are grouped according to their physical maturity rather than age. This has led to a significant reduction in injury levels and a quantifiable improvement in performance.[10]

Ultimately, what we are aiming to ensure is 'automaticity', meaning 'the process of automating repetitive functions so they no longer require conscious thought'. By firmly embedding the physical foundation skills, children can begin to move fluently without having to think about it first – thus creating 'efficiencies in the brain and freeing up processing power for more complex thinking, reasoning, imagining and inventing'. Connell cites the example of handwriting. In the early stages, children have to concentrate hard on correct letter formation rather than the content of what they are writing. As this skill matures, the physical action of writing becomes automatic and creativity may then flourish.

The variables that inform and determine physical development are directly related to two types of physical skills. First, *phylogenetic motor skills*: these are the gross motor (big) movements that emerge naturally as children mature – rolling, crawling, climbing, walking, jumping and running. Of course, environment and opportunity play a significant role in the timing and level of competency acquired, but generally these skills will be gained in a particular order within a recognisable timeframe. They are not skills that are specifically taught but form the absolute bedrock for all future, more complex motor skills. All these large movements demand strength, balance, coordination and agility to perform, and continual practice and repetition ensures the physical foundations are reliable, sound, strong and stable.

Second, *ontogenetic motor skills*. These are physical skills that are influenced by learning and environment. Learning in this context means the phylogenetic skills acquired previously and environment will include geography, opportunities and values. Ontogenetic skills vary widely between countries; certain sports including football, cycling and skating may be highly prized and will therefore be introduced at a very young age or, if safety depends on specific skills such as swimming, running or climbing, these will be promoted.

WHAT DOES 'GOOD' MOVEMENT LOOK LIKE AT THIS AGE?

- Being able to change positions with ease, moving fluently from lying to sitting to kneeling to standing – and back again.

- Managing bodyweight by using appropriate props if necessary, e.g. chairs, stairs.

- Crawling and clambering unaided with coordination, strength and balance over different terrains.

- Being able to stop independently and when asked.

- Making the appropriate connection between a specific task and the required movement skill; choosing the right direction, correct speed and level of energy expenditure.

- Negotiating obstacles with ease – and being aware of possible risks.

- Being able to move slowly and be still if/when necessary.

- Being equally competent and confident moving without shoes or in bare feet.

THE MIDLINES OF THE BODY

From 1–3 years, physical coordination becomes increasingly important. This is intrinsically linked to the three midlines of the body: left to right (horizontal), front to back, and top to bottom (vertical). 'Invisible yet indispensable' midline development ensures that more sophisticated movement patterns are possible to acquire. There are four movement patterns that have a significant impact on physical development.[11]

Bilaterality – 'symmetrical bilateral integration'

Most movements look like this in early infancy, meaning both sides of the body are doing the same thing at the same time, e.g. clapping, reaching with both hands, pushing with two feet on a bike, beating a drum with both hands, using a rolling pin.

Laterality – 'reciprocal bilateral integration'

Required for crawling on hands and knees. When one body part does something in the opposite manner of another part – this also includes marching, climbing, pedalling and using a knife and fork.

Homolaterality – 'asymmetrical bilateral integration'

The ability to move one part of the body while keeping other parts still, e.g. waving goodbye one-handed, climbing foot–foot/hand–hand, writing (keeping one hand still while the other writes), opening a bottle, peeling a banana, sweeping up.

Cross-laterality – 'crossing the midline'

This is one of the most sophisticated movement patterns and an important movement skill to acquire. The body remains still while objects are moved from hand to hand across the midline, or are reached for diagonally across the body. This becomes an essential skill to master for many sports, dance and gymnastics. It is also linked to handwriting and letter formation is dependent on understanding on which side of the midline shapes appear: n, u, c, b and d, m and w, p and q. We are the only species that can work across the vertical midline running down the centre of the body using both hands simultaneously in a coordinated manner.

MOVEMENT SKILLS, CHILDREN'S SELF-CONCEPT AND THE 'KEY ELEMENTS OF EMOTIONAL NEED'

Children's self-concept develops rapidly at 1–3 years. Self-concept begins with self-awareness that in young children is intrinsically related to their physical selves. There are three related elements: personality, competencies and features.[12]

1. Personality

'What am I like?' Much of this will be reflected by adults, particularly when it comes to physical skills. Be aware of the power of the parental narrative here. Children are often designated as being shy/reckless, difficult/easy and as having particular likes, dislikes and competencies. Listen to how often children repeat what adults say about them – it may not be what you have either noticed or experienced. Be aware that obesity issues may emerge even at this age – parents will lay the ground very carefully by saying, for example, that their child 'doesn't like water' so cannot get changed for swimming.

2. Competencies

'What can I do?' Usually much more than we realise. They need time, space and support to acquire skills. This starts off as 'Look at me!' then changes to 'Look what I can do!' We should proactively support their physical abilities, engage in their active play if welcome and continually let them know how much these skills are valued. Any gender bias must be identified and called out. As Manning-Morton reminds us, this may be evident from birth:

> Within the first 24 hours of a baby's life parents/carers behave differently towards boys and girls and have different expectations of their behaviour. Boy babies are handled more vigorously, such as bouncing and holding up in the air, thereby reinforcing any innate predisposition to movement, while girls are held closely and smiled at more, reinforcing social communication.[13]

3. Features

'What do I look like?' Young children are very interested in their changing, developing bodies. They will examine each other closely, particularly hair, clothes and shoes. The adult narrative is critical at this point because children pick up very clear messages as to what merits status, and this often includes deep cultural references. An awareness of possible comparing, contrasting and competing is essential.

The determinants of sound mental health in children are mentioned in Chapter 7. The 'key elements of human emotional need' also appear frequently in social psychology literature, and aligning them with movement practice in the Early Years provides an interesting additional dimension to the field. They are as follows:[14]

The need to feel competent

Not just 'I did it!' but '*I* did it!' Being able to do things physically opens up ever-expanding horizons as children investigate and explore different environments. As their language skills increase they use appropriate language to effect a wider range of outcomes when engaging physically with their peers and adults. Achievements are always unique and personal and may range from very small skills like holding a spoon, to bigger ones including climbing stairs. It is important to understand what this means to each child. Perhaps check your value system here: how much do you allow physical competency to flourish? Is it supported just as long as it is not time-consuming, annoying, messy or risky?

The need to feel autonomous

So much of early childhood involves children having things done *to* them, procedures that are often intrusive and sometimes painful. Practising movement skills gives them a small window of opportunity to be autonomous, to make independent decisions as to when, where, how and with whom to engage. They need time to complete physical tasks independently. How much do you value this and how do you support or prevent? Self-care, including handwashing, teeth-cleaning, toileting and feeding, becomes very important at this age.

The need to feel significant

All children need to feel that they matter. The value we place on their physical skills will have a direct impact on the way they view themselves. Achievements and success during the early years are almost entirely physical. It has been suggested that vocabulary scores at age 5 are a predictor of later curricular success, although the effectiveness of current assessment procedures to support this claim should be seriously questioned. However, to ensure children are confident communicators, and can use a wide range of vocabulary, they need plenty of opportunities to move and work together physically. Not only will they have something to talk about, but language will be rehearsed and refined in a relevant, meaningful context. It is also worth remembering that Article 12 of the UN Convention of the Rights of the Child stipulates that children and young people must be given the right to express their views in all matters affecting them, and requires those views to be given due weight in accordance with the child's age and maturity.

The need to belong

'Belonging' is not well defined in literature and tends to be a taken-for-granted concept – one that everyone agrees is important, but translating this into practice can be a little vague. In the Early Years Framework for Learning in Australia, it features prominently in 'Belonging, Being and Becoming', and in the New Zealand ECEC curriculum, 'Te Whāriki', a main strand is 'Identity and Belonging'. A recent study aimed to determine practitioners' views on ten domains of 'belonging' – emotional, social, spatial, temporal, cultural, legal, ethical/moral, political, physical and spiritual.[15] In this paper, it is suggested that physical belonging 'encompasses physical affinity with the landscape and a deep sensual appreciation of its sights, sounds, smells, tastes and textures'.

It does – but the remit is much wider. In physical terms, 'belonging' implies a profound sense of affinity with self and a peaceful relationship with the body that translates into easy physical engagement with others and the environment. Children also feel a physical sense of belonging by recognising shared attributes and abilities and by having the skills needed to join in, keep up and contribute.

Before we consider the practicalities of planning and provision, there are a few issues to consider.

First, you. There are many and varied ways of supporting children's physical development. It is a question of finding a way that suits your temperament, interests, skills and age and stage of life. Not everyone can do everything. Pool resources as a group. You may find some hidden talents. The main message here is, please find a role. Be an effective movement companion in some way. Support, liaise, use the community and engage with parents.

Second, venue. Where you are moving with the children is very important. You may be using a designated inside movement corner, be outside or you may have to change venue at short notice. Never say, 'No.' Try not to be too precious and make it work – somehow. Check: flooring (hard/soft, rough/smooth, slippery), walls (clear/cluttered), furniture (movable?), temperature (heating off/on). Ideally, 50 per cent of the inside space available should be free to move in.

Third, climate. What sort of overall atmosphere best suits the children, the venue and you? You may work best in a quiet, therapeutic climate or one that is more noisy and energetic. You may be following an activity programme that requires proper organisation or you may need to be more spontaneous. It must work for all of you. The children should feel secure in the environment, familiar with the behaviours required and comfortable with the level of engagement expected.

HOW TO PLAN

Ideally, a significant proportion of children's daily physical experience should be through active play. Public Health Ontario (2015) write that: 'Active play can be defined as unstructured, child-led and often spontaneous physical activity that expends energy well above resting levels. Active play can occur alone, with friends or with family and it most often occurs outdoors. Importantly, active play is perceived as enjoyable by the child.'[16] A range of issues compromises the time, space and opportunities for children to move freely and independently, so designing and delivering effective movement sessions has become an essential addition to practice. The four components may be experienced separately over a day or week – or together in one session if appropriate.

Component 1: Movement experience

- Try to avoid over-planning for this age group. You may be following a prescribed programme, but they are endlessly mercurial and contrary at this age and you may have to react and adapt according to venue, numbers, support and their changing interests.

- 'Planning in the moment' is a skill that requires confidence and a degree of relaxation regarding outcomes. Believe that *all* physical experience for children has value and take every opportunity to provide movement experiences for them. A space may suddenly become available, time freed up unexpectedly, or a new resource may appear.

- Maximise the *incidental* opportunities for movement: arriving and leaving, moving from inside to outside, transitions between activities or changes in the weather.

- Ask yourself if children really need to sit on chairs for any length of time, considering they naturally squat or kneel at this age and keeping still is a challenge. Could they stand around a table to paint or lie on the floor to listen to a story?

- Whatever you decide to include in your sessions, the children must start from a position of physical competence: what they *can* do already – easily and with enjoyment.

THE EARLY YEARS MOVEMENT HANDBOOK

- Remember that 'splinter skills' are fun, but what provides the solid foundations are the big/gross motor/locomotor movements that inform and support all future development.

- Appreciate that progress may not be linear and can pop up in unexpected domains: play at home with siblings, the use of language in different contexts or an increasing confidence to communicate.

- If you need to adopt a more structured approach, you can focus on specific vocabulary (e.g. fast and slow), behaviours (e.g. turn-taking, helping) or particular physical skills (e.g. jump, run, stretch, balance).

What they can do – and when

This is a very loose framework but may be useful to bear in mind when planning for 'Component 1: Movement experience':[17, 18, 19]

- By 18 months, most children can: Roll (both ways). Crawl (competently and fast – forwards and backwards). Walk (with feet apart but beginning to balance well). Run (usually emerges six months after walking). Jump (straight legs, one foot leading and tipping forwards). Push/pull (whatever they can manage and whenever the opportunity arises). Climb (holding on when going upstairs and turning to come down – onto any apparatus using one knee to assist). Clamber (over cushions/different terrains inside and outside). Stretch. Turn and twirl. Clap. Stamp.

- By 2 years, they can (to add to the list above): Walk – forwards, backwards, marching using heel-to-toe gait. Stand on tiptoes. Jump (forwards and especially down from a height – flat feet). Scooter.

- By 2.6 years, they can (to add to the list above): Run (legs a bit straight but the action is fluent and they can stop when required). Climb (onto, into, out of everything and can manage a climbing-frame). Push and pull heavier materials. Start to kick (can kick a ball by walking into it but can't flex the knee yet, so kicking while standing is a challenge). Biking (propel forward with both feet.) Throw overarm.

- By 3 years, children can (to add to the list above): Walk on tiptoes (10 feet in a straight line going forwards), backwards and sideways. Balance (5 seconds on each foot). Jump (very confident now – down from 12 inches, on the spot, on balls of the feet). Run (avoiding obstacles, can change speed and direction and stop). Hop (briefly). Stamp and clap (at the same time). Climb (very confident going up and down stairs using alternate feet). Throw and catch (underhand and with outstretched arms). Kick a ball (from a standing position). Stand still. Pedal a bike or trike.

In the New Zealand Framework, *Sit Less, Move More, Sleep Well: Active Play Guidelines for Under-Fives*, the following data is included:[20]

- 91 per cent of 2-year-olds can run and stop themselves without bumping into things or falling.

- 97 per cent of 2-year-olds can scribble on a piece of paper or crayon.

- 79 per cent of 2-year-olds can kick a ball without holding onto anything.

- 69 per cent of 2-year-olds can jump with both feet leaving the floor at the same time.

What they can't do quite yet

- Process complicated instructions. Two-year-olds only comply with about 50 per cent of parental requests the first time – so also *demonstrating* exactly what you expect is essential – 'arms up/legs straight/lie down'.[21]

- Understand rules. Apart from 'no shouting/keep inside this boundary/ no touching of stuff', that are important, they often can't follow why something must be done in a specific way and forget very quickly.

- Keep going for too long – they will just stop, lie down or wander off. They may have had enough after a few minutes or keep going for much longer. Be sensitive and flexible – each day is different and they have a lot to manage.

- Take turns, unless very carefully introduced – they really don't like waiting, and sharing space and resources can be a challenge.

- Accommodate big groups. A 'sofaful' or 'age plus one' is plenty.

- Go slowly. This becomes easier as they grow stronger and more balanced.

- Sit cross-legged – they are much happier squatting or kneeling.

- Be aware that attention span is usually 2–3 minutes per year of a child's age – for 2-year-olds this will be a maximum of 6 minutes.

What they like to do

- Contribute their own ideas, however random and unconnected.

- Be with older and younger children.

- Talk about themselves.

- Demonstrate what they can do.

- Be sociable – initially from a distance, but progressively getting more intimate.

- Investigate their own and others' bodies, especially small parts: tummy buttons, ears, eyelashes and noses.

- Have time to muse, just to be in the moment and appreciate different sensations.

- Repeat movements – particularly turning and twirling – peeping between their legs.

- Practise skills with others – peers and siblings.

- Have routines and structure: Anticipating what is going to happen, when and how.

- Go fast whenever and wherever possible.

- Take their shoes and clothes off.

What to do – ideas that have worked for me

Many of the following ideas can be adapted for the outdoor environment and accommodate different age groups. They don't need to be followed to the letter, but they may provide some useful tips for planning sessions and, between A and F, you will see how the progression of skills may be carefully supported.

A.

- Designate a specific place where you always begin and end. This may be a movement corner, a blanket spread on the floor, cushions pushed together or some large mats.

- It is very important to have this specific 'home' to return to quickly if necessary.

- You can keep the group safely together if there are distractions or intrusions to accommodate.

- Children will feel comfortable with the parameters, feel safe and secure, and can decide for themselves when/if to move away from their 'home'.

B.

- You need to engage with them immediately. There is no time for complicated explanations and instructions.

- Establish a regular way to begin: a particular song, a clapping sequence, music or tambourine.

- Keep your body and your voice low. Looming over them and talking loudly doesn't work. Sit, kneel or lie. Whisper if necessary and always maintain eye contact.

- Keep all children as close to the floor as possible for as long as possible, even though they may be happily on their feet now and really want to run fast.

C.

- Start by changing positions on the spot: roll from back to front to back; hold their toes; bounce on knees; stand and squat; spin on their bottoms; balance on hands and knees, bottom high in the air, raise one foot off the ground – change feet; knee hop (beginning of bunny hops), take weight on hands – lift knees off the floor.

D.

- Now start to explore the space a bit more. Roll and crawl in different directions. Bear walk, crab walk and try walking on knees (very challenging). Keep close to the floor and your 'home'.

- Make movements bigger and more upright. They love to jump. By age 3, they will enjoy doing this and often hold hands with each other.

- Try a range of different jumps: Feet apart and together – on the spot and going forwards. Arms waving and still. Add music.

- Jump – then add a balance (e.g. hands and feet on the floor – lift one foot in the air), jump and stop (it/lie/kneel down – hold a position, e.g. stand with arms and legs wide – lie on backs and clutch toes). They can also hold your hands and jump as you kneel. Jump on different surfaces (e.g. bubble wrap, mats or large cushion).

- Jump on a large coloured sticker placed on the floor or inside a hoop.

- Place hands on the back of a low chair and jump – feet together and apart.

E.

- Walk: In different directions, on tiptoes or stamping – feeling different surfaces (with hands) around the space.

- Follow a trail of masking tape on the floor – tear into smaller pieces to make stepping stones.

- Make a zigzag or slalom of chairs to walk around: As you narrow the gap, the harder it gets.

- Walk with arms up or arms out, on different surfaces – e.g. carpet/bubble wrap – shoes off if possible.

- Walk up and down an incline if available.

- Change speed – fast/slow.

F.

- Running: what they really, really want to do. Safety is paramount, as they tend to stop suddenly, veer off, look around or forget the direction they are meant to be going in.

- No more than one to two children should run at a time. Others can lie, kneel and clap – keep active somehow. No running while holding toys or with dummies in their mouths.

- They can run in a straight line (you can stop or catch them), in a circle (both directions: this is important – ensures equal strength on both sides of the body).

How to
Extend

- Make the space bigger, the time longer.

- Provide less physical support from adults.

- Use more complex instructions/language.

- Add different tasks to the foundation skills, e.g. directions, balance and positions.

Progress

- There will be progressions, regressions and plateaus. Be aware that progress may appear in other developmental domains – absence of evidence is not evidence of absence in this case.

- There should be no pressure to perform or achieve. They can be very mercurial about their level of engagement, so keep the previous point in mind.

- They need time to observe. They are very able to gauge their own moment of readiness when confident that their body is able to embrace a new skill or gain a new level of competency in one previously acquired.

- It is perfectly acceptable to muse. Doing nothing is a viable option, because something is always going on. They may be getting used to the atmosphere, absorbing new language, watching others and becoming comfortable with the size and properties of the venue.

Vary

- Not too much. They like repetition, anticipating activities and knowing how to behave. Feeling secure, safe and calm is important.

Begin and end in the same way if possible. You may come to a natural conclusion or have imposed time restraints, but use this time at the end to reiterate behaviours, vocabulary, self-care and to talk about how they feel: hot, tired, happy?

Involving parents

- Include activities in your movement sessions that they can repeat at home easily with their children.

- Promote *incidental* movement experience, e.g. stay a bit longer in the bath; take a little longer to change nappies so they can kick freely; get dressed independently; walk or scooter instead of using the buggy.

- Shoes off whenever and wherever possible: wearing shoes does children's feet no favours – they tend to take longer steps with greater ankle and knee motion – the spring action of the arch and the strength required to push off effectively is reduced and the alignment of the ankle, knees, hips and spine is affected. Moving barefoot improves proprioception and children tend to keep their heads up more as the feedback they are getting from the ground means there is less need to look down. Be aware that around 26 per cent of children are wearing the wrong size shoes – and 56 per cent are not measured as recommended every six months.[22]

- Provide lots of opportunities to crawl, walk, climb, run and jump. Focus on the big movements. Remember: a strong child is a safe child.

Component 2: Hand apparatus – ideas for practice

Although children will be handling a range of materials in the natural course of a day, there is definite merit in affording them time and space to use familiar and accessible resources in a movement context. Let's revisit the main differences between engaging with apparatus in curricular and movement contexts.

First, in a movement context, *all* the properties of the apparatus will be considered (size, shape, weight, texture, sound, smell, colour), not just those that apply to their obvious curricular purpose.

Second, the contributions children make through exploration and investigation are of paramount importance. The possibilities are many, varied and equally valued.

Third, maximising movement opportunities is essential as they build on the apparatus skills established during the previous foundation stage. They can now use their increased strength, agility, balance and coordination to extend the range of movement possibilities experienced.

To consider:

- *Time*: Between 5 and 15 minutes, either individually or in small groups. You may want this element to stand alone or to follow on after the movement experience component.

- *Space*: Decide on a designated space that is clean and free from possible risk and distractions.

- *Materials*: Try to use resources that are familiar and easily accessible to children. These resources are often called 'vanilla', 'asensory' or 'neutral'. Unlike sports equipment, there is no specific agenda attached to them. They may be present in a range of environments and are handled by children frequently and naturally.

Always:

- Have plenty of what you choose to use: Remember the 'property laws of the toddler' – sharing is not easy at this age.

- Store carefully as before.

- Remember that turn-taking is challenging and requires frequent practice.

I have selected apparatus here that has the potential to maximise movement experience for young children. All these ideas have been implemented in a wide range of environments (mainly inside), but you can adapt many of these activities to the outside environment.

Balls

The best ones are those made from familiar, easily accessible materials. You can make them different sizes and shapes, ensuring a range of manipulative skills and physical competencies are used as children engage:

- Socks: Roll up large, fluffy sports socks, school socks, baby socks, dolly socks. Choose different textures and colours.

- Tights are also useful: Choose different sizes, colours and textures to roll into a ball.

- Make a larger ball by rolling up a jumper and taping it together.

- Scrunched-up paper bags are light and easy to manipulate.

- Different sized beach balls are also good.

Video boxes

A fantastic resource. Pick them up at car-boot sales. Anything you can do with block play you can do with these. They are light, easy to carry and often have interesting covers to note.

Plastic bottles

Another excellent resource. Collect a selection of different colours and sizes with varying labels – can be used with tops on or off.

Plastic bottle tops

You can ask all adults to collect these – fill a pillowcase or a sports bag of different colours, sizes and shapes.

Masking-tape rolls

Easily available and a really good size, weight and shape for this age group. Collect a mix of wide and narrow rolls.

What to do

Consider including the *properties* of the space you are working in:

- What is the flooring: Carpet, lino or wood?

- Are corners accessible?

- Where is the middle?

- Are walls clear of material?

- What furniture is present?

- Is the space clearly defined?

Try to make the time in which the children engage with apparatus as active as possible. Think of:

- Different ways to *access* the apparatus: Crawl, climb, walk over different surfaces.

- Can children stretch high to reach it or long on their tummies? – Place it on a table or behind a chair.

- What about searching for the apparatus? – Hide it under a cushion/carpet or inside a box.

Balls

All the classic ball skills – throwing, catching and kicking – may be properly embedded through prolonged active engagement with the balls you have made. This will provide an effective base for acquiring the specific skills demanded later for many sporting disciplines.

Balls of different weights, shapes and sizes require a range of physical skills to carry, throw, squeeze, roll, kick and hit. Think about the language children can practise as they engage with the apparatus, particularly prepositions: put the ball(s) on the chair/along the wall/under the table/in the middle/in the corner/on your head/in your lap/under your chin:

- *Throwing*: This emerges in the following order: one hand over and down; two-handed underhand; one-handed underhand; one-handed overhand. *Throw* the balls into a box, up onto a table or along the floor. Remember, small balls are easier to throw.

- *Catching*: There are two parts to this action:

  - Eye-tracking: They will have practised this since tummy time. It is important to now encourage the tracking of a moving object – you can do this by following a feather, balloon or bubble as they fall to the ground.

  - Stopping a moving object: Roll a ball (a large beach ball is best) along the ground while lying, sitting or kneeling opposite each other a short distance apart – stop the ball with both hands. You can also practise this skill by spinning a plastic bottle and stopping it moving with both hands. Graduate to rolling a large ball at eye height along the top of a table while adult and child stand at opposite ends – stop the ball with both hands and push it back. Slowly – as the children gain confidence in the ball coming towards them at speed – you can remove the table and start gently with a 'bounce and catch' and finally throwing the ball.

Catching takes time to master, and giving the rhythm – one–two–three, *catch* – provides a useful support. Both elements need to be practised continually before introducing a ball that may be too large or heavy to manage successfully. Remember, large balls are easier to catch.

- *Kicking*: This is usually mastered by around 3 years, but acquiring the level of balance necessary to perform this action, and the form of the action itself (direction, purpose, contact, timing) takes time and practice. Introducing regular sports equipment too early often leads to frustration and disappointment. Stick to materials that can be kicked with ease and enjoyment.

Video boxes

- Explore the shape of the box – back/front/middle/sides/corners – and the pictures on the covers.

- Carry – they will do a lot of this using one hand/both hands/both arms.

- Stack them up against a wall – lengthways and widthways – there are many different ways to do this.

- Make a 'road' – place them end to end in a line on the floor – walk along and step over.

- Make a zigzag/slalom – place them flat on the floor or balanced on short/long sides – walk around the boxes without knocking them over.

- Make a 'wall' – balance boxes in a line – ends touching or apart.

- Make a tent shape by opening out the boxes and placing ends together to make a tunnel – run cars down the middle.

- Make different sounds by banging, patting, scratching, rubbing, knocking, hitting, beating the boxes on the floor.

- Construct different shapes with the boxes – make a house – a chair – some steps – a tower.

- Put one foot on a box and scooter along or place both hands on a box and push along the floor.

- Stand with both feet on the box and balance – make a tower of boxes and step up – increase the height.

Plastic bottles

These are light, easy to carry and source – children can choose to use one hand or both for these activities – have a good mix of sizes and colours to work with:

- Line them up and place flat on the floor, end to end – or side by side.

- Choose different areas to place them in: behind a chair – against the wall – along the carpet – around the cushions – under the table.

- Make different shapes and patterns – lines, stars, squares – they will have lots of ideas for this.

- Pat and bang the bottles on different surfaces to make rhythms and sounds.

- Roll with both hands – like a rolling pin.

- Spin and stop – the second component of catching – also supports the essential wrist-twisting action for writing.

- Sort into different sizes and colours and place in different containers.

Assorted objects

I have included plastic bottle tops and masking-tape rolls as examples of accessible items that can be collected and replaced with ease.

Bottle tops

- Fill a large box or bag with different coloured bottle tops.

- Children can get into it – sit and paddle the tops back and forth with their hands.

- Tip the tops out – throw out one by one – scoop out – using one hand or both together.

- Make different sounds by swishing the tops around very fast and slow, banging them together – pouring from a height.

- Sort the bottle tops into different colours and sizes.

- Make patterns on the floor.

- Fill a range of small containers with the tops – carry them to a larger one and pour them in.

Masking-tape rolls

Have a bagful that includes both wide and narrow rolls:

- Roll the wider ones along the floor – 'stop'.

- Stack them up to make a tower – alternate wide and narrow rolls.

- Drop a selection of small objects (that they have chosen) down the middle.

- Slide onto arms and carry as bracelets – how many can fit on before they get too heavy.

- Use your space to place the rolls – along the wall – up the wall – (use a mix of wide and narrow rolls).

- Make different shapes and patterns on the floor – a snake – a flower – a river.

- Drop the rolls into a large container – stretch up to place them on a table – or hide under the carpet.

Component 3: Movable large apparatus – indoors

Please review the list of possibilities in Chapter 9 – as any of these ideas may be easily adapted to suit this age group. The following list of apparatus also includes some movement possibilities to consider. Many of these can be adapted to the outside environment. Movable apparatus always offers a wider range of ideas than large fixed equipment. Try to use only resources that are familiar to the children and easily accessible:

- Different sized cushions: To – carry, stack, punch, prod, push, pull, throw, jump on.

- Large beanbags: To – push, pull, dive onto, carry, balance on.

- Pillows: To – walk over, carry, push along, pull, punch, balance on, squash.

- Fluffy throws or bedcover: To – roll on, roll up, carry.

- Large Sports Direct bag: To – get into and out of, push, pull, carry.

- Camping mattress: To – jump on, carry, push, pull, dive onto, roll over, balance on.

- Boxes: To – hide in, push, pull, stack.

You can also add to this list:

- Tunnel (preferably clear and see-through): to crawl into, climb into, roll.

- Chairs (if appropriate to use): to climb onto, crawl under, carry, push along.

- Tables (if appropriate to use): to climb onto, pull along on tummy, crawl under.

I would completely avoid using parachutes with this age group. Duvet covers or sheets are smaller, more familiar and easier to hold. Mainstream parachute activities may be safely and successfully introduced later on if these are used first.

Obstacle courses

Obstacle courses are always popular: use only a maximum of three pieces of apparatus for younger children, six for older.

To consider before you start – indoors:

- Ensure you have a safe, secure space in which to construct your course.

- Discuss with the children what apparatus they would like to include – where it can be found, and who can help.

- They should be appropriately dressed – no shoes if possible, dresses tucked in and trousers pulled up – they need to move their arms and legs easily.

- Ensure they know which direction they are going in and what to do when they come to the end.

- Let them be as independent as possible – be safe, but allow for individual decisions and approaches.

- Some children may need time to get used to managing activities independently – so simply helping to construct and observe is a good start.

- Remember never to put something soft before something hard in case they fall forward.

- Leave adequate space and time between participating children – they can have as many turns as they like.

- Everyone helps to tidy away afterwards.

Some ideas for obstacle courses with a specific focus

- *Strength*: This course will include pushing, pulling, carrying, climbing. A possibility: Climb onto a table – slide or jump down onto a large beanbag – carry a cushion to a designated space (you will have a stack by the end).

- *Speed*: This course needs to look flat and smooth. A possibility: Crawl fast through the tunnel – run and flop onto a large beanbag.

- *Agility*: Children have to manage their own size and weight without support. A possibility: Climb into the tunnel, which is held vertically – climb out – run and stand on the large beanbag.

- *Balance*: Think of uneven surfaces. A possibility: Crawl or run over the camping mattress – walk over the small beanbags placed under a large sheet.

Involving parents

- Encourage parents to use sustainable, accessible apparatus at home – it can be replaced easily and often more opportunities for play are offered than with mainstream toys.

- If appropriate, encourage parents to let their children use the furniture at home to practise their 'big' movements – jump on the bed, go up and down stairs, climb on the sofa, roll on the floor.

Component 4: R&R – Rest and relaxation

Energy levels tend to surge and sink very rapidly at this age. One minute all is well – the next you have an exhausted, furious, tearful, floppy child to deal with who is refusing to cooperate or listen to anyone. Overstimulating sensitive, developing systems often leads to a sense of overload when children simply cannot manage any more demands, questions, noise, bright lights or people. Providing places, times and opportunities for regeneration and recuperation is an essential element to include in your movement 'canopy'.

Daytime sleeps still feature and will be factored in accordingly. During sleep, 80 per cent of the growth hormone, somatotropin, is released, so ensuring children experience the quality and quantity they need is critical. At around 12 months, they will need 2 hours 30 minutes of daytime sleep, at 2 years this reduces to 1 hour 30 minutes and at 3 years this will be down to 45 minutes.

Places

Places in which to be peaceful, calm, quiet – to feel protected, safe and secure – must be known to and accepted by children. These places should remain fixed, unless a mutual decision has been made for a change. They can be comfortable and personal, to be used alone or in company. They may include quiet, dark dens or a comfy sofa in the corner. Whatever form these places take they must be freely available at all times and provide immediate relief and succour.

Allowing children to be alone is important. Sara Maitland believes we are 'underskilled' when it comes to being by ourselves:

> *Everybody says it is natural for the human species to be social – yet we put enormous amounts of effort into training our children to be sociable. We tell them 'don't fight, say thank you, share your toys' – we send them to playgroup. We're depriving them of the skills for being alone.*

She also makes the point that our culture encourages high self-esteem yet discourages us from 'spending time with the one person we ought to like best'.[23]

Opportunities

These should be decided by the children, or you (if specific daytime sleeps are needed). Rest and relaxation are also important to include at the end of movement sessions or if you feel the children would benefit after an exciting event or adventure.

If inside, maximum 2 minutes:

- Turn the lights down.

- Lie on backs or tummies – practise keeping eyes closed.

- Listen to sounds in the environment – who is doing what – what can you hear?

- Feel heartbeats and breathing.

- Wiggle extremities – toes/fingers – nose.

- Add music if appropriate.

HOW THE EIGHT PRINCIPLES APPLY TO PRACTICE
Principle 1: The body is the primary source of learning and development

- Emergence of self-concept is dependent on the acquisition, rehearsal and refinement of physical skills: 'What can I do – how/where can I do it – what does it feel like – can I get better at it – and can I describe it to others?'

- Managing different emotional states: Happiness, enjoyment, frustration, amusement, boredom, determination, despair, fury, exhaustion, embarrassment – and recognising the physical sensations that accompany them.

- Determining likes and dislikes in physical states: Hot/cold, moving/still, free/contained, dressed/undressed, high/low, alone/in company.

- Importance of physical experience to supporting the early understanding of mathematical concepts: Weight, space, direction, forces, pattern, levers, equal and opposite, parallel.

- Language development: Learning vocabulary in relevant and meaningful contexts.

- Communication: Having a range of experiences to describe and discuss with others.

- Movement fosters the sense of 'belonging': An affinity with self, others and the environment.

Parents and carers

All movement experience has value and potential for learning across all domains. Memorable movement experiences are important to children so they can later make meaningful links between their experiences and 2D representations in poems, pictures and stories.

Principle 2: Start where they are

- Milestones should not be millstones. Treat as a useful guide and reference, but all children develop and progress at different rates and there is a very broad range/timescale in which skills emerge, particularly walking (10–20 months).

- Any stages skipped or missed may be revisited, especially crawling.

- There will be endless progressions, regressions and plateaus, some very small, some more significant – all are equally valid, relevant and meaningful.

- Progress may appear in unexpected domains: New friendships or interests, increased verbal communication, greater independence and risk-taking.

- Be mindful that they need time, space and support to continually practise their skills – they will know when they are ready for the next stage and tell you.

- This is the time for big movements: Provide plenty of opportunities for children to gain the strength, agility, balance and coordination that ensure they seamlessly graduate to more complex movements.

Parents and carers

There is no merit in rushing to reach milestones. It is not a competition. Early movement patterns provide essential movement experience that ensures more complex skills will be acquired easily.

Principle 3: The 'enabling' and 'immediate' environments support learning and development

- The primary enabling environment for children is having a strong, agile, balanced, reliably competent, coordinated body.

- This ensures proactive, positive engagement with the immediate environment that includes others, and the physical environment, in which they are growing and developing.

- Remember to trust in the richness of your own context. Recognise and appreciate the positives in your setting and the learning potential contained in your environment.

- Use your space creatively: What do you have already that can support movement experience? Conduct audits for your inside/outside environments.

- Children must learn to trust their physical environment, feel secure and comfortable, and know what behaviours are expected of them during daily rituals. They need to share their space comfortably and manage their bodies easily in relation to others and when navigating furniture.

Parents and carers

Notice the learning possibilities that children's bodies and their physical environment offers. Inside and outside offer a wealth of physical opportunities to extend skills and vocabulary.

Principle 4: Music and rhythm extend opportunities for movement and learning

- Children's bodies and the physical environment are primary sources for experiencing sound and rhythm.

- Songs or rhymes for 'hello/goodbye' when starting and ending sessions are very useful for embedding vocabulary, anticipating, remembering names, sharing and feeling part of a group event.

- Matching gesture to language. Action songs are useful despite the lyrics – children become familiar with the cadence, rhythm, timing and actions they include – but try to invent your own sometimes.

- Moving rhythmically is very energy-efficient and builds up the stamina needed later for more challenging physical activities.

- Rhythmic awareness is an important element when engaging with apparatus, particularly for acquiring the 'timing' ability needed in a range of physical disciplines.

- Exposure to different genres of music raises cultural awareness, especially through songs and lullabies.

- Children love to dance at this age – especially when they discover their hips can move! They tend to stand feet apart and wiggle, twirl, clap and jump.

- Use music that has a steady tempo and be careful of inappropriate lyrics.

- Music to listen, relax, muse and contemplate to is useful – but try not to have it continually burbling away in the background for no reason.

- Silence is to be embraced and enjoyed – and not always used as a control mechanism.

Parents and carers

Sing to children in the bath or any time – the chorus to current songs, lullabies and nursery rhymes from different cultures.

Principle 5: Group work supports communication and language

Children are beginning to notice more what others are doing and form their own little groups based on common interests and sometimes gender:

- Remember ITERS Right to Choose. They don't have to join in.

- The second apparatus component probably offers the most opportunities for encouraging group work at this age. Introduce something they can explore/investigate together, e.g. a large Sports Direct bag, a big box or coloured blanket – and see what emerges. Use a range of hand apparatus that is familiar and accessible.

- The movement context is a very supportive way of becoming familiar with beginnings, endings, rituals, behaviours, and managing self in an enclosed space with others – being a bit less precious – reinforcing the skills needed for nursery life – particularly circle time on the carpet.

- Aim for a few minutes at a time – little and often is plenty at this stage. Be very flexible: a sofaful/age plus 1 as a group is enough.

Parents and carers

It takes time and patience. Some children more naturally join in and share, especially if they have older siblings. Others may need time to watch from the sidelines for a while before they take their first tentative steps.

Principle 6: Apparatus extends opportunities to move and learn

- Working with hand apparatus supports the physical skills that are necessary for later curricular activities: Hand/eye coordination, tracking, foveal focus, manipulative skills and the muscle strength required to stabilise the spine, shoulder, elbow and wrist joints for desk-based learning.

- It mitigates the negative impact of DT and tablet use – particularly regarding hand and eye skills.

- It is essential to maximise the incidental use of hand apparatus throughout the day by using whatever you have available, e.g. if you have a spare plastic cup – blow it across a table, hide a teddy in different places, sort out a box of books or crayons – any activities that require minimal preparation.

- Movable large apparatus: Use any time, individually or with small groups, ensuring all the big movements are practised in preparation for the next developmental phase when more complex physical skills are acquired.

Parents and carers

Encourage little and often. Try not to introduce fiddly apparatus too soon, e.g. scissors. The larger skills must be embedded first, and have fun practising them together. Maybe allow time to help with household tasks – cooking, gardening or washing.

Principle 7: The transfer of skills between environments is actively supported

This is a vital skill and becomes more important and visible as children grow and develop. They begin to manage themselves physically and emotionally in different environments:

- They recognise that doors/stairs/chairs may look different but require the same physical skills to navigate.

- Moving inside to outside: the space may be greater outside and afford different physical opportunities, but similar skills will be needed to manage emotional challenges: 'Do I like it here – what do I need to be comfortable – who will join me – can I remember what to do?'

- Language acquired in a movement context maximises the possibility of repetition at home and elsewhere – particularly useful for Speech, Language and Communication Needs and 'new to English' children.

- Children can recognise 2D representations of movement in stories, poems and art.

- They transfer their knowledge of safety and risk to all environments they experience.

Parents and carers

It is important to recognise how skills transfer to all domains from an initial movement context. Matching action to language, being strong/safe and creating memorable movement experiences to enjoy and share.

Principle 8: A canopy approach to movement provision is created and implemented

All movement experience is valued and recognised as a source of learning, and support for overall health and wellbeing. Opportunities to move should be freely available and continual:

- Accept children's fundamental need to move – however, it may clash with your agenda sometimes.

- Ensure all four components are properly represented in your movement provision.

- Amend the inside physical environment: remove chairs so children stand around tables, suggest different positions for storytime – remember, squatting and kneeling is easier than sitting cross-legged.

- Maximise the potential for incidental movement opportunities: how do children arrive and leave, transition between activities or from inside to outside – how could you make these times more active?

- Current and proposed UK CMO/EY/PA Guidelines recommend 180 minutes as the time recommended for young children's daily physical activity. This can be achieved through a mix of active play, semi-structured sessions, maximising incidental opportunities and encouraging parents to be proactive through using local amenities. Minimise screen time to less than one hour daily.

Parents and carers

Be aware when opportunities arise for the children to move – may be just a few minutes – but use whatever time and available space – and always have something on hand, e.g. a pair of socks to play with. Be confident and proactive.

CONCLUSIONS

- Maximise opportunities for children to move on the horizontal plane, even if up and running.

- Don't be too ambitious about planning for this age group – keep in mind what they can/can't do, what they like to do, where they are practising skills and what their significance is for the individual child.

- Be flexible and spontaneous – plan in the moment. It suits this age group, the wide timescale in which skills are gained and the range of different abilities and interests.

- Be aware of possible outside pressures: Parental expectations and demands, outside providers, marketing fads, media scares, assessments.

- Make the most of outside events at local, national and international level to encourage interest in sports, dance, gymnastics, swimming.

- Find a role to support children's physical development that suits you, your setting and the children you teach and care for.

11

I Move, Therefore I Am

*We all let out a thread, like silkworms. We gnaw at and
fight over the white mulberry leaves, but that thread,
if it crosses over with others and intertwines, can
make a beautiful fabric, an unforgettable cloth.*

Manuel Rivas, *The Carpenter's Pencil*[1]

WHAT YOU WILL LEARN

- How to provide the optimum movement experiences for children
  aged 3–5 years that support their overall learning and development,
  health and wellbeing.

- How hand apparatus and movable large apparatus may be used to
  extend and support movement experience.

- How the eight principles apply to practice and provision.

It seems inevitable that curricular demands will increase. Justifying the
presence of physical development as a 'prime area' and affording time
for children to move, investigate and explore the extraordinary wealth
of learning opportunities that physical activity provides has become ever
more challenging. I am not convinced that nostalgia helps. Continually
looking back to a supposed golden age of unsupervised roaming, productive
investigations of local environments, constructing dams and dens in mixed
age groups: this is rarely useful or positive.

Children's lives have changed immeasurably within a generation, and
childhood has always reflected the zeitgeist – the concerns, priorities,
fads and issues of the day. Instead of wallowing in what was, let's be savvy,

proactive and, in the words of Reinhold Niebuhr, accept the things we cannot change, have courage to change the things we can, and the wisdom to know the difference.[2]

WHAT WE CANNOT CHANGE – MUCH – FOR NOW

- There is increasing top-down pressure for children to acquire formal literacy and numeracy skills at an early age. Testing, baselines, assessments, tweaking the curriculum, all impact on providing time for children to move, space to move in and training opportunities for teachers. There is unrelenting pressure on practitioners to justify their practice – that there must be a quantifiable point to it all.

- Our ability to effect change is currently limited, but we should maximise any and every opportunity to highlight the critical importance of movement skills, not only because they inform children's overall health and wellbeing but also because they support their learning and development.

- Parents have very real concerns about safety. We should acknowledge their fears but be sensible and supportive in providing a rationale for children's risk-taking and pushing boundaries.

WHAT WE CAN TRY TO CHANGE

- The climate in which physical *development* is considered to be something that 'just happens' – and therefore doesn't need to be taken too seriously – and physical *activity* is what children 'just do anyway'. If this were true, childhood obesity statistics may not be so critical and school-readiness would not be such an issue. As David Morley writes in response to the WHO *Obesity Report* (2017): 'For what is often ignored is a child's ability to move effectively. It is one thing to say that a child should be more physically active, but quite another for a child to develop the confidence and competence required to engage in physical activity.'[3] In effect, 'Children's movement development can no longer be left to chance.'

- As educators, teachers and practitioners we can and should play a much more proactive and effective role in supporting children's overall health and wellbeing. Just because the Foundation Stage

Profile data of 2017[4] suggests that 95 per cent of children achieved an 'expected' level in physical development (the highest score for any learning domain), we cannot conclude all is well. The latest obesity statistics for the reception year – 9.6 per cent are obese, 13 per cent are overweight – paint a very different picture.[5] In the USA 45 per cent of 5–8-year-olds are now presenting with at least one heart disease factor, including hypertension and obesity; arteriosclerosis is now appearing in 5-year-olds.

- Parental attitude. We should encourage parents to actively support their children's physical development. Evidence suggests a 68 per cent increase in children's engagement in physical activity if adults join in,[6] but we also know that 30 per cent of children living within a two-mile radius of their school are driven there daily.[7]

Data from the New Zealand State of Play Survey (2018),[8] in which 4095 parents of young children were interviewed, suggests that 65 per cent of mums very often or often let their children take a risk if no major safety threat is involved. It was also found that 75 per cent thought children aged 4–5 years *should*: take part in messy play, use playground equipment, climb trees and play with loose materials (e.g. sticks, tyres, wood, tarpaulins).

However, 51 per cent of these children don't often engage in messy play (mud, dirt, sand, water, paint), 14.8 per cent are not allowed to play in the rain, 71.8 per cent do not often climb trees, 68.4 per cent do not engage in rough-and-tumble games, 53.8 per cent do not often ride bikes, scooters or other non-motorised vehicles. And this is in New Zealand, where we fondly assume that, with the wealth of natural opportunities on offer, parents would be more confident and proactive in providing opportunities for physical activity.

We now know that levels of physical activity start to decline as early as 6 years (not at 13 years as previously thought),[9] so we need to ensure that children arrive at school physically ready to embrace all the opportunities provided, having acquired the positive habits and behaviours around physical activity that ensure long-term engagement and enjoyment.

WHERE DOES THE 'DIFFERENCE' LIE – WHERE IS OUR 'WIGGLE ROOM'?

The possible barriers to young children's engagement in physical activity include obvious factors like housing, geography, finances and time constraints. But there are also hidden issues that we need to be aware of.

Gender bias

Between 3 and 5 years, children become increasingly aware of gender stereotypes and by aged 4 may be quite vocal in their assertions about what girls and boys are good at, can and can't do, and should and shouldn't do. As Julia Manning-Morton writes: '3–6-year-olds may develop stereotypical behaviour in order to be more like their identity group (such as suddenly wanting to wear pink clothes) but they also have a better understanding that their gender will remain always the same.'[10]

We must be particularly observant whenever this occurs. Even a seemingly throwaway remark may have profound implications for individual engagement in physical activity, movement play and their general enjoyment and confidence in their physical abilities. Be as gender-blind as possible and ensure that all children are given equal time, space, support and opportunities to move.

Cultural issues

Although this has not yet been researched thoroughly, there is evidence that 'to some extent cultural determinants link with issues of ethnicity in promoting children's physical activity'. This following statement appears in the latest APPG Report, *Physical Activity in Early Childhood* (2017): 'Parents from Asian, Bangladeshi, Chinese and Yemeni backgrounds value traditional academic achievement over their children being physically active.'[11]

In the same paper, it emerged that the BAME (Black, Asian, and Minority Ethnic) parents 'thought their children enjoyed a high degree of physical activity during the school day, and so did not consider it necessary to supplement this with physical activity at home'.

You may also have encountered the attitude that 'running around and having fun' has nothing to do with learning or development. If and when these opinions are encountered, we should be respectful but determined, and point out the significant learning potential of movement experience and physical activity, particularly if the children are 'new to English'.

The role of DT in children's lives

In the UK, 80 per cent of children aged 3–4 years have access to the Internet through a PC, laptop or netbook, and 65 per cent have access to a tablet. They have often acquired a digital footprint *in utero* and many gain an online presence before they are 2 years old. Among 3–4-year-olds, 12 per cent have a computer, 58 per cent play games weekly, and 20 per cent watch TV on an alternative device. It was found that 50 per cent of pre-school children in Germany and 78 per cent in the Netherlands have access to the Internet. In South Korea, 98 per cent of 3–9-year-olds are online around nine hours a week. In the USA, 25 per cent of 3-year-olds are online daily; this rises to 50 per cent by 5 years. In Australia, 79 per cent aged 5–8 may access online information at home.[12]

> *The prevalence of digital media in children's lives has led to change in the way in which children engage with technology. Children of all ages are spending an increasing number of hours per week in front of different kinds of digital media, which they can control and interact with in an instinctive way and usually through the use of touchscreens.*[13]

Neuroscience is beginning to catch up, but as Mine Conkbayir reminds us, '50 per cent of what we believed about how the brain worked in 1971 has been amended, expanded, re-researched or overturned. Much of what we knew in 1991 has been overtaken by neuroscience and genetics.'[14] We simply do not know for sure yet what effect prolonged use of DT may have on the growing brain. There is anecdotal evidence of concentration levels dropping, communication skills declining, a worrying increase in sedentary behaviours, changing attitudes to friendship, loyalty, failure, authority, and a growing inability to hold or use writing implements correctly.

There is, however, enormous potential to use DT to further children's understanding, not only of their own physical health and wellbeing but in making connections and relationships worldwide through projects related to physical activity. If we take a simple movement like running, children could explore which animals run, why do they run: do they run alone, in a group, for pleasure or, hunting? Why do *we* run? Who are our great runners? What distances do they run? What is the history of the Marathon? What makes a good runner? Can insects run? – some have lots of feet!

Would a rethink of the use of DT to encourage and support physical development and physical activity be beneficial? I think definitely yes. Everyone could be involved – children, colleagues, parents – and all could feed in and find a role. It may also give us an additional tool to allay parental fears of physical activity encroaching into work time, enthuse children who may already be losing interest, and give physical development a broader canvas by making obvious links to other areas of learning and ways of knowing.

Provide a supportive environment for physical development and physical activity

I have included this as a hidden issue because the perceived lack of an optimum environment for physical activity is often used as a reasonable explanation for lack of provision generally. Sally Featherstone writes that:

> A successful educational environment for young children should reflect what children in the wild might experience; an environment that is just enriched enough for natural growth but not so enriched that it has no challenge and overwhelms some children with stimuli.[15]

Linda Pound would agree: 'We denigrate hothousing, yet it seems that at every turn we overstimulate young children, filling their world with noise and bustle, shouting and action.'[16]

So often the reasons given for poor provision around physical activity include a lack of space, time and appropriate resources. Every environment, however small and seemingly challenging, will provide *some* opportunities to move. Movement corners do not have to be full of resources; children are quite happy with a defined space and the chance to take their shoes off. Their bodies alone provide the perfect resource and contain a huge wealth of untapped learning potential. Incidental opportunities to move always emerge – usually when least expected.

MOVEMENT AND LITERACY

The close relationship between movement, communication and language development that was highlighted in Chapter 10 becomes increasingly important during the years 3–5 as children begin to engage with print and achieve literacy.

English is one of the most difficult languages in which to become literate, although, despite stammering being more common, one of the easier to speak. It has a very deep 'orthography', meaning the spelling of English maps imprecisely and inconsistently with sounds and the syllable structure is highly complex. In a 2001 study, evidence suggests that it takes between 2.5–3 years to become literate in English – and only one year for Italian, French, Spanish and Portuguese.[17]

There are four specific ways in which movement experience supports literacy, as follows.

First

Becoming literate is deeply dependent on prior communication and language skills. Being able to contribute verbally is fundamental to childhood in the West and curricula (delivered in spoken language) are supported by children's ability to speak clearly and fluently. By the time they start school they are expected to understand, express, share their feelings and make their needs known.

The following statistic may be relevant. By 4 years, the difference in the number of words that children from advantaged (lucky) and disadvantaged (unlucky) backgrounds have heard is 19 million. By 5 years, a child's vocabulary is considered to predict their educational success and outcomes at 30 years.[18] Again, caution is advisable as this data is frequently used to justify further extension of the literacy component of curricula at the expense of equally valuable areas.

How, where and when children acquire new vocabulary has a significant impact on the ways in which it is used. In turn, this depends on the understanding and use of nonverbal communication skills.

These play an increasingly important role in supporting fluent verbal interactions and may be rehearsed and refined very effectively in a movement context. They include the ability to:

- Sit, or stand still and maintain an empathetic body position.

- Maintain eye contact.

- Be aware of spatial issues: how close is comfortable and when it is appropriate to touch, hug or embrace.

- Wait for a turn to speak – not talking over others or interrupting.

- Anticipate the beginnings and endings of conversations.

- Recognise a common thread – a mutual topic or subject – and sticking to it.

- Maintain a relaxed or tense bodily state depending on the requirements of the situation.

- Display appropriate body language – e.g. crossing arms or legs.

- Use the appropriate tone and volume of voice inside and outside to ask questions, offer support, share confidences, demand, organise, apologise, thank, request, refuse.

- Use appropriate gestures. In English, gestures are linked to words that describe *how* something is done, whereas in Romance languages they are usually related to the verb in a sentence – i.e. *what* is being done.

- Combine expansive and small movements within an interaction to describe and share experiences, to make a specific point, to tell a story, to organise.

Second

Practising whole body movements for letter formation. The Write Dance program[19] was created to support this approach and evidence suggests that children who follow the programme first gain confidence to engage in painting and drawing and then become more motivated to participate in mark-making and writing. Their physical skills and handwriting also improve. There are four distinct movements that support writing:

- Vertical strokes top to bottom: b, d, h and I. ↓↓↓↓ Practise being long/tall, upright, balanced, still – a guard or a soldier.

- Anticlockwise rotational marks: c, d, f and s. It is important to start from the top, practise a whole-body rotation, twirling anticlockwise.

- 'Bouncing' movements: movements that replicate the arches in: n, m, w, u and y.

- 'Doubling back': mmmmmm – uuuuuu. Jumping and skipping are good for this.

- Combinations: twirl and straight (d), twirl left, jump and land.

Third

Accessing print. Mastering the mechanics of reading depends on 'directional reasoning'. All the following elements may be experienced physically to support positive engagement with printed material:[20]

- Books have a front and a back, as do bodies. One side of a two-page spread of text is read before the other. Practise rolling from front to back and standing up one behind the other.

- Pages turn in a specific direction: left for some languages, right for others. Practise turning left and right (a skill usually established by 4 years) in a movement context to reinforce this concept.

- Print begins and ends in different places. Children need lots of experience of linear movement – going in a straight line: e.g. completing obstacle courses, following a masking-tape route on the floor.

- Print is always read in the same direction: left to right or right to left, top to bottom or bottom to top. Practise moving in these directions and align with the particular written language children are working in.

- At the end of a line of print (in English text), the next line starts again underneath. Children need lots of practice of moving around in zigzags and slaloms, weaving in and out and repeating the course when completed.

- Each printed word is a spoken word when read aloud. Providing experience of reacting to and interpreting the written word in a movement context is vital – poems are particularly appropriate.

Fourth

English is a peculiarly idiomatic language – in which meaning is often not deducible from individual words. Expressions like 'What's up with you' or 'Give it a break' make no sense unless the tone of voice, gesture and body language that accompanies them is understood. Lakoff and Johnson claim that the directional metaphors we use are closely linked to emotional states: 'feeling up, feeling down, in a muddle, on good form, beside oneself, getting along'.[21] Movement experience offers a unique opportunity to extend and enhance the understanding and use of emotional vocabulary. Laura Freeman writes of her primary school pupils whose ability to describe their emotions is compromised by reliance on emojis in personal communication:

> *Part of growing up is grappling with your own unruly emotions, impulses and ambitions and tempering your more selfish instincts to the equally unruly needs and feelings of others. You cannot successfully make that leap if you conceive states of mind as only gurning, ready-made cartoons.*[22]

A vast range of everyday expressions have their roots in movement, and their underlying meaning is linked to physical sensations. Consider the following: 'Stand on your own two feet. Jump to conclusions. On a roll. Leap of faith. Running in circles. Bouncing off the walls. Rise and shine. Walking on air. Jog on. Dodging insults. Fingers crossed. Pull yourself together. Scared stiff.'

Success in a formal learning environment is often dependent on making sense of instructions – e.g. 'stand in a circle, sit down, sit up straight, find the middle of the page, read from the top'.

Children will better manage these demands if the language is first experienced and practised in a movement context. This ensures quick reaction times when encountered later at school. Jan White also reminds us that: 'This is also a great context for introducing interesting and unusual words. They can be fascinated by new words, such as *slither, rapid, meandering* and *undulating* when used in a context that makes sense to the moving child and has personal meaning for them.'[23]

KEY ELEMENTS OF EMOTIONAL NEED

How may the 'key elements of emotional need' that we looked at in Chapter 10 apply to this age group?

Being competent

Being physically competent implies a level of skill that supports positive engagement with a range of opportunities. During the years 3–5 this will affect friendship groups, interests, vocabulary acquisition and emotional wellbeing. Being able to join in, keep up and contribute is essential.

Being autonomous

During these years, children become increasingly independent. They start to take an interest in self-care and make personal choices about food, clothes and entertainment. They also develop serious likes and dislikes for people, places and things.

We should be mindful that being autonomous may include an element of solitude. Opportunities to practise skills alone, in their own way, should always be offered, valued and respected.

Being significant

Being physically competent supports children's feelings of significance within their peer group and environment. The level of significance that teachers and parents accord physical skills is very important to children. Stickers and rewards are not necessary – skills should be valued for their intrinsic and not performance value.

Belonging

Moving together, whether inside or outside, provides children with unique and profound opportunities to feel they belong. Offering appropriate activities that encourage negotiation, delegation, collaboration and working on a common task is particularly important; building, digging, constructing, holding hands to make a circle and move around, sharing clapping sequences, moving chairs and tables together – all encourage the feeling of belonging to a group and the physical environment.

WHAT DOES 'GOOD' MOVEMENT LOOK LIKE NOW?

The development of movement is age-related, not age-determined: meaning that children of the same age likely will move differently from each other. Teachers and caregivers should use chronological age as a general guide, not an absolute standard for what to expect from children's movement.[24]

There will be significant variations during these years in terms of height, weight, agility, balance, strength and speed, but overall the following points may be useful:

- Being agile and able to change position at different speeds and levels, from lying (front and back) to kneeling to standing.

- Matching appropriate movement skills to tasks without thinking, e.g. when to run, balance, stretch, jump, hop, clap, skip, stop and start.

- Managing body weight in a range of situations and in different elements, e.g. climbing, swimming, dancing.

- Being able to fluently combine movements to complete tasks, e.g. run and stop, skip and turn, hop and jump, crawl and climb.

- Using increased spatial awareness to move easily in a group, preserving shapes and formations, e.g. circle, lines, scatter.

- Negotiating obstacles and parameters with ease.

- Performing movements to a prescribed rhythm, individually and in groups – with music and percussion.

- Transferring skills between environments with ease, e.g. recognising that the skills needed to climb stairs in one environment will be the same for every set of stairs.

- Children are becoming more proficient when they can perform a movement: without help, faster or slower, with less concentration, show/demonstrate to others, repeat, practise independently and invent personal challenges.

What they can't do quite yet

Some points to be aware of:

- Children this age will rarely keep moving at a high level of intensity for longer than two minutes maximum unless specifically trained to do so. They will flop down, stop, pretend to engage or wander off.

- If running at speed, 10–15 seconds at a time is long enough.

- Processing complex verbal instructions is difficult. Stick to the maxim: *age minus 2* as a manageable number.

- Until 4 years, they will also need visual cues. You need to demonstrate clearly what you want and try not to waffle on. They will end up only hearing the noise and not the instructions. Note that boys need to hear louder voices at this age, particularly if the environment is distracting. Girls' hearing is 35 per cent more acute, so you can vary your voice more. Growth spurts are more dramatic in boys. Their ear canals are affected and the middle ear may become blocked, so they will definitely need added visual reinforcement.

- They hate losing – at anything. Avoid this element until they are at least 5 years old and can process what losing means: what the context is, who is involved, why it has happened.

- They find complex games with rules confusing. Introducing sports may be fun but try not to overload them with minutiae. They need to enjoy physical activity and move as much as possible. Sitting for too long while you explain the rules is a waste of movement time.

- Sitting for any length of time, particularly with legs crossed, is a challenge. Awareness of body sensations is reduced after 10 minutes. Thirty per cent more pressure is placed on the spinal discs when sitting than when standing, which is not beneficial for skeletal growth.

- Concentrate for too long: attention span is usually 2–3 minutes per year of a child's age – for 3-year-olds up to 9 minutes; for 5-year-olds up to 15 minutes.

What they like to do

- Practise movement skills with others of the same ability level and interests.

- Have the time and space to use these skills for a common purpose or project.

- Perform skills accurately. By 4 years, they show an increasing interest in form: being precise, starting and ending movements in defined ways.

- Push personal boundaries by running faster, climbing higher, jumping further.

- Observe older children whose skills are at a slightly higher level – working out how to match them.

- Explore different relationship dynamics in physical terms. This may vary significantly between indoor and outdoor environments. Who is leading/following? Who is making the choices and decisions?

- Feel useful, kind, thoughtful, telling others how they feel, organising activities, helping adults and those younger or less able.

- Make sure everyone is given the same opportunities (they are very wary of show-offs). They can also be quite discriminatory, so be mindful of the gender stereotypes that may emerge: 'Girls can't…', 'Boys are good at…'

- Discuss what they are good at, reflecting on what they've done, describing why it was fun, or what went wrong, what they could do better next time.

- Play games fairly (no cheating) with understandable, manageable and acceptable rules that are simple to organise by themselves, e.g. hide-and-seek, stuck-in-the-mud, hopscotch.

- Talk about and demonstrate what they may be doing physically elsewhere, e.g. football, gymnastics, dancing.

Issues to consider

- Inclusion must be seen to work in practice. Often, movement sessions provide one of the few periods in which SEND children feel truly included. Just being present in a classroom doesn't guarantee real inclusion as curricular demands increase. Find a level at which these children can engage. Create a role for them that is accepted by the whole group and designate a movement companion or buddy to support them.

- Be super-vigilant about the language you use and your tone of voice. Slow down and adopt a calm, quiet approach. Language-wise, terms like 'find a space', 'run a lap', 'stand on your toes' or 'freeze' are meaningless unless you have demonstrated and practised them first. Try not to use the expression 'Can you…?' all the time – someone will always say, 'No, I can't.' Some alternatives: 'I wonder – how could we – let's try – shall we – what about…?'

- Be very careful when linking movements to imaginary characters or animals. Being a guard, a princess, an elephant or snake may be confusing, particularly for children new to English or who have language difficulties.

- You can't win them all. There will always be children who don't gain as much enjoyment and pleasure from physical activity and movement as you would expect. Try to accommodate and don't let them affect the whole group. It is not a reflection on you, and they may well find opportunities elsewhere that are mainly solitary, in a different element or more competitive that suit them better.

- Rewards. You don't need to provide stickers and badges. Be specific when giving praise – what *exactly* was good, interesting or innovative? Saying 'Good job' means nothing really. Be positive in avoiding negatives. Try not to say, 'Don't do…,' but rather, 'Keep between the lines,' 'Sit here.'

- Link success to effort, not just ability.

- Movement experience offers endless opportunities to learn through mistakes. We tend to think of mistakes as failures, whereas in Japan and China they highlight what needs to be learnt. Be positive – children can try again immediately and practise elsewhere.

- Relating movement experience to other media – literature, poetry, painting, sculpture and film – is very important for extending the understanding of concepts.

- DT – through Twitter, tablets, cameras and mobiles – may be very useful in forming a community of companions in movement. Be sensible: take the good parts.

SOME PRACTICALITIES
You

Whatever approach you take to providing movement experiences for children must suit your personality, interests, skills and physical ability. There is no point in trying to adopt a more sporty, direct approach if you would much rather be moving freely to music. Children are generally accepting of a range of experiences. You can share provision between colleagues to ensure they have as varied a movement canopy as possible. Bear in mind that you may change and how you feel about yourself will be reflected in whatever approach suits you best at any one time.

Venue

Try not to be too precious about this. The more ambitious the plan, the less flexible you can be. Keep provision simple and manageable so you can adapt and react to all eventualities.

Climate

What sort of climate for movement suits you and the children best? Undoubtedly, as they mature they will be more accepting of a direct approach, but it has to work for you also. You must be comfortable with your role and how you are a companion to children in and through movement.

Time

This may be as brief as a few minutes' mainly incidental opportunities, longer movement sessions of up to 20 minutes inside or extended active play up to a few hours outside. The 180 minutes' daily physical activity recommendation for the early years provides a benchmark. With a bit of thought – e.g. extend active outdoor sessions, remove chairs for the day, encourage walking or scootering to and from your setting – it should be manageable on most days.

Numbers

How many children are you happy to move with: are you confident enough to manage a large group with adequate support or are you better with a smaller group of up to four, or even one-to-one? Ideally, children should not operate in groups larger than twice their age. This is not always possible to effect but a good rule of thumb.

Be very strict about sticking to what you can manage. Being landed with more children just because they happen to be around is unacceptable, unless you are sure you can cope. Also, be careful how many SEND children are involved: will they be properly supported for the entire time? Be mindful they don't end up with you as an easy option.

Safety

Before starting any movement session, you must check the venue (wherever it is) very carefully, every time, especially if there has been a sudden change of plan. This is critical.

Check for risks: anything on the floor (staples are always lurking), pins sticking out of the walls, anything obviously distracting that could be picked up, tweaked or pulled (displays and carpets offer lots of possibilities here), any obvious hazards or things that could topple over, be pushed or pulled.

A major source of safety issues is clothing and footwear. Ensure that clothing is suitable to move in (long dresses and tight jeans are the usual culprits here) and that footwear doesn't compromise movement (e.g. moon-boots, wellies, flip-flops). Hoop earrings, bangles and necklaces must also be noted and removed if necessary.

The non-participant

You won't please everyone all the time, and in some educational approaches (e.g. Montessori), it is entirely acceptable to make a personal choice whether to join in or not. Never, ever force anyone to engage and be aware there may be particular reasons for their behaviour. Check the following:

- Are they getting used to the setting and taking time to settle, or are new to English and therefore struggling to understand verbal instructions?

- Are they unused to being in a group and finding the energy and noise level overwhelming?

- Are they not feeling very well; need the loo but forgot; something is going on at home; sleeping badly; a new baby; an injury you can't see – they've fallen over and have bumps or bruises?

Very few children opt out just to seek attention but, if they do, don't offer an alternative. They can observe or help you. Remember, children will always be learning something, e.g. exposure to new vocabulary, watching others move and how to do things well.

Disruptive behaviour

Reiterate your rules before you begin, so everyone knows what is acceptable behaviour and what is not, e.g.:

- No shouting; use only 'inside' or quiet voices.

- No deliberate bumping, pushing or shoving – however enjoyable.

- Who is the movement companion or buddy for any SEND children today – what is the plan if an additional level of support is suddenly needed?

- Entering/exiting, beginning/ending – what are the expected behaviours and routines?

- Identify known combinations of children that may cause disruption – separate if necessary.

PLANNING OVERALL
Long term
Note the dates in your diary for any events that may provide stimuli for physical activity: sports (e.g. Olympics), gymnastics, football (e.g. World Cup). Are there any community or charity events you could support or encourage parents to join in? Are there less confident children that may need help with specific issues around school performances or sports days?

Knowing what is expected of children in terms of physical development and movement as they start school is very important to determine. Identify any specific skills that must be in place and how best to include them in provision for physical activity.

Medium term: Term to term
Keep notes for each term – an overview of practice. You can then compare children's progress at the same point each year and identify any significant changes. From this information you will be prepared to address possible issues before they may become evident.

Short term: Weekly
Respond to any observed issues, new enthusiasms, feedback from parents or colleagues, ideas from children or changes in the weather.

Daily: In the moment
Be flexible and embrace spontaneity. The four components may be experienced separately over a day or week – or together in one session if appropriate. Provision is based on the foundation movement skills that ensure children have the strength, agility, balance and coordination to embrace all movement opportunities.

Component 1: Movement experience
The four possible modes of delivery are: incidental, semi-structured, structured and free play.

Incidental

This is where you can build up time towards the 180 minutes CMO recommendation. 'Incidental' movement opportunities are those you can slide under the radar, ones that don't require too much planning, that all adults can support and children may engage in. Consider the following possibilities:

- Arriving and leaving (note that many children arrive at settings in buggies and sit down immediately, having barely moved since they woke up – the same happens when they leave – back into buggies and home to mainly sedentary activities.):

  - Stick masking-tape on the floor in a long line from the entrance and explore different ways of walking along it – tiny steps on tiptoes, heel-to-toe steps, sideways steps, long steps.

  - Tear off smaller pieces and step, jump or leap from one to the next – place them wide apart in a line or scatter.

  - Place a bench inside the entrance: pull along, crawl along, walk along – unaided if safe to do so.

  - Arrange a tunnel at the entrance to crawl through – try not to touch the sides and go as fast as possible.

  - Jump and pat a balloon hanging from the ceiling as they enter.

  - Have a pile of old telephone directories handy: as each child arrives, carry one to make another pile somewhere else.

- Take time in the movement corner to explore own movement skills with shoes off.

- Plan for 'no-chair' periods or days. Encourage children to try different positions for activities: lying down to draw, kneeling to construct or standing to paint.

- Ensure the transitions between activities and moving from inside to outside are as active as possible: crawl, jump, slither, walk on knees/heels/toes.

- Make circle time more active. E.g. briefly sit cross-legged and push bottoms off the floor with both hands – hold this position. Squat and

I MOVE, THEREFORE I AM

stand at speed. Clapping sequences – fast and slow. Lie on tummies or backs and hold toes. Sit on knees – bounce up and down.

- Top and tail circle time with something active, simple and fun: e.g. 'swimming' on dry land – practise different strokes.

Semi-structured
Plan for 10–20 minutes and follow a similar structure to that suggested in Chapter 10: build up slowly from moving close to the floor to running. All the 'big', gross motor and locomotor movements will be practised.

To begin
Define your space as before. Have a designated 'home' that you start and end at. Children can sit on chairs, under tables, on a blanket/carpet or against the wall. They need to be 'anchored' before starting and you need to ensure that all are toileted, dressed appropriately and there are no obvious health issues. Reinforce any rules: no shouting/pushing; be careful of smaller children; who are the movement companions and buddies today?

Start immediately. Give them something to do. Keep it very simple. Demonstrate. Keep your voice low and maintain eye contact. Some ideas:

- Cross legs, straighten legs very fast.

- Bend knees, straighten legs. Both together, one at a time.

- Drum feet on floor: heels, toes, flat feet.

- Feet together. Let knees flop out. Bring together fast.

- With crossed legs and straight legs, push bottom off the floor or chair

- Rock from one side to the other, one hand in the air, balance on one hand, then the other, cross-legged and straight.

- Slide backs up and down the wall, no hands.

- Clapping sequences – ones they know that include a rhyme, or those they create themselves.

- Spinning on bottoms or tummies if the flooring is appropriate.

The middle
This will be the main section of your session – when the 'big' movements are practised and children aim for the mature version of each skill. Space may

be limited – but there are always ways to adapt – and many of these ideas also work in the outside environment. Keep children as close to the floor as possible for as long as possible.

Rolling

This action should be practised frequently, both inside and outside, on flat surfaces and inclines, at different speeds and over varying terrains:

- Rolling is a challenging movement to perform precisely and correctly. The mature version requires a high degree of whole-body strength and coordination to keep the toes pointed, with the legs and arms straight and in line with the head.

- The classic version is often known as a pin- or logroll and is a useful preparation for learning forward and backward rolls.

- Children must trust their bodies, as they cannot rely on visual input when rolling. They need to adjust their weight to manage different terrains and directions.

- By 5 years, a classic roll should be performed confidently and precisely.

Crawling – hands and knees

Practise as often as possible as children can crawl safely in a group and in a limited space:

- Prior to crawling on hands and knees, children can practise 'seal-crawling' – on their tummies with feet together – and 'worm-crawling' without using their arms or legs.

- Crawling is challenging to perform either very fast or very slow and demands a high degree of strength and balance to maintain the correct position.

- It is excellent preparation for establishing the whole-body strength, balance, agility and coordination needed for climbing, and in ensuring the stability of the shoulder joint that is essential for later writing. It may be practised inside, outside, in small groups and in a limited space.

- There is no determined mature version of crawling.

- *Extend*: Change the speed: there is an optimum speed to be reached before falling over – go as slow as possible – very challenging. Change direction: forwards and backwards, turn both ways in a circle, scuttle right and left. Crawl in and out of a slalom through chairs and tables. Add apparatus: a tunnel or a box. Be precise: 'Don't touch the sides.'

- *Progress*: Crawl in groups, within a specific timescale, in a longer or wider area or up and down inclines. Practise different types of crawls: monkey-crawl (walking with bottom off the floor, with opposite hands and feet); bear-crawling (bottom up, use hands and feet on the same side); beetle-crawling (on elbows and knees); crab-crawling (tummy up, on hands and feet going sideways).

- *Vary*: Progress to sliding bunny-hops, walking on knees very fast and very slow (take long and short slides).

- *Games*: Crawl and pat scrunched-up paper bags, rolled-up socks or a beach ball around the floor – use both hands. Add goals or targets.

Walking

Children don't use this skill very much in their play but it works well in a limited space – and is a safe skill to practise with a larger group:

- Missing the crawling stage will not have a negative effect on walking ability.

- The body straightens up at around 3 years and there is a significant increase in lower body strength at 4 years:

  - When walking, the toes should be pointing straight ahead, with the weight evenly distributed between all five toes.

  - Children should walk as much as possible, with and without shoes on different terrains and surfaces.

  - Using different parts of their feet – e.g. toes, heels.

- *Extend*: Create a track to follow using masking-tape on the floor or create a slalom with chairs to challenge balance and agility. Add something to carry, e.g. a marble in a spoon. Inclines are especially useful for challenging strength and balance – walk up and down unaided. Explore different types of walks:

- On tiptoes/heels.

- Heel to toe.

- One foot flat, one on tiptoe – swap sides.

- Ankle to ankle, going sideways.

- Shuffle – so feet don't leave the ground.

- Penguin-walking – feet facing out and heels touching.

- Duck-walking – keep bottom close to the floor.

- *Progress*: Children can begin to manage changes in speed and direction, holding hands and walking with a group in a circle, in and out, left and right, changing places, passing an object (e.g. teddies or beanbag) when walking around in a group, walking to music – keeping to a steady beat and clapping at the same time.

- *Vary*: They enjoy repeating movements, and continual practice ensures the action becomes automatic, fluent and coordinated. Walking is not an interesting movement skill for children – but it provides a safe and manageable way to build the strength, agility, balance, coordination and stamina needed for more challenging physical skills.

Jumping

There is something about jumping that is joyful and energising. It seems a generic reaction by all children of any age to excitement or pleasure:

- Around 3 years, most children can jump successfully from two feet to two feet.

- Jumping down from a height is easier than jumping up onto something.

- Jumping up and down on the spot is more difficult than jumping forwards.

- Jumping requires balance, strength and coordination:

    - Hips must be aligned in the horizontal plane.

- Joints need to be extended from ankles, knees and hips.

- The body must be held in the correct level of overall tension and evenly balanced.

- Arms must swing upwards and stop between eyes and ears.

- Toes are the last part of the foot to leave the ground and the first part to land.

Many different jumps may be practised:

- Small bounces with heels just leaving the floor.

- As high as possible.

- As far forward as possible.

- Feet together, feet apart.

- Star-jumps – on the spot and turning.

- Spotty-dog (scissor jumps) – feet forward and back.

How to

- *Extend*: Try different directions – forward and back, side to side, in a circle. Practise jumps with hands on the table or hold the back of a chair – jump very fast on tiptoes, very slowly on flat feet – quietly or stamping.

  Jump down from a height or jump up onto a bench. Use music. Create combinations of jumps to a steady beat, to remember and perform. Add a rhyme, e.g. 'teddy bear, teddy bear, turn around/touch the ground'.

- *Progress*: Add apparatus. Jump on a sticker in the centre of a hoop. Jump over a rope. Ensure feet are neat – arms provide appropriate support and landings are balanced and secure.

- *Vary*: Use jumping apparatus – pogo sticks, trampolines, skipping ropes, French-skipping elastic.

- *Games*: Musical Bumps/Statues.

Running

Fluent running is entirely dependent on getting the basics right. It may be practised inside and outside if carefully organised and safety considerations are properly addressed:

- Children start trying to run at around 18 months, and by 2 years they can run quite competently. At 4–6 years running will be the most used skill in their independent play.

- Strength is needed in the muscles surrounding the hips and knees and ankles to keep the joints aligned and stable.

- Arms and legs must coordinate to ensure maximum forward propulsion.

- Even muscle tension is necessary throughout the body to maintain the correct position in flight.

- The stride of the action lengthens as the children mature.

INSIDE

If space is tight, put tables together in a line. Children place one hand on the table. They can run around the table but must keep the hand in contact. Go both ways. Ensure you have a signal or sound they respond to immediately – a 'freeze' or stop position that never changes. Always check they remember what this is before you start:

- Place both hands on the table and practice jogging on the spot – lift legs as high as possible.

- No more than three children should run inside at any one time because they are easily distracted, can stop suddenly or wait for their friends.

HOW TO

- *Extend*: If you have an appropriate venue. Explore different directions. Mainly forwards at this age, but they can run in a circle (both ways), slalom or straight line. Be very clear and demonstrate exactly what you are looking for. Change speed and stop, accelerate/decelerate. Set time limits.

- *Progress*: Relays, add music, run with apparatus – passing, throwing and catching. Outside environments will offer greater opportunities to push personal boundaries.

- *Vary*: Always plan the running element for the end of a session. Build up to this. Reiterate safety every time. Give everyone a go. Create an incline to run up and down.

- *Games*: Be mindful that some children find being chased and caught very frightening. Source games that involve running without a chasing or catching element.

Hopping

As children mature, they will choose to hop as part of their independent movement repertoire – something they practise happily and frequently:

- Hopping is a highly complex, homolateral (one part of the body moves while the other is still) movement that is an essential component of martial arts and racquet sports.

- By 40 months, most children can hop on their preferred leg, and by aged 5 they can perform ten continuous hops and travel forwards two to three metres. Hopping is usually acquired around two years after walking.

- As the same leg is used for take-off and landing, this movement requires a high degree of strength, balance, coordination and timing to perform successfully.

- Initially, children will hop slightly bending over and the arms will not be used. The body will barely leave the floor.

- In the mature version, the body remains relatively upright and the arms will be used to assist balance. This can be seen in the dodging action required in many sports and the flooring movements seen in martial arts.

- They will hop forwards on their preferred leg, then from side to side but rarely backwards.

To practise hopping on the spot, use the tables again as in the *Jumping* and *Running* sections. Keep hands flat on the table. Hop on one leg, then the other. This is very safe to do and ensures both sides are used equally. If possible, practise this movement barefoot – it strengthens the muscles around the ankle joint, which may become stressed in certain sports.

How to

- *Extend*: Aim for ten hops on each foot without support. Hop on the spot and also moving forwards along a prescribed route. Change speed and distance between hops – smaller hops need tiptoes; larger hops will need flat feet to perform successfully.

- *Progress*: Use music. Hop to steady beat. Add to movement combinations, e.g. hop twice both sides – repeat – run and stop.

- *Games*: Add apparatus. Play hopscotch inside by marking the course with masking tape. Chalk or hoops may be used outside. Hopscotch requires a high degree of timing, rhythm, balance, agility and sequencing.

Skipping

Once skipping has emerged (teaching it rarely works), girls will practise it independently and it quickly becomes a valued element of their movement repertoire. This is often not the case for boys – so, it is important that all children are provided with opportunities to rehearse this skill:

- Skipping emerges at around 43 months, and by 5 years has become a reasonably fluent movement for most children.

- Curiously, by 5.6 years, 91 per cent of girls are competent and confident skippers, yet only 55 per cent of boys are.

- Skipping is an important component in many forms of dance and is present in a variety of playground games.

- The *form* of skipping is very important: feet can be neat and precise, with arms discretely used for balance and head up – as seen in a dance context – or the skipping action may be bold and athletic – as practised in a run up to score in basketball.

- The rhythm of skipping is challenging, combining a step-hop with the emphasis on the hop. A one-two rhythm is needed with the accent on the *two*: the lift-off.

- This may be extended to galloping sideways later on.

How to

- *Extend*: In a dance or movement context, practise changing directions: skip forwards and backwards (this is an important component of many cultural dances), in a circle (both ways) and eventually on the spot. In an athletic context, practise the approach to a goal and skip to score.

- *Progress*: Skip to music. Keep to a steady beat. Create combinations of movements (e.g. skip – stop – clap) that children can perform and repeat easily. Change places. Skipping is very useful to include in group activities as they cannot go too fast.

- *Vary*: Perform with and without music or percussion to ensure the challenging rhythm of skipping is embedded. Introduce more complex floor patterns and combinations to memorise and perform. Work in larger groups that challenge spatial awareness and timing ability.

- *Games*: That require running may simply be adapted to skipping.

Non-locomotor 'axial' movements

These are the 'frilly' bits that may be added to all the 'big' foundation movements as automaticity is established. They add further challenges to strength, balance, coordination and agility and stimulate proprioceptive and vestibular functioning.

Stretch

Children stretch quite naturally whenever necessary, but as they mature they enjoy performing specific stretches for different muscles and may also be engaging in yoga sessions. Stretching in different positions (on tummy, back, sitting, kneeling, standing) offers many opportunities to learn new vocabulary and embed maths and science concepts: how long, how wide, tall or high – how much space can I take up? It also provides challenging positions to begin and end a movement sequence. Holding a position (maximum six seconds) supports overall strength and balance.

Bend

Bending can be performed at different speeds and directions as preparation for large movements – and is particularly present in dance forms. There are many language possibilities to explore as bending also implies: tipping, melting, collapsing, falling, swaying and shaking.

Turn

As children become stronger and more balanced, you can combine the foundation movement skills with turning. They will always enjoy twirling as a separate movement and spinning on their tummies and bottoms, but can now begin to walk, turn 360 degrees and keep going – hop and turn, skip and turn. They will turn right and left at speed, on the spot, and with legs wide. This is a basic movement for dance, gymnastics and many sports and so needs to be frequently practised.

Twist

This is an essential component for all racquet sports, particularly when performing backhands. Twisting challenges overall body strength and is the action that produces the most force to hit and throw. Different body parts twist differently: the screwdriving action is performed one-handed; a wringing action with both hands; digging a hole with one foot only; playing Twister.

Stillness

Stillness implies being alert, tense, watchful and ready. This is quite different from feeling calm, rested, relaxed and quiet. There are different forms of stillness. It may be a preparation for action or required in holding a specific position at the end of an action. Different levels of stillness may be experienced when standing, lying or kneeling.

To end

- If you need to stop a session early for whatever reason (not going well, injury, interference, tiredness), have your 'home' ready. This is critical. You can bring the group safely together fast.

- End in the same place or position as you began – sitting, kneeling or lying together as a group.

- Always allow enough time to wind down and be calm.

- Children need to end feeling energised and pleased with themselves – not tired and fractious.

- It's a good moment to review any new vocabulary: Body parts, systems, muscles, bones – introduce the formal terminology.

- Highlight any particularly good or poor behaviour and reflect as a group.

- Are there any individual performances the group noticed: E.g. a great jump, somebody gained a new skill or joined in for the first time?

- Be sparing with your praise: 'I notice,' 'I see,' 'I like' – not continual 'Good job.'

- Have a particular way of ending/saying goodbye: A clapping sequence or a rhyme. I always say (as we all touch the correct body parts), 'Head, shoulders, tummy, knees, toes. Big, big stretch! (Arms stretched above heads) And (three claps) thank you very much.'

Structured

As children mature they can process more complex verbal instructions without needing additional demonstration. Many will attend sports clubs or dance studios where they are expected to respond immediately to rapid verbal direction. Structured sessions work best if there is a specific focus, they are short (10 minutes) and infrequent (weekly is enough). You may have noticed a specific skill or behaviour that needs attention (e.g. catching, climbing, balancing; waiting a turn, being in a circle, sharing resources), vocabulary that needs rehearsing (e.g. prepositions), or maths concepts that require a review (e.g. more/less, same/different).

Free play

The ideal environment for children's active play is probably a beach. Most of us don't have easy access to one but we can try to give children the freedom, space and security to explore movement possibilities in a range of environments.

Movement corners provide opportunities inside for free movement play, but try not to over-clutter with resources. All they really need is a comfortable surface and a safe space to practise skills without instruction or intrusion from adults. Provide access whenever possible: a few times a week or daily.

A range of spaces and resources is usually available for children to enjoy active play outside. Aim for at least 45 minutes in all weathers. Again, try not to over-clutter. Use lots of natural resources and present possibilities to explore and investigate, construct and dig, to make their own decisions to collaborate or not, to be busy or not.

Free active play often provokes different individual responses. Some children enjoy projects within a committed group, being energetic and proactive. Others need time to pootle around, musing and deciding where, when and with whom to engage. Remember, absence of evidence is not evidence of absence: something is always going on. Value, appreciate and respect the individual response to freedom.

Component 2: Hand apparatus

As with the previous age groups, the use of hand apparatus is a vitally important component of the overall provision for children's physical development. Successful engagement with resources at 3–5 years is heavily dependent on automaticity being gained through continual practice of the foundation movement skills. Body systems may then be freed up to work with apparatus in interesting, varied and innovative ways.

This starts with the 'discovery' stage of the foundation year, during which infants explore and investigate the innate properties of materials. Entering the 'developing' stage means children become increasingly competent and confident to engage with a wide variety of apparatus. The 'consolidating' phase further reinforces and extends the skills required for successful long-term participation in many physical disciplines.

In Chapter 6, we explored the importance of hand apparatus in supporting children's learning, particularly the development of communication and language skills. Reviewing the section 'Conversations with a paper bag' reminds us of the breadth and depth of learning possibilities that using accessible, manageable materials affords. In Chapters 9 and 10, the use of apparatus is further explored and 'handling' skills are highlighted. All the activities suggested in Chapter 10 may be adapted for this older age group.

The four modes of delivery: incidental, semi-structured, structured and free play.

Incidental

These opportunities emerge throughout the day. You may have a few minutes to spare between activities, or the children suddenly engage in an unexpected way with materials, e.g. make a pattern with their plates, line up pencils, make sounds with their cups. Always have resources available that can be used quickly and easily in a small space with varying numbers, and ideas for activities that don't demand too much support or organisation, e.g. blowing tissue balls or patting paper cups across a table.

Semi-structured

The approach that is most applicable to this age group. There may be a particular focus: a specific skill (e.g. passing), a behaviour linked to a group game (e.g. waiting a turn) or vocabulary that relates to a certain activity (e.g. aim, shoot). Allow time for children's independent contributions and be aware of variations in levels of competence and capability.

Structured

Some children will be attending sports clubs and will be familiar with a structured, skill-based approach, repetitive drills, complex instructions, frustration and failure. For our purposes, little and often works best. The extended use of a wide range of familiar and manageable resources prior to engagement in mainstream activities ensures that children develop the confidence and competence to engage in whatever physical activities are offered when they start school.

Free play

The quality and quantity of free play with apparatus that children experience during these years has a significant impact on their response to more structured activities. Through engagement with a range of materials, personal preferences and abilities emerge that will inform future choices.

Ball skills

Ball skills now become particularly important. Most children will have experience of throwing, catching, batting and kicking in a variety of environments with a range of materials by 3 years.

Becoming confident and competent with a ball opens up a world of physical activities that may include families and communities, extends friendship groups and provides further possibilities to explore specific interests and abilities.

The more carefully ball skills are introduced (e.g. separating tracking and handling skills for catching) and the broader the range of materials offered, the more successful children will be in using these skills independently for their own enjoyment. There will always be children who are naturally adept, have innate hand–eye/foot coordination and find teamwork fun. Others may struggle to master the basics and take any interest at all. But all children should gain a level of competence as the contexts in which ball skills apply are so many and varied – e.g. football, gymnastics, dance, table tennis, the circus.

Throwing

To recap: throwing progresses as follows: one hand over and down, two-handed underhand, one-handed underhand, one-handed overarm. Young children need a variety of opportunities to practise all types of throwing action as they build up slowly to the mature version of single overarm throwing. This requires:

- Starting in a sideways standing position to effect maximum thrust through a rotating action.

- Body weight needs to be transferred from the back to the front leg, keeping eyes focused and forward.

- Strength and control are needed to provide a stable base.

How to

- *Extend*: Provide a range of accessible materials (socks, paper bags, shower puffs, rolled-up tights) to practise throwing upwards and along. Add an aiming element – low down (into a hoop, tunnel, box or bag), high up (onto a shelf, up the stairs). Make the targets smaller – stand further away.

- *Progress*: The ability to process more complex verbal instructions is important. Coaching points provoke a faster response once visual cues are removed. Children begin to understand the point of rules and when and how they apply. What being in a team means, how teams work, who makes the decisions. Why goals matter – winning and losing. They are also becoming more precise and aligning skills to specific tasks – when to run, when to throw and pass, when to be still but remain alert and aware.

- *Vary*: Sound foundation movement skills ensure the necessary strength, balance, coordination and agility on which basic ball skills depend. Introduce larger apparatus to throw – frisbees, beach balls, wellies, pillows, cushions.

- *Games*: Children enjoy repetitive activities: throw materials into water or sand – large and small containers, onto different surfaces, hoopla.

Catching

The two separate elements that inform catching – eye-tracking and stopping a moving object – should be practised continually, especially with children who are finding this skill difficult to master:

- Eye-tracking: Use feathers, bubbles, small pieces of tissue or light fabric. Track the materials as they fall to the ground – try to catch or pat.

- Stopping a moving object: Spin a plastic bottle or beach ball on the spot – stop it. Roll a ball along a table at eye level – stop with both hands.

Build up slowly to a mature catching action. This requires:

- The body to be stable, slightly leaning forward, with hips flexed, ready to catch.

- Eyes focused forward. Watch the object to be caught.

- Feet placed apart and pointing towards the object.

- Knees soft, slightly bent in preparation.

- Arms apart, elbows flexed and ready to extend.

- Hands: Palms open and fingers extended ready to close around the object.

- Accurate timing is needed as the object is drawn towards the body.

How to

- *Extend*: This is the most challenging ball skill to acquire and the one least likely to be enjoyed if early experiences are negative or painful. It is essential that tracking and stopping skills are reliably in place before children are faced with larger, heavier balls coming towards them fast at eye level. They should be completely comfortable with objects being rolled towards them on the floor and along a table. Only then attempt an airborne stop. Initially, use large, light balls (jumper, beach ball) and build up to more challenging variations. Change the direction the ball is coming from and vary the speed.

- *Progress*: Reaction times will get faster and more reliable. Find incidental opportunities and use unexpected apparatus, e.g. hats or teddies, that they won't mind missing or dropping. Practise catching high and low and eventually with one hand at a time. Combine passing, catching and throwing within a small group.

- *Vary*: Try to keep variations accessible and manageable so children can practise independently or with their peer group. Roll or throw a ball against a wall or to each other. Include possibilities for outdoor practice that are safe and simple to organise.

- *Games*: Don't be too ambitious – form can quickly disappear if a game is too complex or fast. Start sitting with simple passing games, e.g. pass-the-parcel or rolling a ball across the circle – graduate to passing teddies or cushions while walking.

Batting, striking

Some children demonstrate a natural aptitude for this action from the moment they hold a spoon in their hand, and progress easily to using a range of bats and racquets. Others find it harder to develop the level of balance, strength and coordination needed to successfully engage in activities that include batting and striking.

To maximise the level of participation, children need extensive experience of using only their hands as batting implements before formal racquets, sticks or bats are introduced. This ensures the requisite level of hand–eye coordination is achieved, the rhythm and timing of the action is familiar, and children have the confidence to give it a go and accept that mistakes are part of the learning process.

Build up slowly to the mature batting action. This requires:

- Wrist and finger strength to grasp an implement for an extended period of time.

- Overall body strength to maintain the optimum body position to connect with balls of different weights, sizes and shapes.

- A high degree of hand–eye coordination to aim at and hit goals/ targets.

- A high degree of balance and agility to change position at speed, to connect with moving balls.

- Choosing the correct shots to hit a target, score a goal, evade an opponent, attack and defend becomes faster and more automatic/ instinctive.

How to

- *Extend*: Use the foundation movement skills as a base: crawl, walk on knees or walk – bat scrunched-up paper bags, paper cups or semi-pumped balloons (if appropriate) around the floor. Create a slalom course to bat materials around – use both hands equally.

  Introduce familiar implements to bat and strike with: Wrapping-paper rolls, short plastic rulers, small wooden spoons – children may use a preferred hand. Provide a range of outdoor opportunities and resources that may be batted, patted, banged or hit. Aiming is a very important component of batting technique. Construct goals or targets of different sizes – change their size and the distance to aim from.

- *Progress*: Batting skills can be practised individually, in pairs or in groups. Progression happens when different skills are used successfully in various contexts and environments – these may include a range of sports that include bats or racquets.

- *Vary*: Provide a wide range of batting possibilities inside and outside that children can use in their own time and in their own way. They will probably find their natural implement and individual way of practising skills.

- *Games*: Many catching games you can adapt to support batting skills – children need only a suitable bat that they are comfortable with and can use easily. They enjoy creating their own games with rules that change frequently according to the participants.

Kicking

This action is an established component of most children's movement portfolios by aged 3, and by 4 years it has become quite fluent and coordinated. For obvious reasons, it is a skill best practised outside, but the different elements that ensure successful kicking is achieved may be rehearsed in all environments with a range of resources.

Build up slowly to a mature kicking action. This requires:

- A high degree of balancing ability. Children must be able to balance on one leg. The kicking leg must flex in a backswing before driving forward and connecting with the ball.

- The inside of the preferred foot must connect with the ball.

- Arms should be spread for balance.

- Ultimately, both body and ball will be travelling at speed. This challenges dynamic equilibrium, the ability to balance while moving.

How to

- *Extend*: Children need lots of practice with familiar, accessible, manageable apparatus, (rolled-up jumpers, socks, tights, paper bags) before standard-sized balls are introduced. These resources have no specific agenda attached – no one can dominate or show off – but they all demand a high-level skill to control successfully.

  Dribbling any of these balls around a slalom course using both feet is a good way to promote balance and control. Moving obstacles closer together creates a greater challenge. Introduce goals and targets to encourage more precise and focused kicking, increased speed and faster changes of direction.

- *Progress*: Begin to practise kicking skills in small group situations, sharing one ball between all participants. Rules and the correct kicking form are becoming important. Kicking backwards and sideways may be introduced.

- *Vary*: Provide different situations and environments in which kicking skills may be practised, not just for football reasons.

- *Games*: Inside, construct mini-slaloms and kick paper bags, socks or tights around obstacles – introduce goals and teams. Outside, football!

Component 3: Movable large apparatus – indoors

Engaging with large apparatus provides a wealth of opportunities to further consolidate the foundation movement skills that support the strength, balance, agility and coordination necessary to engage successfully in a range of physical disciplines.

Before you begin, check the following:

- Venue: Do you have enough space? Will there be any disruption? Is it safe?

- Time: Variable – 5–15 minutes.

- Numbers: One-to-one or a small group.

- Resources: Determine what the possibilities are in the immediate environment: tables, chairs, cushions. Add: large cushions, beanbags, camping mattress, a clear tunnel, a large Sports Direct bag, blanket.

The four modes of delivery are: incidental, semi-structured, structured and free play.

Incidental

Often these moments emerge organically. Children suddenly do something quite unexpected: drape themselves over a table and lift up both legs; lie under a chair and attempt to lift it; jump onto a beanbag and land on their knees. Sometimes new equipment is delivered in a large box that provides opportunities to get in and out, push and pull, fill up, or hide in. A parent may bring in an unusual resource, e.g. a long rope that may be coiled into different shapes, jumped over or become a washing line. Prepare to be flexible and adjust agendas to accommodate these moments.

Semi-structured

You may have noted a particular issue – physical, behavioural or cognitive – that you aim to address, e.g. upper-body strength may be lacking so climbing is proving difficult; certain personalities are not gelling; a particular concept or vocabulary seems challenging to grasp or parents may have reported a concern. Working together on physical tasks/activities provides a positive way of addressing a range of issues.

Structured

This works well if you have a very specific issue to address with particular children: usually these sessions are short interventions that are useful for observation/evaluation purposes. Can a child do something in a movement context that has not been evident elsewhere, e.g. cooperate, collaborate, turn-take, share?

Free play

The outdoor environment presents more exciting opportunities, more space and freedom to choose what, how and with whom to engage. Free play with large apparatus can work well inside if you have determined acceptable boundaries around the resources and everyone agrees that, for a certain period, children may use the apparatus in different ways, e.g. climb on tables, jump on cushions.

Obstacle courses

All the resources used to construct obstacle courses may be used as individual pieces with small groups. The following ideas for using a large flat cushion highlight the range of skills that may be supported through very simple activities using just one piece of apparatus:

- With both hands, everyone help pick the cushion off the floor – lift as high as possible, then drop.

- Pat the cushion very hard with both hands – make a tower of hands in the middle.

- Stamp on the cushion – then jump and hop.

- All sit, holding onto the cushion with legs underneath – pull outwards as hard as possible.

- Try to lift the cushion using legs only.

- All kneel, holding the cushion tightly – wave up and down very fast.

- Lie on tummies, holding on and move the cushion right and left.

- Hide someone underneath.

- Pull individual children around as they sit on the cushion.

- Children will often create their own activities if afforded the time and opportunities to do so.

Allowing time for them to engage with single pieces of large apparatus as a group is important. It gives less confident children a chance to handle resources in preparation for completing obstacle courses independently.

Use six pieces or less for your obstacle course and remember never to put something soft before something hard. Construct in a *linear* formation.

To consider before you start:

- Don't make them too long or complicated. Children need to feel challenged but not intimidated.

- Clothing: Tuck in long dresses and pull up tight jeans – shoes off if inside.

- Safety: Be very clear about your expectations. They can be quite reckless around 4 years as lower-body strength increases. Separate larger children from younger, smaller ones.

- Be very clear what direction they're going in: What to do when the course is completed.

- Always ask for their assistance in setting up and clearing away.

- Children should always try to complete the course unaided.

Courses may be constructed to highlight the following: strength, speed, agility, balance.

Strength

Focus on climbing, pulling and pushing. It is important to include an element of upper-bodywork as the lower body is gaining strength naturally:

- Climb onto a table.

- Pull along on tummy – turn and slide off.

- Push large cushion along the floor.

- Crawl over a large beanbag.

Speed

Useful to practise rolling, crawling, walking and running. Keep this course as flat as possible and combine different surfaces:

- Crawl through the tunnel.

- Crawl under the chairs.

- Run over the flat cushions.

- Dive onto a large beanbag.

Agility

Focus on in-and-out and slaloms. This challenges the ability to manage body weight at speed. Place three chairs in a line (gaps can get smaller as they get more proficient):

- Run in and out.

- Crawl under a blanket.

- Climb into the tunnel – held upright.

- Lift it over the head and escape.

- Crawl to the Sports Direct bag.

- Climb in and sit still.

Balance
Focus on uneven surfaces and holding positions without support:

- Scatter small beanbags on the floor. Cover with a sheet or blanket – walk over unaided.

- Run to a large beanbag. Stand on it with arms up and balance.

- Flop onto the mattress. Stand and walk on tiptoes to the end.

Component 4: R&R – Rest and relaxation

This component may come at the end of a semi-structured session or experienced as a stand-alone whenever children need time to rest and relax. There should be special places where they may go to independently to feel peaceful, calm and secure – inside and outside, in company or not.

If you are planning a specific time *inside* for a group, consider the following:

- Children may choose a comfortable position: baby pose, on backs, sides or tummies. Some children like to lean against something solid (e.g. a wall), be in a corner, or cover themselves.

- Aligning the physical sensations of being calm, relaxed, peaceful, secure and quiet with the relevant vocabulary increases understanding of language and concepts.

- Children may tune into their bodies and become more aware of personal rhythms – heartbeat and breathing – and the extremities of fingers and toes.

- Listen to the sounds of the environment – traffic, voices, deliveries, telephones.

- Play soothing music from different genres – cultural and classical.

- Read an appropriate poem or listen to a recording.

I MOVE, THEREFORE I AM

Reflections

This element works best with small groups:

- Lie on tummies or backs with hands touching in the middle of the circle.

- Sit in a circle with straight legs and toes touching in the middle.

It is a good opportunity to talk about what they have done in the session, what they most enjoyed (or not) and why. What they could repeat at home and with whom, and some ideas for next time.

This is also a time when health and self-care topics can be introduced, e.g. why being active makes them hot – the importance of water – taking shoes off – how to be calm and manage tempers.

Noticing and recognising

Physical development practice crosses all boundaries, supporting, underpinning and informing all areas of provision. 'Noticing' should be continual and not just applied to times when children are obviously physically active. 'Spiky' development is the norm and progress in physical development may emerge in a different domain – new friends, interests, use of language, increased confidence to interact or practise specific skills in other environments. 'Recognising' will be more specific and often linked to particular issues or difficulties you have identified, e.g. catching a ball, climbing, group work, turn-taking.

Incidental opportunities

Did you find any opportunities or miss any? Did the children create their own?

Encourage children to 'notice' and 'recognise' for themselves. Many are well used to ipsative (self-) assessment through DT use. They will become more specific and realistic in terms of their physical development: 'Where am I now? Where would I like to be? What do I need to do to get there?' They can record themselves in different ways – draw and paint, photograph, film and model.

Jan White has created a very effective template for 'noticing' and 'recognising' children's outside physical play that may be easily adapted for the inside environment.[25]

Semi-structured and structured activities

How did the actual outcomes reflect planning? Anything specific to highlight: behaviours, skills, language. What to revise for next time. How did the children contribute; what ideas did they have?

Free physical play

Focus on: What they did and why, where they did it and why, how they did it and why, who did they do it with and why. You may include visual evidence, input from colleagues and parents and brief notes.

HOW THE EIGHT PRINCIPLES APPLY TO PRACTICE
Principle 1: The body is the primary source of learning and development

- Children's self-concept is formed and supported through varied physical experience – 'What can I do now – why can I do it – how can I do it better – and who can I share it with?'

- Physical skills extend the possibilities for positive engagement and communication with people, places and things – particularly through active play.

- Physical experience fosters the sense of 'belonging' – an affinity with the body (the 'enabling environment'), and a peaceful relationship with the 'immediate' environment.

- Language acquisition is supported through exposure to vocabulary in relevant and meaningful contexts.

- Spoken language is encouraged through vestibular stimulation and manipulative activities.

- Children are able to memorise, describe, evaluate and record movement experiences using a range of media: spoken and written word, drawing and painting, re-enacting.

- Resilience is developed through managing mistakes and setbacks, using the properties of the body (weight, shape, size, length) to overcome physical challenges.

- Self-regulation is supported by aligning relevant vocabulary with physical and feeling states.

- Concept of risk: what this means for individual children and how they react and adapt to different circumstances, environments and agendas.

Parents and carers

Movement experience and opportunities play a critical role in the development of self-concept, resilience and self-regulation. Try not to 'swoop and scoop' all the time; they can manage their own risks quite well, given the chance.

Principle 2: Start where they are

- The quality and quantity of movement experiences afforded to children will impact on how and where physical skills are acquired.

- The 'big' foundation movements should remain an integral component of movement provision throughout the reception year and beyond. They provide the ideal opportunities to ensure 'automaticity' is achieved, freeing up other body systems to acquire more complex skills.

- Progress is frequently nonlinear. Children need time, space and support to grow into a new skill and use it with confidence in a range of environments. Regressions and plateaus provide equally valuable learning opportunities.

- Inclusion is very important: Children should recognise that some start from a different point for whatever reason and have alternative priorities and needs. Movement buddies must be an integral part of provision.

- Acknowledgement of what their aspirations are regarding physical skills (e.g. to be on a team, win a prize, join a club) is important to factor into practice.

- They are managing many profound bodily changes during this time: Height, weight, shape, teeth fall out, shoes get tighter and some may be wearing glasses or hearing aids. Be aware that for some children (and their parents) accepting physical changes may be a challenge.

Parents and carers

Childhood is not a race or competition and all development is 'spiky' in some way. They will all get to where they want to be at a pace and in a manner that suits *them*. Be sensitive to likes and dislikes about physical experience. Children feel these deeply. Never force a child to do anything they are clearly averse to or afraid of.

Principle 3: The 'enabling' and 'immediate' environments support learning and development

- The 'enabling' environment becomes increasingly important to children during these years as they explore and investigate what their bodies can do, why they can perform certain movements and how their bodies relate to others and the physical environments they encounter.

- They become increasingly adept at navigating different environments using a range of transferable skills. They can move seamlessly from inside to outside, home to setting – accommodating different elements – land, water.

- Using all the properties of the immediate physical environment in a movement context fosters 'belonging', trust, security and familiarity.

- Using the 'enabling' and 'immediate' environments as a learning aid encourages children to understand, value and nurture the richness of their own context.

Parents and carers

You don't need expensive equipment to support children's physical development. There is huge learning potential within the resources you have already. Maximise incidental opportunities – bedtime, bathtime, washing, cooking – all these will anchor children's movement experience in a place they respect and value.

Principle 4: Music and rhythm extend opportunities for movement and learning

- Children are becoming aware of different genres of music (cultural, classical, popular) heard in a range of environments through various media.

- They often memorise and repeat words to current releases and watch music videos that they mimic quite accurately.

- They are becoming familiar with their own voices and can identify a personal recording. This adds another element to the growth of self-concept.

- They enjoy shouting and pushing their ('outside') voices to the limit.

- Rhythmical awareness informs and supports successful nonverbal and verbal communication. A range of opportunities to enhance rhythmical awareness should be provided, e.g. simple clapping/ jumping games, with and without music, time and space to move freely to music.

- It also supports positive engagement in a range of sports through 'timing' ability.

- Provide opportunities to raise awareness of personal rhythms, e.g. heartbeat, breathing, sleeping and digestion and how these are affected by physical activity.

- Patterning and sequencing in movement is linked to mathematical thinking. Understanding of shape, space and pattern is supported through moving to music.

Parents and carers
Dance together. Be silly. Sing choruses loudly. Make up your own rhymes. Try to be rhythmical in all your physical interactions with children.

Principle 5: Group work supports communication and language

- Moving in a group with and without music is a powerfully bonding experience. It reinforces spatial awareness, turn-taking, anticipating, cooperating and supporting. All differences may be accommodated and groups will find an inner dynamic or rhythm that works best for them.

- Moving to music supports all children to find a meaningful place within a group; that their presence is noted and contributions valued. Moving in a group accommodates emotional issues of aggression, envy, shifting friendships, showing off. It provides a secure environment in which spoken language is not pre-eminent and other priorities and skills may be highlighted.

- Working together with apparatus encourages children to speak. All are able to contribute, cooperate, collaborate and decide on outcomes. Children begin to understand the concept of teams, enjoy the camaraderie and appreciate the rules and forms of engagement.

- Include a reflecting time for the group if appropriate: What did they enjoy most or didn't? What went well? Include their contributions for future planning and provision. Moving and engaging with apparatus provides them with a wealth of relevant and meaningful material to talk about.

Parents and carers

Not all children are natural team players. It takes time to acquire the skills to manage. Try not to expect too much too soon and never place children in large groups before they decide they are ready.

Principle 6: Apparatus extends opportunities to move and learn

- Acquiring effective curricular skills is dependent on the 'big' foundation movement skills that ensure children have the strength, balance, coordination and agility to embrace all learning opportunities, especially as they start school.

- Engaging with familiar, accessible resources builds confidence and competence in the reliable use of skills in a range of environments and contexts, particularly sport.

- Using a variety of materials encourages mathematical thinking to be approached as a useful, living, embodied discipline.

- Engagement with large apparatus supports overall body strength, balance, coordination and agility. It encourages personal risk-taking, assessment and identifying personal boundaries.

- Using familiar, accessible materials encourages responsibility towards resources and the environment.

Parents and carers

Familiar, accessible resources present a wide range of possibilities to move and learn. Suitable resources may be identified, sourced, collected, recycled and valued.

Principle 7: The transfer of skills between environments is actively supported

- The ability to transfer skills acquired in a movement context to other environments and opportunities maximises the use and value of physical competencies.

- Achieving 'automaticity' through continual practice of the foundation movement skills ensures children can acquire new, more specific skills. They can and adapt and react easily to changing circumstances, demands, agendas and environments.

- Children manage their own perception of risk. They can trust their physical skills and make the right decisions for themselves.

- Children transfer their communication skills: waiting a turn, being supportive, caring, sharing – all important elements for school preparation.

- Cognitive skills are supported by making connections between the initial physical experience and representations in other media: stories, art, poetry, sculpture, film.

Parents and carers

The foundation skills are important to ensure children can manage transitions between environments with ease. Being physically confident, competent and capable affects all domains of learning and development.

Principle 8: **A canopy approach to movement provision is created and implemented**

- Ensure all four components are properly represented in practice.

- Continuous provision for movement experience should be available for children throughout the day, from home to setting, back to the home environment.

- Identify/determine where (inside/outside), when and how movement opportunities may be provided: aim for children to be active for 180 minutes and highly active for 60 minutes of this time (accumulative) during waking hours.

- Aim for a mix of incidental, semi-structured, structured and free play opportunities with and without apparatus, individual and group, with and without music.

- Rest and relaxation is an important component to include in provision either as a final section of a movement session or as a stand-alone.

- Look out for community possibilities, parental interests, events, free sessions from outside providers or franchises that could support your practice.

- Use DT wisely to support physical development and physical activity projects and minimise screen time – less than one hour daily.

- Use the strengths of your learning community to support and encourage practice.

Parents and carers

Encourage the increase of children's physical activity at home. Support their independence when dressing, eating, washing up and helping with household chores. Make the best use of community amenities – parks, pools.

CONCLUSIONS

- Movement experience and physical activity provide the optimum opportunities for children to acquire a range of skills that support and inform physical, cognitive and emotional development – 'I move, therefore I am.'

- Positive early movement experience ensures long-term engagement and enjoyment of a variety of physical activities that support overall health and wellbeing.

- Supporting EY Physical Activity guidelines mitigates the negative impact that changes in lifestyle and environment have on children's levels of physical activity.

- The teacher/practitioner role is critical in supporting children's physical activity, health and wellbeing and in ensuring proactive parental engagement in this field.

- Determine *why* movement is important – and *how* you plan to support children's physical skills.

- *What* you do – is up to you.

I will leave the final word to the Chilean poet Lucila Godoy Alcayaga (Gabriela Mistral), who won the Nobel Prize for Literature in 1945:

We are guilty of many errors and many faults, but our worst crime is abandoning the children, neglecting the foundation of life. Many of the things we need can wait. The child cannot. Right now is the time his bones are being formed, his blood is being made, and his senses are being developed. To him we cannot answer, 'Tomorrow.' Their name is today.

Gabriela Mistral, Nobel Laureate (1889–1957)[26]

Useful Resources

GENERAL INFORMATION

American Academy of Pediatrics. www.aap.org
Centre for Longitudinal Studies. www.cls.ioe.ac.uk
Children's Society. www.childrenssociety.org.uk
Current Education and Children's Services Research. www.ceruk.ac.uk
Every Disabled Child Matters. www.edcm.org.uk
Harvard University Centre for the Developing Child.
    www.developingchild.harvard.edu
Health and Biology. www.journals.elsevier.com
Health and Safety Executive. www.hse.gov.uk
Healthy Start Scheme. www.healthystart.nhs.uk
Millpond Children's Sleep Clinic. www.millpondsleepclinic.com
Pikler. www.pikler.co.uk
Public Health England (PHE). www.noo.org.uk
Slow Education. www.sloweducation.co.uk
Start Active Stay Active: infographics. www.gov.uk
The HENRY Programme. www.henry.org.uk
University of Wollongong, Australia: Early Start. www.earlystart.uow.edu.au

PLAY

www.earlyeducation.org.uk
www.freeplaynetwork.org.uk
www.londonplay.org.uk
www.ncb.org.uk
www.playengland.org.uk

OUTDOORS

www.creativepartnerships.com
www.forestschools.com

www.inspiringlearningforall.gov.uk
www.ltl.org.uk
www.outdoor-learning.org

VISUAL MATERIAL

'Babies Know When a Cuddle is Coming.' Professor V. Reddy, University of
    Portsmouth. http://uopnews.port.ac.uk/2013/06/25/babies-know-when-a-
    cuddle-is-coming
'Rolling – Feldenkrais with Baby Liv.' www.youtube.com/watch?v=D9Ko7U1pLlg
'The Power of Physical Play.' https://www.sirenfilms.co.uk/product/power-physical-
    play
'Early Years Inspections: Challenge or Opportunity? Professor Ferre Laevers Talks
    to Early Years Scotland.' (2016) (*Wellbeing and Involvement Can Be Improved in
    a Short Time*). https://www.youtube.com/watch?v=5RZDYK8tsvk
'Freedom to Move on One's Own.' www.pikler.co.uk/shop
'Play, Learning and Development (0–12 Months): Babies Outdoors.'
    www.sirenfilms.co.uk
'Play, Learning and Development (12–24 Months): Toddlers Outdoors.'
    www.sirenfilms.co.uk
'Play, Learning and Development: Two-Year-Olds Outdoors.' www.sirenfilms.co.uk
The Children's Project. www.socialbaby.com
Young Explorers. Jacob Krupnik. www.youngexplorers.club/home

USEFUL WEBSITES

www.activematters.org

A vibrant, popular site for practitioners, parents and all those involved with young
children – in whatever professional capacity. 'activematters' is the 'go to' site for all
things related to EY physical development/activity/health/wellbeing. Frequent blogs
and postings keep users well-informed and engaged with the field.

www.babybwell.co.uk

The best 'ages and stages' information I have come across. They are known primarily
for car safety initiatives – but it's definitely worth browsing through other materials
here.

www.bhfactive.org.uk

Early Movers resources – give essential underpinning knowledge and some excellent
practical tips to encourage movement and active play throughout the day. From
babies to reception age.

www.movingsmart.co.nz

Gill Connell is well-known internationally for her work in EY/PD. This website provides much-needed resources and information and very useful blogs.

www.raepica.com

Useful material for practice – and an excellent weekly blog.

www.sportnz.org.nz

Excellent resources for EY physical activity – very accessible and usable – look under 'Active Movement'.

www.surreycc.gov.uk

Very useful resources for physical activity – look under 'Move with Me' – all downloadable – very clear and concise – good for parents.

www.theplaydoctors.co.uk

Primarily aimed at older children on the autism spectrum – but all their resources are adaptable for EY/PA and are excellent.

Endnotes

Introduction

1   United Nations International Children's Emergency Fund (UNICEF) (1990) *United Nations Convention on the Rights of the Child (UNCRC)*, www.unicef.org.uk/what-we-do/un-convention-child-rights.

2   UNESCO (2000) *Education for All (EFA)*, www.unesco.org/new/en/education/themes/leading-the-international-agenda/education-for-all.

3   WHO (2015) 'Country Data, Universal Accountability: Monitoring Priorities for the Global Strategy for Women's, Children's and Adolescents' Health (2016–2030): Survive, Thrive, Transform,' *Every Woman Every Child*, www.everywomaneverychild.org/wp-content/uploads/2016/11/gs-monitoring-readiness-report.pdf.

4   WHO (2013) 'Obesity and Overweight,' Factsheet No. 311, www.who.int/mediacentre/factsheets/fs311/en.

5   Department for Education (DfE) (2017) *Early Years Foundation Stage (EYFS): Setting the Standards for Learning Development and Care for Children from Birth to Five*, London: DfE.

6   Manners, L.M. (2018) *Moving Right from the Start: The Importance of Physicality in the Early Years, Introduction*, London: Pre-school Learning Alliance, p.6.

Chapter 1

1   Robinson, Sir Ken (2007) 'Do Schools Kill Creativity?' TED Talks, 6 January, www.ted.com/talks/ken_robinson_says_schools_kill_creativity.

2   Claxton, G. (2015) *Intelligence in the Flesh: Why Your Mind Needs Your Body Much More than It Thinks*, New Haven, CT, and London: Yale Univesity Press, p.3.

3   Tobin, J. (2004) 'The Disappearance of the Body in Early Childhood Education,' in L. Bresler (ed.) *Knowing Bodies, Moving Minds: Towards Embodied Teaching and Learning*, Dordrecht: Kluwer Academic, p.111.

4   Burkitt, I. (1999) *Bodies of Thought: Embodiment, Identity & Modernity*, London: Sage, p.18.

5   Merleau-Ponty, M. (1962) *Phenomenology of Perception* (trans. C. Smith), Abingdon: Routledge. pp.26-27.

6   Bowman, W. (2004) 'Cognition and the Body: Perspectives from Music Education,' in L. Bresler (ed.) *Knowing Bodies, Knowing Minds: Towards Embodied Teaching and Learning*. Dordrecht: Kluwer Academic, p.29.

7   Whitehead, M. (1990) 'Meaningful Existence, Embodiment and Physical Education,' *Journal of Philosophy of Education* 24, 1.

8   Tanyhill, A. (2016) 'John Locke vs Jean-Jacques Rousseau: Comparison of Theories of Government,' 27 October, accessed 3 November 2018, www.academia.edu/30465184/John_Locke_vs_Jean-Jacques_Rousseau_Comparison_of_Theories_of_Government.pdf.

9   Schorsch, A. (1979) *Images of Childhood*, New York: Mayflower Books, p.43.

10 Pound, L. (2014) *How Children Learn*, London: Practical Pre-School Books, p.11.

11 Ibid.

12 Ibid.
13 Steiner Waldorf Education (2009) *Guide to the Early Years Foundation Stage in Steiner Waldorf Early Childhood Settings*, Cambridgeshire: White Horse Press, www.foundationyears.org.uk/files/2011/10/Guide_to_the_EYFS_in_Steiner_Wardorf_settings1.pdf.
14 Standing, E.M. (1957) *The Montessori Revolution in Education*, New York: Schocken Books.
15 Shilling, C. (1993) *The Body and Social Theory*, London: Sage, p.9.
16 Bowman (2004), p.36.
17 Claxton (2015), p.41.
18 Lloyd, R.J. (2016) 'Becoming Physically Literate for Life: Embracing the Functions, Forms, Feelings and Flows of Alternative and Mainstream Physical Activity,' *Journal of Teaching in Physical Education* 35, 107–116.
19 Whitehead, M. (ed.) (2010) 'Introduction,' *Physical Literacy: Throughout the Lifecourse*, Oxon: Routledge, p. 5.
20 Mandigo, J., Francis, N., Lodewyk, K. and Lopez, R. (2009) 'Physical Literacy for Educators,' *Physical Health and Education Journal* 75, 3, 27–30.
21 Haydn-Davies, D. (2010) 'Learning and Teaching Approaches,' in M. Whitehead (ed.) *Physical Literacy Throughout the Lifecourse*, Abingdon: Routledge, p.173.
22 Ward, G. (2018) 'Moving Beyond Sport in Primary Education,' in G. Griggs and K. Petrie (eds) *Routledge Handbook of Primary Physical Education*, Abingdon: Routledge, p.19.
23 Thom, J. (2017) 'Embodied Learning,' *Nursery World*, 27 November, pp.17–21.
24 Gallagher, S. (2005) *How the Body Shapes the Mind*, Oxford: Clarendon Press.
25 Burkitt (1999) *Op. cit.*, p.19.
26 Sheets-Johnstone, M. (1999) *The Primacy of Movement*, Amsterdam and Philadelphia, PA: John Benjamins.
27 Wolpert, D. (2011) 'The Real Reason for Brains,' TED Talks, July, www.ted.com/talks/daniel_wolpert_the_real_reason_for_brains.
28 Davis, B. and the Spatial Reasoning Study Group (2015) *Spatial Reasoning in the Early Years: Principles, Assertions, and Speculations*, New York and Abingdon: Routledge.
29 Ross, J. (2004) 'The Instructable Body: Student Bodies from Classrooms to Prisons,' in L. Bresler (ed.) *Knowing Bodies, Knowing Minds: Towards Embodied Teaching and Learning*. Dordrecht: Kluwer Academic, p.171.
30 Moravec, H.P. (1999) *Robot: Mere Machine to Transcendent Mind*, Oxford: Oxford University Press.

Chapter 2

1 Connell, G. and McCarthy, C. (2014) *A Moving Child is a Learning Child: How the Body Teaches the Brain to Think*, Minneapolis, MN: Free Spirit Publishing, p.222.
2 Manners, L.M. (2014) 'Hang On,' *Nursery World*, 27 July, p.36.
3 Palaiologou, I. (2010) 'Personal, Social and Emotional Development,' in I. Palaiologou (ed.) *The Early Years Foundation Stage. Theory and Practice*, London: Sage, p.130.
4 Walsh, D.J. (2004) 'Frog Boy and the American Monkey,' in C. Bresler (ed.) *Knowing Bodies, Moving Minds: Towards Embodied Teaching and Learning*. Dordrecht: Kluwer Academic, p.100.
5 Shilling, C. (1993) *The Body and Social Theory*? London: Sage, p.21.
6 Ibid., p.23.
7 Ibid., p.22.
8 Center on the Developing Child (2010) *The Foundations of Lifelong Health Are Built in Early Childhood*, Cambridge, MA: Harvard University.
9 Pound, L. (2014) *How Children Learn*, London: Practical Pre-School Books, p.33.
10 Field, F. (2010) *The Foundation Years: Preventing Poor Children Becoming Poor Adults: The Report of the Independent Review on Poverty and Life Chances*, London: HM Government.
11 Allen, G. (2011) *Early Intervention. The Next Steps*. London: HM Government.
12 Tickell, C. (2011) *The Early Years: Foundations for Life, Health and Learning. An Independent Report on the Early Years Foundation Stage.* London: Cabinet Office.
13 Timmons, B.W., Leblanc, A.G., Carson, V., Connor Gorber, S. and Glover, V. (2012) *Systematic Review of Physical Activity and Health in the Early Years (0–4 Years)*, in Allen+Clarke (2015) *Review of Physical Activity Guidance and Resources for Under Fives: Final Report for the Ministry of Health*,

Wellington: New Zealand Ministry for Health, p.21, www.health.govt.nz/system/files/documents/publications/review-physical-activity-guidance-resources-for-under-fives-apr16.pdf.

14 Black, M.M. and Hurley, K.M. (2014) 'Investment in Early Childhood Development,' *The Lancet* 384.

15 Weisner, T. (1998) 'Human Development, Child Well-Being and the Cultural Project of Development,' in D. Sharma and K.W. Fischer (eds) *Socioemotional Development Across Cultures*, San Francisco, CA: Jossey-Bass, pp.69–85.

16 O'Connor, A. and Daly, A. (2016) *Understanding Physical Development in the Early Years: Linking Bodies and Minds*, Abingdon: Routledge.

17 Laevers, F. (ed.) (1994) *Well-Being and Involvement in Care: A Process-Oriented Self-Evaluation Instrument for Care Settings*, Leuven: Centre for Experiential Education, Kind & Gezin, https://www.kindengezin.be/img/sics-ziko-manual.pdf.

18 Giske, R., Ugelstad, I.B., Meland, A.T., Kaltvedt, E.H. *et al.* (2018) 'Toddlers' Social Competence, Play, Movement Skills and Wellbeing: An Analysis of Their Relationship Based on Authentic Assessment in Kindergarten,' *European Early Childhood Education Research Journal* 26, 3, 362–374.

19 Gesell, A. and Thompson, A. (1943) *Infant Behaviour: Its Genesis and Growth*, New York: McGraw-Hill.

20 Pound, L. (2015) *Child Development: A Unique Child Series*, London: Practical Pre-School Books, p.4.

21 Walsh (2004) *Op. cit.*, pp.97–109.

22 Anonymous post (2016) on BishopBlog, 13 November. Accessed on 16/12/18 www.deevybee.blogspot.com/2016.

23 Jones, L., Barron, I., Powell, J. and Holmes, R. (2005) 'Concluding Remarks,' in L. Jones, R. Holmes and J. Powell (eds) *Early Childhood Studies: A Multiprofessional Perspective*, New York: Open University Press, McGraw-Hill Education, p.211.

24 Shilling (1993) *Op. cit.*

25 Cannella, G.S. (2005) 'Reconceptualizing the Field (of Early Care and Education),' in N. Yelland (ed) *Critical Issues in Early Childhood Education*, New York: Open University Press, McGraw-Hill Education, p.18.

26 Walsh (2004) *Op. cit.*

27 Walsh (2004) *Op. cit.*

28 LeVine, R.A. and LeVine, S. (2016) *Do Parents Matter? Why Japanese Babies Sleep Soundly, Mexican Siblings Don't Fight, and American Families Should Just Relax*, New York: PublicAffairs: Perseus.

29 Blakeslee, S. and Blakeslee, M. (2008) *The Body Has a Mind of Its Own: How Body Maps in Your Brain Help You Do (Almost) Everything Better*, New York: Random House.

30 Goddard Blythe, S. (2004) *The Well-Balanced Child: Movement and Early Learning* (rev. edn), Stroud: Hawthorn Press.

31 Ibid., p.12.

32 O'Connor and Daly (2016) *Op. cit.*, p.115.

33 Ibid.

34 Ibid.

35 Sherrington, C.S. (1906) *The Integrative Action of the Nervous System*, Oxford: Oxford University Press, p.10.

36 Bastian, H.C. (1880) *The Brain as an Organ of the Mind*, Boston, MA: D. Appleton & Company.

37 Dearborn, G.V.N. (1913) 'Kinesthesia and the Intelligent Will,' *American Journal of Psychology* 24, 2, 204–255.

38 Connell, G. and McCarthy, C. (2014) *A Moving Child Is a Learning Child: How the Body Teaches the Brain to Think*, Minneapolis, MN: Free Spirit Publishing, p.93.

39 White, J. (2015) *Every Child a Mover: A Practical Guide to Providing Young Children with the Physical Opportunities They Need*, London: British Association for Early Childhood Education, p.31.

40 Gallagher, S. and Cole, J. (1995) 'Body Schema and Body Image in a Deafferented Subject,' *Journal of Mind and Behavior* 16, 4, 369–390.

41 Schilder, P.F. (1935) *The Image and Appearance of the Human Body*, Abingdon: Routledge.

42 Greenfield, S. (2008) *ID: The Quest for Identity in the 21st Century*, London: Hodder & Stoughton, p.117.

43 Leach, P. (2018) 'Fifty Years of Childhood,' in P. Leach (ed.) *Transforming Infant Wellbeing. Research, Policy and Practice for the First 1000 Critical Days*, Abingdon: Routledge, pp.3–10.

44   Balbernie, R. (2018) 'Circuits and Circumstances: Importance of Earliest Relationships and Their Context,' in P. Leach (ed.) *Transforming Infant Wellbeing. Research, Policy and Practice for the First 1000 Critical Days*. Abingdon: Routledge, pp.19–27.

45   Karr-Morse, R. and Wiley, M.S. (1997) *Ghosts from the Nursery: Tracing the Roots of Violence*, New York: Atlantic Monthly Press, p.227.

46   Balbernie (2018). *Op. cit.*

47   Vandenbroeck, M. (2014) 'The Brainification of Early Childhood Education and Other Challenges to Academic Rigour,' *European Early Childhood Education Research Journal* 22, 1, 1–3.

48   Tobin, J. (2004) 'The Disappearance of the Body in Early Childhood Education,' in L. Bresler (ed.) *Knowing Bodies, Moving Minds: Towards Embodied Teaching and Learning*. Dordrecht: Kluwer Academic., pp.111–124.

49   Conkbayir, M. (2017) *Early Childhood and Neuroscience: Theory, Research and Implications for Practice*, London: Bloomsbury Academic, p.30.

50   Carson, V., Hunter, S., Kuzik, N., Wiebe, S.A. *et al.* (2016) 'Systematic Review of Physical Activity and Cognitive Development in Early Childhood,' *Journal of Science and Medicine in Sport*, http://dx.doi.org/10.1016/j.jsams.2015.07.011.

51   Swain, J. (n.d.) 'Pikler's Trust in the Wise Infant: A Warm and Nurturing Welcome,' *Wisconsin Education Career Access Network (WECAN)*.

52   Marlen, D. (2017) 'All about Pikler,' *Nursery World*, 6 March, 23–27.

53   Marlen, D. (2014) 'Respect, Care, Wisdom,' *Early Years Educator* 16, 6, 28–30.

54   Ibid.

55   Swain, *Op cit.*

56   Sumner, E. and Hill, E.L. (2016) 'Are Children Who Walk and Talk Early Geniuses in the Making?' *The Conversation*, 4 February, http://theconversation.com/are-children-who-walk-and-talk-early-geniuses-in-the-making-54069.

57   Brazelton, T.B. and Sparrow, J. (2003) *The Touchpoints Model of Development*, Brazelton Touchpoints Centre, www.touchpoints.org.

58   Conkbayir (2017) *Op. cit.*

59   Hall, S.S. (1998) 'Test Tube Moms,' *New York Times Magazine*, 5 April, pp.22–28.

Chapter 3

1   Lakoff, G. and Johnson, M. (1999) *Philosophy in the Flesh: The Embodied Mind and Its Challenge to Western Thought*, New York: Basic Books, Hachette, p.566.

2   Fortunati, A. (2014) in M. Pace, *I Love Forest School*, London: Featherstone Education, p.22.

3   Christensen, P.H. (2000) 'Childhood and the Cultural Constitution of Vulnerable Bodies,' in A. Prout (ed.) *The Body, Childhood and Society*, Basingstoke: Macmillan Press, p.40.

4   Pearce, A., Scalzi, D., Lynch, J. and Smithers, L.G. (2016) 'Do Thin, Overweight and Obese Children Have Poorer Development than Their Healthy-Weight Peers at the Start of School? Findings from a South Australian Data Linkage Study,' *Early Childhood Research Quarterly* 35, 2, 85–94.

5   Lindon, J. (2012) *Understanding Child Development 0–8 Years* (3rd edn), Basingstoke: Hodder Education, p.6.

6   O'Sullivan, J. (2009) *Successful Leadership in the Early Years*, London: Featherstone Education, p.90.

7   Tassoni, P. (2014) *Getting It Right for Two-Year-Olds*, Basingstoke: Hodder Education, p.35.

8   Solly, K. (2015) *Risk, Challenge and Adventure in the Early Years: A Practical Guide to Exploring and Extending Learning Outdoors*, Abingdon: David Fulton, Routledge, p.64.

9   Aubrun, A. and Grady, J. (2002) *Promoting School-Readiness and Early Child Development: Findings from Cognitive Elicitations*, FrameWorks Institute, http://docplayer.net/12188098-Promoting-school-readiness-and-early-child-development-findings-from-cognitive-elicitations.html.

10   Pace, M. (2014) *I Love Forest School: Transforming Early Years Practice through Woodland Experiences*, London: Featherstone Education, p.9.

11   Bronfenbrenner, U. (1994) 'Ecological Models of Human Development,' in T. Postlewaite and T. Husén (eds) *International Encyclopedia of Education*, Vol. 3 (2nd edn), Oxford: Elsevier, pp.1643–1647.

12 Bronfenbrenner, U. and Morris, P.A. (2006) 'The Bioecological Model of Human Development,' in W. Damon and R.A. Lerner (eds) *Handbook of Child Psychology*, Vol. 1: *Theoretical Models of Human Development* (6th edn), New York: Wiley, pp.793–828.

13 Paquette, D. and Ryan, J. (2012) 'Bronfenbrenner's Ecological Systems Theory,' Dropout Prevention, http://dropoutprevention.org/wp-content/uploads/2015/07/paquetteryanwebquest_20091110.pdf.

14 Clements, R. (2004) 'An Investigation of the Status of Outdoor Play,' *Contemporary Issues in Early Childhood 5*, 1, 68–80.

15 Hocker, P. (2018) 'City Hall Briefing: Play Attrition Since 2013,' London Play, www.londonplay.org.uk.

16 Lindon (2012) *Op. cit.*

17 Coleridge, S.T. (1802) Cited in Coleridge, H. (1836) *The Literary Remains of Samuel Taylor Coleridge*, Vol. 1, London: William Pickering.

18 Goddard Blythe, S. (2004) *The Well-Balanced Child. Movement and Early Learning* (rev. edn). Stroud: Hawthorn Press, p.5.

19 Claxton (2015) *Intelligence in the Flesh: Why Your Mind Needs Your Body Much More than It Thinks*. New Haven & London: Yale University Press, p.264.

20 Conkbayir (2017) *Early Childhood and Neuroscience: Theory, Research and Implications for Practice*, London: Bloomsbury Academic.

21 National Academies of Sciences, Engineering and Medicine (2016) 'Obesity in the Early Childhood Years: State of the Science and Implementation of Promising Solutions: Workshop Summary,' Washington, DC: National Academies Press, doi: 10.17226/23445.

22 Glover, V. (2018) 'Stress in pregnancy can change fetal and child development,' in P. Leach (ed.) *Transforming Infant Wellbeing. Research, Policy and Practice for the First 1000 Critical Days*. Oxon: Routledge, pp.98–106.

23 Sarkar, P., Bergman, K., Fisk, N.M., O'Connor, T.G. *et al.* (2007) 'Ontogeny of Foetal Exposure to Maternal Cortisol Using Mid-Trimester Amniotic Fluid as a Biomarker,' *Clinical Endocrinology 66*, 5, 636–640.

24 Drugli, M.B., Solheim, E., Lydersen, S., Moe, V., Smith, L. and Berg-Nielsen, T.S. (2017) 'Elevated Cortisol Levels in Norwegian Toddlers in Childcare,' *Early Child Development and Care*, http://dx/doi.org/10.1080/03004430-12.78368.

25 Watamura, S.E., Coe, C.L., Laudenslager, M.L. and Robertson, S.S. (2010) 'Child Care Setting Affects Salivary Cortisol and Antibody Secretion in Young Children,' *Psychoneuroendocrinology 35*, 1156–1166.

26 Goddard Blythe (2004) *Op. cit.*

27 Gill, S. (2011) 'The Primacy of Movement and Gesture: Brain Body Movement,' *Sam Gill*, 11 January, www.sam-gill.com.

28 Kagan, J. and Snidman, N. (2004) *The Long Shadow of Temperament*, Cambridge, MA: Harvard University Press.

29 Caspi, A., Harrington, H., Milne, B., Amell, J.W., Theodore, R.F. and Moffitt, T.E. (2003) 'Children's Behavioural Styles at Age 3 are Linked to Their Adult Personality Traits at Age 26,' *Journal of Personality 71*, 4, 496–513.

30 Tsaneva-Atanasova, K., Słowiński, P., Zhai, C., Alderisio, F. et al. (2015) 'Dynamic Similarity Promotes Interpersonal Coordination in Joint Action,' *Journal of the Royal Society, Interface*, http://rsif.royalsocietypublishing.org/content/13/116/20151093.

31 O'Connor, A. and Daly, A. (2016) *Understanding Physical Development in the Early Years: Linking Bodies and Minds*, Abingdon: Routledge, p.28.

32 Reunamo, J. (2017) 'Physical Activity: Some Lessons from Finland,' *Nursery World*, 3 April, p.15.

33 O'Sullivan (2009) *Op. cit.*

34 Kálló, É. and Balog, G. (2005) *The Origins of Free Play*, Budapest: Pikler-Lóczy.

35 Janssen-Vos, F., Pompert, B. and Schiferli, T. (1998) *HOREB: Activity-Oriented Observation, Registration and Evaluation of Basic Development*, Utrecht: APS.

36 Fortunati in Pace (2014) *Op. cit.*

37 Ter Laack, J., de Goede, M. and Aleva, A. (2005) 'The Draw-a-Person Test: An Indicator of Children's Cognitive and Socioemotional Adaptation,' *Journal of Genetic Psychology 166*, 1, 77–93.

38 Naglieri, J.A. (1998) *DAP. Draw a Person Test: A Quantitative Scoring System Manual*, San Antonio, TX: Psychological Corporation, Harcourt Brace-Jovanovich.

39 Davies, M. (1995) *Helping Children Learn through a Movement Perspective*, London: Hodder & Stoughton.

40 Katz, L. (1993) 'ERIC ED360104: Dispositions: Definitions and Implications for Early Childhood Practices: Perspectives from ERIC/EECE: A Monograph Series, No. 4.' *ERIC*, https://archive.org/details/ERIC_ED360104.

41 Lindon (2012) *Op. cit.*

42 Thompson, W. (2010) 'Meeting EYFS Outcomes Outside of the Early Years Setting, in Palaiologou (ed.) *The Early Years Foundation Stage*, pp.106–120.

43 Ibid.

44 Sargent, M. (2015) 'Going Public,' *Nursery World*, 5 October, www.bricproject.org.

45 Weaver, T. (2015) 'Returning to the Poetic,' *EYE (Early Years Educator)* 17, 7, November, 28–30.

46 Johnson, M. (1967) *The Body in the Mind: The Bodily Basis of Meaning, Imagination and Reason*, Chicago, IL: University of Chicago Press, p.15.

Chapter 4

1 de Lamartine, A. (1820) *Méditations poétiques*, France.

2 Roth, Gabrielle (1941–2012).

3 Cross, I. and Morley, I. (2010) 'The Evolution of Music: Theories, Definitions and the Nature of the Evidence,' in S. Malloch and C. Trevarthen (eds) *Communicative Musicality: Exploring the Basis of Human Companionship*, Oxford: Oxford University Press, p.63.

4 Bowman, W. (2004) 'Cognition and the Body: Perspectives from Music Education,' in L. Bresler (ed.) *Knowing Bodies, Knowing Minds: Towards Embodied Teaching and Learning*. Dordrecht: Kluwer Academic, p.47.

5 Ibid.

6 Cross and Morley (2010) *Op. cit.*, p.63.

7 Ibid., p.65.

8 Bowman (2004) *Op. cit.*, p.31.

9 Ibid.

10 Clayton, M., Sager, R. and Will, U. (2004) 'In Time with the Music: The Concept of Entrainment and Its Significance for Ethnomusicology,' *ESEM CounterPoint* 1, 1–82.

11 Lefebvre, H. (2004) *Rhythmanalysis: Space, Time and Everyday Life*, London: Continuum, p.4.

12 Ruckmich, C. (1913) 'The Role of Kinaesthesis in the Perception of Rhythm,' *American Journal of Psychology* 24, 3, 305–359. In P. Crespi (2014) 'Rhythmanalysis in Gymnastics and Dance: Rudolf Bode and Rudolf Laban,' *Body and Society* 20, 3–4, 30–50, Sage. Doi: 10.1177/1357034X14547523.

13 Bowman (2004) *Op. cit.*, p.37.

14 Lazarev, M. (2007) *Mamababy*, Moscow: Olma Media Grupp, p48.

15 Tomatis, A. (1991) *The Conscious Ear: My Life of Transformation through Listening*, New York: Station Hill Press.

16 Goddard Blythe, S. (2004) *The Well-Balanced Child: Movement and Early Learning* (rev. edn), Stroud: Hawthorn Press, p.69.

17 Dissanayake, E. (2010) 'The Evolution of Music: Theories, Definitions and the Nature of the Evidence,' in S. Malloch and C. Trevarthen (eds) *Communicative Musicality: Exploring the Basis of Human Companionship*. Oxford: Oxford University Press, p.22.

18 Powers, N. and Trevarthen, C. (2010) 'Voices of Shared Emotion and Meaning: Young Infants and Their Mothers in Scotland and Japan,' in S. Malloch and C. Trevarthen (eds) *Communicative Musicality: Exploring the Basis of Human Companionship*. Oxford: Oxford University Press, p.209.

19 Malloch, S. and Trevarthen, C. (2010) 'Musicality: Communicating the Vitality and Interests of Life,' in S. Malloch and C. Trevarthen (eds) *Communicative Musicality: Exploring the Basis of Human Companionship*. Oxford: Oxford University Press.

20 Ibid.

21 Mazokopaki, K. and Kugiumutzakis, G. (2010) 'Infant Rhythms: Expressions of Musical Companionship,' in S. Malloch and C. Trevarthen (eds) *Communicative Musicality: Exploring the Basis of Human Companionship*. Oxford: Oxford University Press, p.190.

22 Stern, D.N. (2000) *The Interpersonal World of the Infant: A View from Psychoanalysis and Developmental Psychology* (2nd edn), New York: Basic Books: Hachette, p.232.

23 Froebel, F. (1895) *The Mottoes and Commentaries of Friedrich Froebel's Mother Play* (trans. H.R. Eliot and S.E. Blow, 1902), New York: Appleton & Company.

24 Powell, S., Goouch, K. and Werth, L. (2013) 'Seeking Froebel's "Mother Songs" in Daycare for Babies,' New York: CReaTE, Canterbury Christ Church University, http://tactyc.org.uk/pdfs/Sacha%20 Powell.pdf.

25 Steiner Waldorf (2009) *Guide to the Early Years Foundation Stage in Steiner Waldorf Early Childhood Settings*, Cambridgeshire: White Horse Press, www.steinerwaldorf.org.uk.

26 Steiner, R. (1981) *The Renewal of Education through Science of the Spirit*, Forest Row, East Sussex: Kolisko Archive Publications for the Steiner Waldorf Schools Fellowship.

27 Weikart, P. (1986) *Movement Curriculum Improves Children's Rhythmic Competency*, Ypsilanti, MI: High Scope Educational Research Foundation.

28 Ibid.

29 *The Telegraph* (2012) 'Music Helps Children Learn Maths,' 22 March, www.telegraph.co.uk/ news/9159802/music-helps-children-learn-maths.html.

30 Ockelford, A. (2013) *Music, Language and Autism: Exceptional Strategies for Exceptional Minds*, London: Jessica Kingsley Publishers, p.9.

31 Happé, F. (2013) 'Foreword,' in A. Ockelford (ed.) *Music, Language and Autism: Exceptional Strategies for Exceptional Minds*. London: Jessica Kingsley Publishers, p.70.

32 Cross and Morley (2010) *Op. cit.*, p.39.

33 Bowman (2004) *Op. cit.*

34 Malloch and Trevarthen (2010) *Op. cit.*

35 Eckerdal, P. and Merker, B. (2010) '"Music" and the "Action Song" in Infant Development: An Interpretation,' in S. Malloch and C. Trevarthen (eds) *Communicative Musicality Exploring the Basis of Human Companionship*, Oxford: Oxford University Press, pp.241–262.

36 Roth, Gabrielle (1941–2012) Poem.

Chapter 5

1 Malloch, S. and Trevarthen, C. (eds) (2010) *Communicative Musicality: Exploring the Basis of Human Companionship.* Oxford: Oxford University Press, p.8.

2 Adams, S. (2013) 'The 10 Skills Employers Most Want in 20-Somehing Employees,' *Forbes*, 13 October, www.forbes.com/sites/susanadams/2013/10/11/the-10-skills-employers-most-want-in-20-something-employees/#4bebd35a6330.

3 Youth Employment UK (2017) 'Employability Review,' Youth Employment UK, www. youthemployment.org.uk/dev/wp-content/uploads/2017/07/Youth-Employment-UK-Employability-Review-June-2017.pdf.

4 Boyce, S. (2012) *Not Just Talking: Identifying Non-Verbal Communication Difficulties – A Life-Changing Approach.* Abingdon: Speechmark Publishing, Routledge.

5 Howard, S. (2010) 'Pedagogy in Context,' in I. Palaiologou (ed.) *The Early Years Foundation Stage: Theory and Practice.* London Sage, p.49.

6 Gianoutsos, J. (2006) 'Locke and Rousseau: Early Childhood Education,' *The Pulse* 4, 1, 1–23, Waco, TX: Undergraduate Journal of Baylor University.

7 LeVine, R.A. and LeVine, S. (2016) *Do Parents Matter? Why Japanese Babies Sleep Soundly, Mexican Siblings Don't Fight, and American Families Should Just Relax.* New York: Public Affairs: Perseus Books, p.114.

8 Ibid.

9 Powers, N. and Trevarthen, C. (2010) 'Voices of Shared Emotion and Meaning: Young Infants and Their Mothers in Scotland and Japan,' in S. Malloch and C. Trevarthen (eds) *Communicative Musicality: Exploring the Basis of Human Companionship.* Oxford: Oxford University Press, p.219.

10 Cain, S. (2012) *Quiet: The Power of Introverts in a World that Can't Stop Talking*, London: Penguin, p.190.

11 Bruner, J. (2000) 'Foreword,' in J. de Loache and A. Gottlieb (eds) *A World of Babies: Imagined Childcare for Seven Societies*, Cambridge: Cambridge University Press, p.5.

12 Penn, H. (1998) 'Does it Matter What Country You Are in? Are All Children the Same Everywhere or Does it Matter Where You Are?', in S. Smidt (ed.) *Key Issues in Early Years Education* (2nd edn), Abingdon: Routledge, p.21.

13 Brooker, L. (2005) 'Learning to be a Child: Cultural Diversity and Early Years Ideology', in N. Yelland (ed.) *Critical Issues in Early Childhood Education*, New York: Open University Press, McGraw-Hill Education, p.118.

14 Private correspondence with EY practitioner.

15 DfE (2017) *Statutory Framework for the Early Years Foundation Stage (EYFS): Setting the Standards for Learning, Development and Care for Children from Birth to 5*, London: DfE.

16 Pace, M. (2014) *I Love Forest School: Transforming Early Years Practice through Woodland Experiences*, London: Featherstone Education, p.28.

17 Ibid., p.5.

18 Steiner Waldorf Education (2009) *Guide to the Early Years Foundation Stage in Steiner Waldorf Early Childhood Settings*. Cambridgeshire: White Horse Press. www.steinerwaldorf.org.uk

19 Standing, E.M. (1957) *The Montessori Revolution in Education*. New York: Schocken Books.

20 Knauf, H. (2016) 'Interlaced Social Worlds: Exploring the Use of Social Media in the Kindergarten', *Early Years: International Research Journal* 36, 3, 254–270, www.tandfonline.com/doi/abs/10.1080/09575146.2016.1147424?scroll=top&needAccess=true&journalCode=ceye20.

21 Boxall, M. (2002) *Nurture Groups in Schools: Principles and Practice*, London: Sage, p.54.

22 Lindon, J. (2012) *Understanding Children's Behaviour 0–11 Years*, Basingstoke: Hodder Education, p.57.

23 Mosley, J. (1996) *Quality Circle Time in the Primary Classroom: Your Essential Guide to Enhancing Self-Esteem, Self-Discipline and Positive Relationships*, Cambridge: LDA.

24 Solly, K. (2015) *Risk, Challenge and Adventure in the Early Years: A Practical Guide to Exploring and Extending Learning Outdoors*, Abingdon: David Fulton, Routledge, p.57.

25 Lindon (2012) *Op. cit.*, p.101.

26 Connell, G. and McCarthy, C. (2014) *A Moving Child is a Learning Child: How the Body Teaches the Brain to Think*, Minneapolis, MN: Free Spirit Publishing, p.93.

27 O'Connor and Daly (2016) *Op. cit.*, p.115.

28 Ayers, A.J. (2005) *Sensory Integration and the Child: 25th Anniversary Edition*, Los Angeles, CA: Western Psychological Services.

29 Hannaford, C. (1995) *Smart Moves: Why Learning is Not All in Your Head*, North Carolina: Great Ocean Publishers, p.41.

30 Boyce (2012) *Op. cit.*

31 Plummer, D.M. (2008) *Social Skills Games for Children*, London: Jessica Kingsley Publishers, p.26.

32 Lindon (2012) *Op. cit.*

33 Trevarthen, C. (2017) 'Foreword', 'Relating the Miracle of Young Life to the Mysteries of the Growing Brain', in M. Conkbayir (ed.) *Early Childhood and Neuroscience: Theory, Research and Implications for Practice*. London: Bloomsbury Academic, p.8.

34 Claxton, G. (2015) *Intelligence in the Flesh: Why Your Mind Needs Your Body Much More than It Thinks*, New Haven, CT, and London: Yale Univesity Press, p.57.

35 Cocozza, P. (2018) 'Losing Our Touch', *The Guardian*, 8 March, p.8.

36 Silin, J.G. (2005) 'Who Can Speak? Silence, Voice and Pedagogy', in N. Yelland (ed.) *Critical Issues in Early Childhood Education*, New York: Open University Press, McGraw-Hill Education, p.84.

37 Wolf, M. (2007) *Proust and the Squid: The Story and Science of the Reading Brain*, New York: HarperCollins, p.213.

38 Solly, K. (2016) 'All about Trust', *Nursery World*, 31 October, pp.31–34.

39 Tutu, D.M. (2000) *No Future without Forgiveness: A Personal Overview of South Africa's Truth and Reconciliation Commission*, London: Rider, Ebury Press.

Chapter 6

1 Pre-school Learning Alliance (PSLA) (2013) *Patterns of Care: How Playful Relationships Enable Brain Development and Support Learning in the First Years of Life*, London: Early Years Publications & Resources, p.106.

2 Ibid., p.124.

3 Claxton, G. (2015) *Intelligence in the Flesh: Why Your Mind Needs Your Body Much More than It Thinks*. New Haven & London: Yale University Press, p.8.

4   Wilson, F.R. (1998) *The Hand: How Its Use Shapes the Brain, Language and Human Culture*, New York: Vintage Books, p.37.

5   Ibid.

6   Ibid., p.238.

7   Boyd, C. and Bee, H. (2014) *The Developing Child*, London: Pearson Education.

8   Pound, L. (2014) *How Children Learn*. London: Practical Pre-School Books.

9   Tovey, H. (2016) *Bringing the Froebel Approach to Your Early Years Practice* (2nd edn), Oxon: Routledge.

10 Bruce, T. and Dyke, J. (2017) 'Learning from Froebel: The Gifts,' *Nursery World*, 23 January, pp.27–30; and Bruce and Dyke (2017) 'Learning from Froebel: Occupations,' *Nursery World*, 20 February, pp.27–30.

11 Montessori (n.d.) *Montessori Primary Guide: Introduction to Sensorial*, www.infomontessori.com/sensorial/introduction.htm.

12 Standing, E.M. (1957) *The Montessori Revolution in Education*. New York: Schocken Books, p.35.

13 Montessori (n.d.) *Montessori Primary Guide: Introduction to Practical Life*, www.infomontessori.com/practical-life/introduction.htm.

14 Kallo, E. and Balog, G. (2014) *The Origins of Free Play* (trans. M. Holm). Budapest: Pikler-Lóczy.

15 Ibid., p.16.

16 Ibid., p.10.

17 Ibid., p.29.

18 Ibid., p.6.

19 Goldschmied, E. and Jackson, S. (2004) *People Under Three: Young Children in Day Care* (2nd edn), Abingdon: Routledge.

20 Cousins, J., Hughes, A.M. and Selleck, D.Y. (2014) 'Elinor Goldschmied: A Life Revised,' *Nursery World, Learning and Development*, posted 5 May, www.nurseryworld.co.uk.

21 Goldschmied and Jackson (2004) *Op. cit.*

22 Tassoni, P. (2011) 'A Parent's Guide to Heuristic Play,' *Nursery World*, posted 22 August, www.nurseryworld.co.uk.

23 Page, J. (2007) 'All about Heuristic Play: Children Start to Understand the World by Exploring Objects,' *Nursery World*, posted 6 June, www.nurseryworld.co.uk.

24 Gascoyne, S. (2012) *Treasure Baskets and Beyond: Realising the Potential of Sensory-Rich Play*, Maidenhead: Open University Press.

25 Weaver, T. (2015) 'Returning to the Poetic,' *EYE (Early Years Educator)* 17, 7, November, 28–30.

26 Lindon, J. (2012) *Understanding Child Development 0–8 Years* (3rd edn), Basingstoke: Hodder Education, p.196.

Chapter 7

1   Larson, Doug (1926–2017)

2   Gardner, H. and Davis, K. (2013) *The App Generation: How Today's Youth Navigate Identity, Intimacy and Imagination in a Digital World*, New Haven, CT & London: Yale University Press, p.179.

3   Connell, G. and McCarthy, C. (2014) *A Moving Child is a Learning Child: How the Body Teaches the Brain to Think*, Minneapolis, MN: Free Spirit Publishing, p.105.

4   Center on the Developing Child (2016) *Building Core Capabilities for Life: The Science Behind the Skills Adults Need to Succeed in Parenting and in the Workplace*, Cambridge, MA: Harvard University Press, p.3, www.developingchild.harvard.edu.

5   Tassoni, P. (2016) *Reducing Educational Disadvantage: A Strategic Approach in the Early Years*, London: Featherstone Education, p.170.

6   Goddard Blythe, S. (2004) *Attention, Balance and Coordination: The ABC of Learning Success*, Chichester: John Wiley & Sons.

7   Katz, L.G. (2010) 'A Developmental Approach to the Curriculum in the Early Years,' in S. Smidt (ed.) *Key Issues in Early Years Education*, Abingdon: Routledge, pp.11–17.

8   Carr, M. (2001) *Assessment in Early Childhood Settings*, London: Paul Chapman Publishing.

9   Silin, J.G. (2005) 'Who Can Speak? Silence, Voice and Pedagogy.' in N.Yelland (ed) *Critical Issues in Early Childhood Education*. New York: Open University Press: McGraw-Hill Education, p.85.

10 Csíkszentmihályi, M. (1997) *Finding Flow: The Psychology of Engagement with Everyday Life*, New York: Basic Books, Hachette.

11 Laevers, F., Daems, M., De Bruyckere, G., Declercq, B. *et al.* (2005) *Wellbeing and Involvement in Care: A Process-Oriented Self-Evaluation Instrument for Care Settings*, Belgium: Centre for Experiential Education, Leuven University.

12 Saljo, R. (1979) *Learning in the Learner's Perspective, 1: Some Common-Sense Conceptions*, 76, Gothenburg: Institute of Education, University of Gothenburg, https://eric.ed.gov/?id=ED173369.

13 Lindon, J. (2012), *Understanding Child Development 0–8 Years*, Basingstoke: Hodder Education, p.240.

14 CMO (2011) 'UK Physical Activity Guidelines – Early Years,' Fact Sheets 1 and 2, London: CMO, www.gov.uk/government/publications/uk-physical-activity-guidelines.

15 Department of Health (DoH) (2017) 'Guidelines for Healthy Growth and Development for Your Child,' *Australian 24-Hour Movement Guidelines*, Canberra, www.health.gov.au/internet/main/publishing. nsf/content/FCE78513DAC85E08CA257BF0001BAF95/$File/Birthto5years_24hrGuidelines_ Brochure.pdf.

16 Tremblay, M.S., Chaput, J.-P., Adamo, K.B., Aubert, S. *et al.* (2017) 'Canadian 24-Hour Movement Guidelines for the Early Years (0–4 Years): An Integration of Physical Activity, Sedentary Behaviour and Sleep,' *BMC Public Health* 17, 55, 1–32, doi: 10.1186/s12889-017-4859-6.

17 Draper, C. (2018) 'Here's How Much Kids Need to Move, Play and Sleep in Their Early Years.' *The Conversation*. Accessed on 18/12/2018 at www.theconversation.com/heres-how-much-kids-need-to-move-play-and-sleep-in-their-early-years-107024.

18 Mental Health Foundation (1999) *Bright Futures: Promoting Children and Young People's Mental Health*, London: Mental Health Foundation.

19 Young, E. (2015) *Home-Start: Big Hopes – Big Futures: Evaluation Report, England Pilot Study*, Leicester: British Association of Social Workers (BASW), p.10, www.basw.co.uk/resource/?id=4413.

20 National Association for the Education of Young Children (NAEYC) (1995) *Position Statement: School Readiness*, NAEYC, www.naeyc.org/sites/default/files/globally-shared/downloads/PDFs/ resources/position-statements/PSREADY98.PDF.

21 New Mexico PreK (2006) 'PreK Policy Brief #1: Readiness,' *High Horizons: New Mexico's Educational Readiness Framework*, Santa Fe, NM: Public Education Department, State of New Mexico, p.6, https:// prek.ped.state.nm.us/Docs/PolicyMaterialsLib/PolicyBriefs/PreK%20Policy%20Brief1.pdf.

22 Peckham, K. (2017) *Developing School-Readiness: Creating Lifelong Learners*, London: Sage.

23 Rhode Island KIDS COUNT (2005) *Getting Ready: Findings from the National School Readiness Indicators Initiative, A 17 State Partnership*, Providence, RI: BASW, p.6, www.rikidscount.org.

24 Korkodilos, M. (2015) *Improving School Readiness: Creating a Better Start for London*, London: PHE, www.gov.uk/government/publications/improving-school-readiness-creating-a-better-start-for-london.

25 PACEY (2013) *What Does 'School-Ready' Really Mean? A Research Report from Professional Association for Childcare and Early Years*, Bromley: PACEY, p.43, www.pacey.org.uk/Pacey/media/ Website-files/school%20ready/School-Ready-Report.pdf.

26 PACEY (2015) *Parents Anxious about Children Starting School*, Bromley: PACEY, www.pacey.org.uk/ news-and-views/news/archive/2015-news/august-2015/parents-anxious-about-children-starting-school.

27 DfE and Department of Health and Social Care (DHSC) (2011) *Supporting Families in the Foundation Years*, DfE and DHSC, www.gov.uk/government/publications/supporting-families-in-the-foundation-years.

28 Ofsted (2014) 'Are You Ready? Good Practice in School-Readiness,' Manchester: Ofsted, p.7, https://assets.publishing.service.gov.uk/government/uploads/system/uploads/attachment_data/ file/418819/Are_you_ready_Good_practice_in_school_readiness.pdf.

29 Australian Early Development Census (AEDC) (2015) Australia, www.aedc.gov.au.

30 Hamerslag, R., Oostdam, R. and Tavecchio, L. (2018) 'Inside School Readiness: The Role of Socioemotional and Behavioural Factors in Relation to School, Teachers, Peers and Academic Outcome in Kindergarten and First Grade,' *European Early Childhood Education Research Journal* 26, 1, 80–96.

31 Goddard Blythe, S. (2012) *Assessing Neuromotor Readiness for Learning*, Chichester: John Wiley and Sons, p.5.

32 Ibid.

33 Hansen, K., Josh, J.H., and Dex, S. (eds) (2010) *Children of the 21st Century: The First Five Years*, Bristol: Policy Press, p.5.

34 Duncombe, R. and Preedy, P. (2018) 'Movement for Learning,' in P. Preedy and Sir C. Bell (eds) *Early Childhood Education Redefined: Reflections and Recommendations on the Impact of Start Right*, Abingdon: Routledge, pp.48–60.

35 Hartley, C., Rogers, P., Smith, J., Peters, S. and Carr, M. (2012) *Crossing the Border: A Community Negotiates the Transition from Early Childhood to Primary School*, Wellington: NZCER Press.

36 Greeno, J.G. (2006) 'Authoritative, Accountable Positioning and Connected, General Knowing: Progressive Themes in Understanding Transfer,' *Journal of the Learning Sciences* 15, 4, 537–547.

Chapter 8

1 Weiler, R., Allardyce, S., Whyte, G.P. and Stamatakis, E. (2013) 'Is the Lack of Physical Activity Strategy for Children Complicit Child Neglect?', *British Journal of Sports Medicine* 48, 13, 11 December.

2 Ibid.

3 BHF (2011) 'Evidence Briefing: Physical Activity for the Early Years, – Making PE a Priority,' National Centre, July, BHF.

4 CEDAR (2015) 'Evidence Brief 10: Sitting out Physical Activity – Children's Sedentary Behaviour, Health and the Family Environment,' CEDAR, 10 November, www.cedar.iph.cam.ac.uk/resources/evidence/eb-10-children-sedentary-family.

5 EEF (2015) 'Physical Development Approaches,' EEF, https://educationendowmentfoundation.org.uk/evidence-summaries/early-years-toolkit/physical-development-approaches.

6 Queen Margaret University (2010) 'Reliability of a Modified Version of the Children's Activity Rating Scale (CARS) as a Measure of Physical Activity in Preschool Children,' Master's thesis, posted 8 March 2011, depositing user: Isabel Bentley, https://etheses.qmu.ac.uk.

7 Hager, E.R., Gormley, C.E., Latta, L.W., Treuth, M.S., Caulfield, L.E. and Black, M.M. (2016) 'Toddler Physical Activity Study: Laboratory and Community Studies to Evaluate Accelerometer Validity and Correlates,' London: BioMed Central, 6 September, https://www.ncbi.nlm.nih.gov/pubmed/27600404.

8 Lewicka, M. and Farrell, L. (2007) 'Physical Activity Measurement in Children 2–5 Years of Age,' Report No. CPAH06-002, Sydney, NSW: Centre for Physical Activity and Health, http://citeseerx.ist.psu.edu/viewdoc/download;jsessionid=7837C2A7CCADE57515C3E060E6A1E75D?doi=10.1.1.535.1533&rep=rep1&type=pdf and www.asph.sc.edu/USC_CPARG/pdf/OSRAC_Manual.pdf.

9 Cardon, G., Van Cauwenberghe, E. and de Bourdeaudhuij, I. (2011) 'Physical Activity in Infants and Toddlers,' *Encyclopedia on Early Childhood Development*, Quebec: CEECD/SKC-ECD, January, www.child-encyclopedia.com/physical-activity/according-experts/physical-activity-infants-and-toddlers.

10 NLSCY (2011) 'Physical Activity Recommendations for Early Childhood. Setting the Stage for Lifelong Healthy Habits,' Parenting Series, *Encyclopedia on Early Childhood Development*, Quebec: CEECD/SKC-ECD. www.excellence-earlychildhood.ca/documents/Parenting_2011-04.pdf.

11 PHE (2015) 'Patterns and Trends in Child Physical Activity,' PHE Publications Gateway No. 2015143, PHE, www.noo.org.uk.

12 BHF (2015) 'Evidence Briefing: Physical Activity Guidelines for the Early Years,' BHF, www.bhfactive.org.uk.

13 Ibid.

14 Lewicka and Farrell (2007) *Op. cit.*

15 Ministry of Education and Culture (2016) 'Joy, Play and Doing Together: Recommendations for Physical Activity in Early Childhood,' Helsinki: Ministry of Education and Culture, p.15, http://julkaisut.valtioneuvosto.fi/bitstream/handle/10024/78924/OKM35.pdf.

16 Lewicka and Farrell (2007) *Op. cit.*

17 Ibid.

18 Cliff, D.P. and Janssen, X. (2011) 'Levels of Habitual Physical Activity in Early Childhood,' *Encyclopedia on Early Childhood Development*, www.child-encyclopedia.com.

19 CMO (2011) 'UK Physical Activity Guidelines – Early Years: Fact Sheet 1,' London: CMO, www.gov. uk/government/publications/uk-physical-activity-guidelines.

20 Ministry of Health (2017) 'Sit Less, Move More, Sleep Well: Active Play Guidelines for Under-Fives,' Wellington: Ministry of Health, www.health.govt.nz/publication/sit-less-move-more-sleep-well-active-play-guidelines-under-fives.

21 World Health Organization (2019) 'Guidelines on physical activity, sedentary behaviour and sleep for children under 5 years of age,' World Health Organization, www.who.int/iris/handle/10665/311664.

22 Ministry of Education and Culture (2016) *Op. cit.*

23 Hinkley, T. and Salmon, J. (2011) 'Correlates of Physical Activity in Early Childhood,' Centre for Physical Activity and Nutrition research (C-PAN), Victoria: Deakin University.

24 White, J. (2015) *Every Child a Mover: A Practical Guide to Providing Young Children with the Physical Opportunities They Need*, London: British Association for Early Childhood Education, p.104.

25 Brodie, K. (2018) *The Holistic Care and Development of Children from Birth to Three*, Abingdon: David Fulton, Routledge.

26 Duncombe, R. *et al.* (2014) *Physical Literacy/Development, Pathway Research: Report*, Leicestershire & Rutland Sport (LRS).

27 Pettavel, M. (2018) 'One Size Doesn't Fit All,' *Nursery World*, 20 August, p.16.

28 Leitschuh, C.A., Harring, J.R. and Dunn, W. (2014) 'A Monitoring Tool of Infant and Toddler Movement Skills,' *Journal of Early Intervention* 36, 1, 18–36.

29 Solly, K. (2015) *Risk, Challenge and Adventure in the Early Years: A Practical Guide to Exploring and Extending Learning Outdoors*, Abingdon: David Fulton, Routledge, p.80.

30 RoSPA (2010) 'Advice on Outdoor Risks,' Birmingham: RoSPA, www.rospa.com/school-college-safety/teaching-safely/government-stakeholder/outdoor-risks.

31 Child Alert (n.d.) 'Safety,' thebabywebsite.com, www.cdalert.co.uk/safety.php?tab=Safety.

32 Hedström, E.M., Svensson, O., Bergström, U. and Michno, P. (2010) 'Epidemiology of Fractures in Children and Adolescents,' *Acta Orthopaedica* 81, 1, 148–153.

33 Rosin, H. (2014) 'The Overprotected Kid,' *Atlantic*, April, www.theatlantic.com/magazine/archive/2014/04/hey-parents-leave-those-kids-alone/358631.

34 Hanscom, A.J. (2016) *Balanced and Barefoot*, Oakland: New Harbinger Publications Inc, p.21.

Chapter 9

1 Fisher, J. (2016) *Interacting or Interfering? Improving Interactions in the Early Years*, Maidenhead: McGraw-Hill Education, p.15.

2 Purves, L. (1999) *Tuning into Children: Understanding a Child's Development from Birth to Five Years*, London: BBC Education, p.3.

3 Angermeier, P. (2013) 'Infant Positioning and Development: Research Reinforces the Need for Tummy Time and Close Caregiver Interaction,' *ADVANCE for Occupational Therapy Practitioners* 29, 1, 7, www.occupational-therapy.advanceweb.com, posted 8 January, www.advanceweb.com/web/AdvertisingPromos/2014/Circulation/NonSubscriberDigitalEditionAlert/OT/OT011314_Interactive.pdf.

4 Manier, J. (2008) 'Canadian study, "Experts Say Tummy Time Key for Tots,"' *Chicago Tribune*, 27 January, p.266.

5 PHE (2018) 'Our Approach to Newborn and Infant Physical Examination Screening Standards,' 21 March, PHE, www.gov.uk/government/publications/newborn-and-infant-physical-examination-screening-standards.

6 Ibid.

7 O'Connor, A. and Daly, A. (2016) *Understanding Physical Development in the Early Years. Linking Bodies and Minds*. Abingdon: David Fulton: Routledge.

8 Angermeier (2013) *Op. cit.*

9 American Physical Therapy Association (2008) 'Lack of Tummy Time Leads to Motor Delays in Infants,' CBS News Release, 6 August.

10 BabyBWell (n.d.), '90 Minute Rule,' Wellington: Ministry of Health, www.babybwell.co.uk.

11 Ministry of Health (2017) 'Sit Less, Move More, Sleep Well: Active Play Guidelines for Under-Fives,' Wellington: Ministry of Health. http://www.health.govt.nz/publication/sit-less-move-more-sleep-well-active-play-guidelines-under-fives.

12 Garrett, M., McElroy, A. and Staines, A. (2002) 'Locomotor Milestones and Baby Walkers: Cross-Sectional Study,' *British Medical Journal* 324, 494; and Talebian, A., Honarpisheh, A., Taghavi, A., Fakharian, E., Parsa, M. and Mousavi, G.A. (2008) 'Do Infants Using Baby Walkers Suffer Developmental Delays in Acquisition of Motor Skills?', *Iranian Journal of Child Neurology* 2, 3, 15–18.

13 Jones Russell, M. (2017) 'A Cambridge Nursery has Introduced Babywearing to Improve Wellbeing for Babies and Staff,' www.nurseryworld.co.uk, posted 29 September.

14 Marlen, D. (2014) 'Respect, Care, Wisdom,' *Early Years Educator* 16, 6.

15 Pasch, J. (2017) 'What Happens When We Move and Play Together with Our Infants?', *Early Education Journal* 81, 4–6.

16 Siegel, A. and Burton, R. (1999) 'Effects of Baby Walkers on Motor and Mental Development in Human Infant,' *Journal of Developmental & Behavioral Pediatrics* 25, 355–361, and in C. Davies, 'Who are the Sub-Level-4 Students Going into English Secondary Schools Aged 11 years? What are the Fundamental Underlying Causes of Their Failure to Thrive as Effective Learners by the End of Primary School?', www.fit-2-learn.com, accessed 15 March 2018.

17 Anderson, T. (n.d.) 'Regain and Build Your Original Strength through Crawling,' www.breakingmuscle.com/uk/fitness/regain-and-build-your-original-strength-through-crawling, accessed 29 September 2017.

18 Goswani, U. (2014) *Child Psychology: A Very Short Introduction*, Oxford: Oxford University Press, p.25.

19 Gascoyne, S. (2014) *Summary of Preliminary Research Findings*, www.playtoz.co.uk, accessed 13 December 2014.

20 'Things I Wish I'd Known about Babies,' (2013) www.whataboutthechildren.org.uk, posted 1 February, accessed 29 July 2013.

21 Harms, T., Clifford, R.M. and Cryer, D. (2003) *Infant/Toddler Environmental Rating Scale: Revised (ITERS-R)*, New York: Teachers College Press.

Chapter 10

1   Manning-Morton, J. (2017) *Foundations of Being: Understanding Young Children's Emotional, Personal and Social Development*, London: British Association for Early Childhood Education, p.40.

2   Fisher, J. (2016) *Interacting or Interfering? Improving Interactions in the Early Years*. Maidenhead: McGraw-Hill Education, p.19.

3   Tassoni, P. (2016) *Reducing Educational Disadvantage: A Strategic Approach in the Early Years*. London: Featherstone Education, p.49.

4   Manning-Morton (2017) *Op. cit.*

5   O'Connor, A. and Daly, A. (2016) *Understanding Physical Development in the Early Years. Linking Bodies and Minds*. Abingdon: David Fulton: Routledge.

6   Childwise (2014) *The Monitor Pre-School Report (2014): Key Behaviour Patterns among 0–4 Year Olds*, London: Childwise.

7   Preedy, P., Sanderson, K. and Ball, Sir C. (eds) (2018) *Early Childhood Education Redefined: Reflections and Recommendations on the impact of Start Right*. Abingdon: Routledge, p.21.

8   National Academies of Sciences, Engineering and Medicine (2016) 'Obesity in the Early Childhood Years: State of the Science and Implementation of Promising Solutions – Workshop Summary,' Washington, DC: National Academies Press, doi: 10.17226/23445.

9   Connell, G. and McCarthy, C. (2014) *A Moving Child is a Learning Child: How the Body Teaches the Brain to Think*, Minneapolis, MN, Free Spirit Publishing. p.176.

10 Doward, J. (2018) 'Size Matters, Not Age, for Football's Stars of the Future: Biobanding – or Coaching by Height – Can Bring out the Best in Young Players,' *The Observer*, 2 September.

11 Davies, C., Healy, M. and Smith, D. (2018) *The Maze of Learning: Developing Motor Skills*, Croydon: Fit-2-Learn CIC.

12 Oakley, A. (2015) *Sex, Gender and Society*, Abingdon: Routledge.

13 Manning-Morton (2017) *Op. cit.*, p.44.

14 Fox, K. (2010) 'The Physical Self and Physical Literacy,' in M. Whitehead (ed.) *Physical Literacy Throughout the Lifecourse*. Abingdon: Routledge, p.79.

15 Tillett, V. and Wong, S. (2017) 'An Investigative Case Study into Early Child Educators' Understanding about "Belonging",' *European Early Childhood Education Research Journal* 6, 1, 37–49.

16 Jarvis, J. and Oei, T. (2015) *Evidence Brief: Promoting Active Play for Children 0–12: A Review of Community-Based Interventions*, Toronto: Ontario Agency for Health Protection and Promotion (Public Health Ontario), Queen's Printer for Ontario.

17 Surrey County Council (2014) *Move with Me: Physical Development Tips: 12–18 Months, 18–24 Months, 2–3-Year-Olds, 3–4-Year-Olds*, Kingston upon Thames: Surrey County Council, www.surreycc.gov.uk/people-and-community/family-information-service/publications-for-families/move-with-me-physical-development-tips-leaflets.

18 Lindon, J. (2012) *What Does it Mean to Be Two?* London: Practical Pre-School Books

19 Lindon, J. (2012) *What Does it Mean to Be Three?* London: Practical Pre-School Books.

20 Ministry of Health (2017) 'Sit Less, Move More, Sleep Well: Active Play Guidelines for Under-Fives,' Wellington: Ministry of Health, www.health.govt.nz/publication/sit-less-move-more-sleep-well-active-play-guidelines-under-fives.

21 Manning-Morton (2017) *Op. cit.*, p.67.

22 Murphy, S. (2010) 'Why Barefoot is Best for Children,' *The Guardian*, 9 August; and White, J. (2015) *Every Child a Mover: A Practical Guide to Providing Young Children with the Physical Opportunities They Need*, London: British Association for Early Childhood Education.

23 Maitland, S. (2018) in E.Buist, 'How to Be Alone: "I Feel Most Alive When I'm with My Own Thoughts,"' *The Guardian Weekend Magazine*, 28 April, www.theguardian.com/lifeandstyle/2018/apr/28/how-to-be-alone-having-things-do.

Chapter 11

1   Rivas, M. (1998) *The Carpenter's Pencil* (trans. J. Dunne), New York: Overlook, p.6.

2   Sifton, E. (2003) *The Serenity Prayer: Faith in Times of Peace and War*, New York: Norton.

3   Morley, D. (2017) 'Overweight Kids: Tackling Obesity is about More than Diet and Exercise,' *The Conversation*, Sheffield: Sheffield Hallam University, https://theconversation.com/overweight-kids-tackling-childhood-obesity-is-about-more-than-just-diet-and-exercise-85616, 23 October.

4   Department of Education (2017) *Early Years Foundation Stage Profile Results in England, 2017*, London: DfE, SFR/60/2017, posted 19 October, https://assets.publishing.service.gov.uk/government/uploads/system/uploads/attachment_data/file/652602/SFR60_2017_Text.pdf.

5   House of Commons Library (2018) *Obesity Statistics*, London: House of Commons, https://researchbriefings.parliament.uk/ResearchBriefing/Summary/SN03336.

6   All-Party Parliamentary Group (APPG) (2017) *Physical Activity in Early Childhood: A Report by the All-Party Parliamentary Group on a Fit and Healthy Childhood*, London: House of Commons, p.55, www.neytco.co.uk/wp-content/uploads/2017/10/Physical-Activity-in-Childhood-Report-.pdf.

7   Ibid.

8   Auckland University of Technology (AUT) (2015) *State of Play Survey: Executive Report*, Auckland: AUT.

9   Adamson, A.J., Basterfield, L., Farooq, M.A., Hughes, A.R. *et al.* (2016) 'Timing of the Decline in Physical Activity in Childhood and Adolescence: Gateshead Millennium Cohort Study,' *British Journal of Sports Medicine*, doi: 10.1136/bjsports-2016-096933.

10 Manning-Morton (2017) *Op. cit.*, p.44.

11 APPG (2017) *Op. cit.*, p.55.

12 Kay, L. (ed.) (2017) *Supporting Learning and Development with Technology in the Early Years*, Abingdon: Routledge.

13 Ibid.

14 Conkbayir, M. (2017) *Early Childhood and Neuroscience. Theory, Research and Implications for Practice*, London: Bloomsbury Academic, p.115.

15 Featherstone, S. (2017) *Making Sense of Neuroscience in the Early Years*, London: Featherstone Education, p.13.

16 Pound, L. (2016) 'All about Calm,' *Nursery World*, 4 April, pp.21–24.

17 Seymour, P.H.K. (2001) 'How do Children Learn to Read? Is English More Difficult than Other Languages?', Paper presented at the BA Festival of Science, Glasgow.

18 Tassoni, P. (2016) *Reducing Educational Disadvantage: A Strategic Approach in the Early Years*, London: Featherstone Education, p.87.

19 Barrons, N. and Strauss, D. (2017) *Don't Stop the Song and Dance: An Evaluation of Write Dance Practices in Schools and Early Years Settings*, Canterbury: Canterbury Christchurch University.

20 Connell, G. and McCarthy, C. (2014) *A Moving Child is a Learning Child: How the Body Teaches the Brain to Think*, Minneapolis, MN: Free Spirit Publishing, p.172.

21 Johnson, M. and Lakoff, G. (1980) *Metaphors We Live By*, Chicago, IL: University of Chicago Press.

22 Freeman, L. (2018) 'Children Need More than Just a Smiley Face to Communicate,' *The Spectasor*, 12 May.

23 White, J. (2015) *Every Child a Mover. A Practical Guide to Providing Young Children with the Physical Opportunities They Need.* London: The British Association for Early Childhood Education, p.76.

24 National Association for Sport and Physical Education (n.d.) *Appropriate Practices in Movement Programs for Children Ages 3–5* (3rd edn), Sewickley, PA: NASPE/AAHPERD Publications, www.naspeinfo.org.

25 White (2015) *Op. cit.*, pp.106–109.

26 Mistral, G. (1889–1957) *Their Name Is Today*.

Subject Index

Author Index